Thomas Hardy

'Hardy and Wolfreys make a delicious match. What's finest about this book is Wolfreys' ability to prod us into play, opening up new possibilities for wandering inside a Hardy text.' – **James R. Kincaid,** *University of Southern California*

'An invaluable introduction to the writing of Thomas Hardy.' – **Lawrence Phillips** *University of Northampton*

No other major author of the nineteenth century has arguably produced as much critical activity as Thomas Hardy. This stimulating and timely new study offers fresh perspectives on his work, exploring the various philosophical views of critics, with close textual analysis of Hardy's novels.

Thomas Hardy:

- presents detailed readings of all of the novels, moving beyond the ever popular *Tess of the D'Urbervilles* and *Jude the Obscure* to provide original analyses of other key works such as *Desperate Remedies, Under the Greenword Tree, Far from the Madding Crowd* and *The Mayor of Casterbridge*
- includes discussion of Hardy's poems where relevant in order to serve as a counterpoint to the main texts and to highlight particular issues
- sets forth a provocative argument that Hardy is not of his time but anticipates modernism and contemporary philosophical questions of being, historicity and subjectivity, as these are in turn inflected by material concerns of the late nineteenth century.

Focusing on the tensions between the archaic and the modern in Hardy's novels, this insightful book is essential reading for anyone interested in the work of this fascinating and widely-studied author.

Julian Wolfreys is Professor of Modern Literature and Culture in the Department of English and Drama at Loughborough University. He has published numerous books on literary theory and nineteenth- and twentieth-century English literature.

CRITICAL ISSUES

General Editors

John Peck & Martin Coyle

Critical Issues

Published

Mary Shelley	*Graham Allen*
Jane Austen	*Darryl Jones*
George Eliot	*Pauline Nestor*
Virginia Woolf	*Linden Peach*
Charlotte Brontë	*Carl Plasa*
Charles Dickens	*Lyn Pykett*
Joseph Conrad	*Allan H. Simmons*
John Donne	*Richard Sugg*
Henry James	*Jeremy Tambling*
John Keats	*John Whale*
William Wordsworth	*John Williams*
Thomas Hardy	*Julian Wolfreys*

In preparation

D. H. Lawrence	*Rick Rylance*

Critical Issues Series
Series Standing Order
ISBN 1–4039–2158–X hardcover
ISBN 1–4039–2159–8 paperback
(outside North America only)

You can receive future titles in this series as they are published by placing a standing order. Please contact your bookseller or, in case of difficulty, write to us at the address below with your name and address, the title of the series and the ISBN quoted above.

Customer Services Department, Macmillan Distribution Ltd
Houndmills, Basingstoke, Hampshire RG21 6XS, England

Critical Issues

Thomas Hardy

Julian Wolfreys

palgrave
macmillan

No portion of this publication may be reproduced, copied or transmitted
save with written permission or in accordance with the provisions of the
Copyright, Designs and Patents Act 1988, or under the terms of any licence
permitting limited copying issued by the Copyright Licensing Agency,
Saffron House, 6–10 Kirby Street, London EC1N 8TS.

Any person who does any unauthorized act in relation to this publication
may be liable to criminal prosecution and civil claims for damages.

The author has asserted his right to be identified as the author of this
work in accordance with the Copyright, Designs and Patents Act 1988.

First published 2009 by
PALGRAVE MACMILLAN

Palgrave Macmillan in the UK is an imprint of Macmillan Publishers Limited,
registered in England, company number 785998, of Houndmills, Basingstoke,
Hampshire RG21 6XS.

Palgrave Macmillan in the US is a division of St Martin's Press LLC,
175 Fifth Avenue, New York, NY 10010.

Palgrave Macmillan is the global academic imprint of the above companies
and has companies and representatives throughout the world.

Palgrave® and Macmillan® are registered trademarks in the United States,
the United Kingdom, Europe and other countries

ISBN-13: 978–0–333–92249–1   hardback
ISBN-10: 0–333–92249–2   hardback
ISBN-13: 978–0–333–92250–7   paperback
ISBN-10: 0–333–92250–6   paperback

This book is printed on paper suitable for recycling and made from fully
managed and sustained forest sources. Logging, pulping and manufacturing
processes are expected to conform to the environmental regulations of the
country of origin.

A catalogue record for this book is available from the British Library.

A catalog record for this book is available from the Library of Congress.

10 9 8 7 6 5 4 3 2 1
18 17 16 15 14 13 12 11 10 09

Printed and bound in China

For
J. Hillis Miller
(and Woolfrey, the draper)

Contents

Abbreviations and a Note on References

The following abbreviations for Hardy's works are used throughout. Bibliographical details are given in the Bibliography.

CP	*Collected Poems*
D	*The Dynasts*
DPOT	*The Distracted Preacher and Other Tales*
DR	*Desperate Remedies*
FMC	*Far from the Madding Crowd*
FN	*Thomas Hardy's 'Facts' Notebook*
HE	*The Hand of Ethelberta*
JO	*Jude the Obscure*
L	*A Laodicean*
LTH	*The Life of Thomas Hardy*
MC	*The Mayor of Casterbridge*
PBE	*A Pair of Blue Eyes*
PWB	*The Pursuit of the Well-Beloved*
RN	*The Return of the Native*
TD'U	*Tess of the D'Urbervilles*
TM	*The Trumpet-Major*
TT	*Two on a Tower*
SP	*Selected Poems*
UGT	*Under the Greenwood Tree*
W	*The Woodlanders*
WB	*The Well-Beloved*

While I have consulted Hardy's own final, edited versions of the novels, published as the Wessex Edition (1912–13), I have cited throughout the Penguin Classics editions for two reasons: first, these are amongst the most readily available to all Hardy readers; second, under the general editorship of Patricia Ingham, the editors have based their editions on Hardy's first volume publications, before his revisions, initially in 1895, and then subsequently (as distinct from those editions available as Oxford World's Classics, which follow, more or less, the Wessex Edition). These present the reader with a good deal of material that Hardy revised, edited, or, on a number of occasions, deleted. In a few cases the result was to remove whole sentences and even paragraphs. While I do not go into any particular comparative detail about such passages, I have found them worthy of critical attention, in the greater context of reading Hardy, and do comment on occasions on what was removed or changed.

NOTE ON REFERENCES

Throughout, all references are given parenthetically, following Harvard-style citation. These are keyed to the Bibliography at the end of the book. For those using different editions of the Hardy texts, the abbreviations above are followed by chapter and page numbers. Where Penguin has followed volume or other division, so reference is to volume (book, part, or, as in *Tess*, 'phase'), chapter and page.

Acknowledgements

This book has taken a long time getting to this point. That it arrives at all is perhaps an acknowledgement of the significance of Thomas Hardy for me, in ways that are expressed everywhere in this volume, on the surface and in encrypted fashion also. I'd like to thank those students whose own enthusiasm for Hardy helped to sustain the writing of this volume and the ideas behind it. Two students particularly brought new insight to my understanding of Hardy, and I gratefully acknowledge Daniella Draughon and Cameron Moxley for their contribution and enthusiasm.

At Loughborough University, three colleagues in particular brought to the chapters particularly keen and sympathetic critical acuity, with a generosity of spirit that goes beyond all collegiality. Nick Freeman, Brian Jarvis and Bill Overton deserve thanks beyond this formal, and because of that, insincere acknowledgement, but which, I hope, they hear in this meagre statement. Whatever the failings of this volume, they would have been immeasurably worse, had it not been for the generous readings and editorial advice Nick, Brian and Bill have offered.

There are of course always those unrepayable debts of gratitude. I would like to thank John Peck and Martin Coyle for inviting me to write this volume. Additionally, and for all those intangibles, thanks go to Caroline Blomfield, David Blomfield, John Brannigan, Sudipto Chatterjee, Tom Cohen, Claire Colebrook, Roger Ebbatson, Regenia Gagnier, Jane Goldman, Elaine Hobby, Juliet Flower MacCannell, Alex Murray, Lawrence Phillips, Arkady

Plotnitsky, Jean-Michel Rabaté, Avital Ronell, Nick Royle, Ashley Tauchert, Dan Watt, Keith Wilson, and Kenneth Womack.

I would, finally, like to thank the dedicatee of this volume, J. Hillis Miller, whose work, along with the ethical commitment to literature and the humanities he embodies and performs, offer every scholar, without doubt, the singular exemplar of all that is best and right concerning the profession of literature.

Parts of Chapters 1 and 6 originally appeared in *The Mayor of Casterbridge: Contemporary Critical Essays*, ed. Julian Wolfreys (Basingstoke: Macmillan, 2000), and reappear here extensively amended and revised. I am grateful to the editors of the New Casebooks Series, John Peck and Martin Coyle, and to Palgrave Macmillan, for permission to reprint.

Introduction: Dwelling on Hardy

Thomas Hardy is at once amongst the most constantly read of novelists of the nineteenth century, and yet, at the same time, the most challenging and misread of authors. He lends himself to popular adaptation, as the BBC's 2008 production of, predictably, *Tess of the D'Urbervilles* demonstrates. Yet, as faithful as such adaptation – or what I would term 'translation' – might be to the narrative, that which is most arguably 'Hardy' is occluded, if not erased almost entirely. With Hardy (and, indeed, almost any novelist), there is so much which does not translate. In Hardy's case, though, the untranslatable is of greater significance, and so remains, encrypted and in full view, on almost every page. *Tess* and *Jude the Obscure* excepted, Hardy's dozen or so other novels still receive less attention than is their due (unless by some Hardy critics), and it is in part the purpose of this book to redress that balance a little. To this end, *Tess* and *Jude* are given less attention than some might think they deserve, and I explain, without justifying, my reasons for this in the last chapter.

With Hardy, whose texts bear witness to a daunting eclecticism in reading, thought and epistemology, touching on everything from English folklore to the thought of Arthur Schopenhauer and Henri Bergson, it seems all the more important to respect the singularity of the text, in order that we begin to mine that which is embedded so densely, and without which Thomas Hardy is not Thomas Hardy. For this, and other reasons, I have not presented a central argument beforehand in this introduction, concerning the nature of what is to be read in Hardy. In every chapter I seek to respond to that which Hardy's text imposes, to greater or lesser degrees. The

result, I hope, is that this volume will be read as having an organic development, in which motifs, tropes, concepts and so on come to reiterate themselves, returning with different emphases, approached from different perspectives, and given different degrees of scrutiny. Inevitably, this will result in certain tensions for the reader, which, I believe, are not simply unresolved problems, but rather a response to the paradoxes, aporia, and undecidables which are encountered as that which takes place in the text of Thomas Hardy.

Because novelists are not systematic – not necessarily, not merely systematic – in the organization of their materials, except where the dictates of narrative development and logic demand certain trajectories, it seems inappropriate to explicate one's reading in too schematic or formalized a manner. With Hardy, whose texts bear witness to a daunting eclecticism touching on everything from English folklore to the thought of Schopenhauer and Bergson, it seems all the more important to respect the singular nature of the text. For this reason, I have not presented beforehand a central argument concerning what is to be read in Hardy's text. In every chapter I have sought to respond to that which Hardy's text imposes, to greater or lesser degrees. In short, this volume is written – if it is produced with any shadowy figure in mind at all – for the good reader of Thomas Hardy, who apprehends how in the phenomena of repetition and return, it is difference and not the same which is of significance. This may result for some readers in a sense of being immersed in an argument, only to find that abruptly terminated, as Hardy determines another direction, or demands another mode of critical perception. Inevitably, this results in certain tensions, which I believe are not simply unresolved problems in the process of analysis (if indeed, they are this at all), but rather that the tensions, paradoxes and concomitant aporia which are encountered, are mediations or translations, if you will, of what takes place already in Hardy's text.

In proceeding in this manner, I have organized the chapters more or less according to the order in which Hardy's novels were published. Where I depart from chronological order, this is dictated by the demands of particular novels, their insistence on being heard. In pursuing a roughly chronological order though, from earliest to the latest novel, I am not proposing a development or some seamless trajectory to be read from *Desperate Remedies* (1871) to *Jude the Obscure* (1895). I do, however, pursue readings of the texts in this manner in order to work, however silently and in small, local ways, against Hardy's revisionary categories, introduced first in 1895, whereby he divided the novels into three 'sets': 'Novels of

Character and Environment', these being: *Under the Greenwood Tree*; *Far from the Madding Crowd*; *The Return of the Native*; *The Mayor of Casterbridge*; *The Woodlanders*; *Wessex Tales* (a collection of short stories, published in 1888); *Tess of the D'Urbervilles*; another collection of short stories, *Life's Little Ironies* (1894); and *Jude the Obscure*; 'Romances and Fantasies', the next category, includes *A Pair of Blue Eyes*, *The Trumpet-Major*, *Two on a Tower*, *The Well-Beloved* and the collection of short stories, *A Group of Noble Dames* (1891); the last group of novels, *Desperate Remedies*, *The Hand of Ethelberta*, and *A Laodicean* are given by Hardy the collective title 'Novels of Ingenuity'. Despite such categorization and the logic by which Hardy makes these decisions retrospectively, novels from one group share obsessions and interests with novels from another, and these may be more effectively highlighted in the manner I have chosen.

I. DWELLING IN HARDY

Between 1882 and 1886 Thomas Hardy published no major work. Having been seriously ill in 1881 when he was forced to dictate much of *A Laodicean* to Emma, his first wife, Hardy moved back to Dorset, in the following year, first to Wimborne and subsequently to Dorchester, when the building of Max Gate, Hardy's final home, began. A 'Laodicean' is someone who is lukewarm or half-hearted, particularly concerning matters of doctrine or ideology in religion or politics; the very opposite of Hardy, in fact. Yet this, his sixth novel, has less to do with such indecision than it might be said to be interested in interrogating an obsessive ambivalence concerning the relative values of modernity and the past, the ways in which the former persists in the latter, or the manner in which particular members of late Victorian society are driven by a sense of the past. *A Laodicean* asks a question underlying Hardy's writing: how can the archaic and modern coexist? Is such a thing imaginable, or is it perhaps the case that the constant collision between the traces of the past and experience of the present cause chaos and crisis, precipitating fateful decisions on the modern subject in the face of the undecidable in the historical present?

In *Two on a Tower*, Hardy forces the old and the new together in a number of ways. A folly built on what may have been either a Roman fortress or a pagan burial mound or barrow becomes the site for the practice of astronomy. However, the origin of the site remains unknown, Hardy informing us of this. Such unknowability or, as Hardy calls it, in an inflection that situates responsibility in human

consciousness, 'forgetfulness' (*TT* I.I.6) extends to the origin of the faux-Tuscan tower itself, as 'Probably not a dozen people within the district knew the name of the person commemorated, while perhaps not a soul remembered whether the column were hollow or solid, whether with or without a tablet explaining its date and purpose' (*TT* I.I.6). Certainty concerning the past, along with matters of verification and authenticity, cannot be gained. What this yields is the confrontation, through the latest astronomical technology, with an undecidability in the face of the limits of human knowledge, culminating in nothing less than the ageless age of the universe, its temporal abyss. With that arrives a 'coming-to-consciousness' for astronomer Swithin St. Cleve, possibly Lady Constantine, on whose estate the tower is situated, and perhaps for the reader also: the most singular 'modern' understanding is the absolute insignificance of human perception when confronted with the apprehension of the abyssal and the infinite. If the light that reaches us comes from a star already extinguished, in effect we are receiving that which only remains as a trace, and which no longer exists as such. This being the case, we glimpse in the abyss our own-having-become-extinct.

What to do in the face of this appalling recognition except to stop writing perhaps, as does Hardy? Admittedly, this is merely hypothesis, a convenient fiction structured by the equal convenience of hindsight in collusion with the force of narrative. However, in reading or 'inventing' this creative 'hiatus' as a place from which to start a study of Hardy, what one is given to read in the literary silence of Hardy is the possibility that there is a secret at the heart of his writing. Such a secret is not necessarily recuperable. It cannot be unearthed as such. Yet, the secret of Hardy is everywhere in his writing. It moves in different eddies; it flows throughout his narratives as an inevitable, and invisible force shaping novel and poem alike. A late poem such as 'Silences' (*CP* 865–66), from *Winter Words* (1928), captures the persistence of the secret, in its repetition of the different silences that inform place, silence being the signifier of a present haunted by memory. Of the various silences, the silence of the house is the most strident in its call; for it brings to the poet's mind the human past, of lost songs, 'music-strains', the sounds of friends – all in fact that constitutes for Hardy the experience of what it means to dwell[1] as a being conscious of one's material existence on the earth, rather than simply to exist. Hardy, we might say, dwells on dwelling, as both material existence and a privileged metaphor for one's being as it bears the burden of memory. As Hardy has it: 'we two kept *house*, the Past and I' (*CP* 308–9; emphasis added). In 'Silences', the work of memory, figured through the silence, has

powerful properties; the silence transforms the house into a 'tomb' and, therefore, the merely living witness into one who is more truly dead than those who are simply deceased. Mourning and memory, closely interlinked here, are the proper work of literature for Hardy, and both are caught in a web with the question of what it means to dwell on the earth.

Hardy's 'secret' has to do, therefore, with dwelling, not as a given place or structure, but instead as the manner in which human beings exist historically and culturally. Reflecting on dwelling in a philosophical sense given it by Martin Heidegger, I would define dwelling in the following manner: to dwell means to orientate oneself with regard to one's being, and the historicity of being. Mindful merely of the modern or the present, one forgets the true nature of one's being, and so one's dwelling. This is the 'secret' that each of Hardy's characters and his narratives seek to negotiate or by which they are confronted in moments of crisis and *contretemps*. Hardy's 'secret' is thus marked on the text through the *amaterial* – neither material nor immaterial in any simple empirical sense – traces or remains that inform, shape and determine action, identity and the historicity of any present moment. Silence gives the world if not meaning, then a place for meaning to be inscribed. It thus gives meaning to human apprehension, even if that understanding is of one's true self bereft of any theological or metaphysical comfort. This gift bears in it the double bind, such a gift being given at a price. This is the sense for Hardy that dwelling is marked indelibly with a necessary material and historial finitude: figured in the loss of sound, and the space concomitantly opened by silence in 'Silences'. In this space will be written significance for the reader, who bears witness to that silent space. Such loss acknowledges the historicity of being itself, and with that the inevitable finitude by which being is informed.

Winter Words is the work of an old man aware acutely of his own mortality. It might be argued that a sense of one's finitude, however indirect or implicit in a poem which mourns loss and records silence as the place in which memory gives shape to one's phantasms, and which spectres, in turn, illuminate the nature of being, is inevitable. Nevertheless, it is not mortality that is troubling. It is the burden of memory, and, with that, the inescapable sense of the extent to which one's being is bound up with this responsibility in relation to the act of dwelling; dwelling not simply in a place, at a given time, but dwelling as consciousness, as specific and reflective singular consciousness of the ways in which being and dwelling, though non-synonymous, are interchangeable.

Were we to consider briefly each of Hardy's novels, the interest in notions of being and dwelling, the traces of the past and the materiality of modernity, the role of memory and the responsibility of story-telling, all are seen to inform a vast and complex web, a generative matrix that performs even as it questions what is for Hardy the modern condition in the 1880s and 1890s. Whatever the particulars of such singular narratives, however, each may be read as coming down through particular perspectives to an interrogation of the meaning of being and what it means, moreover, to dwell, if being is, in its reflective consciousness and responsibility for the remains of the past, a mode of dwelling. It should come as no surprise, therefore, to reflect on the fact that, while 'Silence' is one of Hardy's last poems, one of his first extant works is also a poem concerned with the idea of the house, dwelling and memory: 'Domicilium' (CP 3–4). Of this first poem, it is perhaps worth noting, at least in passing, that the very title, the Latin for dwelling place or place of habitation, marks and remarks itself with both distancing irony, historical anachrony and untranslatability (the loss, or breakdown, of communication). There is thus a sense of something foreign in and about the idea of home. There is a foreign guest, if you will, and an apperception also of what haunts the familiar, of what disturbs in the most familiar location, home. The unfamiliar, the strange, returns from within the most familiar locations. A dead language, Latin, defines home and, in being this trace of the dead, signifies that which is always unassimilable, irrecuperable, and other. A title in another's tongue, it remains on the page as a boundary resistant to domestication, as well as a threshold one will never cross. At the same time it also signals through the trace of the tongue the historical colonization of England. Its trace remains, then, as a remainder of the ghosts of the past, of history itself as a history of colonial possession and dispossession, and, in that one word, a history also of place, of the historical event taking place, and of displacement. The present home, with identity familiarly defined through place in the present, is always interrupted in this fashion for Hardy. It is always troubled by a communication from some other time, some other place, which has fallen into partial or complete ruin and untranslatability, and yet which is intimately bound up in that which gives identity a home, and which makes us who we are.

From the title to the poem: first published in 1918, it was, we discover from a note written by Hardy on the occasion of a private printing given to Florence Hardy, composed 'somewhere between the years 1857 and 1860, while he was still living with his parents at the charming cottage described in the verses, the

birthplace of both himself and his father' (*SP* 248). Beginning with a representation of a present scene, opening out from the cottage to a description of the immediate landscape, the poem moves back, at the beginning of the fourth stanza, to a past of 'days bygone – /long gone' and 'my father's mother'. Memory presents the scene to the mind's eye, bringing to light and thereby illuminating the moment with another representation folded inside the present poem, and the present of the poem. Hardy thus recollects his younger, other self, but in dwelling on that memory, calls forth another, still older scene, by which the present is haunted, by which it is touched, and which remainder of the past continues to touch in the present, thereby maintaining the connection. This in turn is opened from within, in a moment of potentially abyssal unfolding and revelation as the grand-mother's voice emerges, recorded on Hardy's memory as if it had left an impression like a stylus on wax, but here given a material pros-thetic projection, to enact its own anamnesiac witness to a past fifty years before Hardy's childhood: 'Fifty years/Have past since then, my child, and change has marked/The face of all things'. Dwelling as reflective memory and dwelling as existence in a given location, on the earth, in which past and present, earth, sky and existent being are connected, come together through the act of witness that is literature. But attestation does not offer closure. From within rep-resentation, from within the stable and supposedly fixable image or snapshot, the self is exposed to the memory of the other, who returns to open yet again another memory, and with that let in, through the rift in the present, the remains of a past otherwise inaccessible. This is what is understood as authentic dwelling in Hardy's text; and this is Hardy's secret.

II. HARDY, WHO HE?

All questions concerning being and identity give one pause to reflect: Who was Hardy? Who *is* Thomas Hardy, today? Is it more accur-ate to speak of him as a poet or a novelist, a poet who wrote novels and short stories, or a novelist who happened to write a great deal of poetry, some of it of the very finest in the English language? Is he a Victorian author, properly speaking, or, conceivably, a modernist, albeit one *avant la lettre*? Or is Hardy someone who, working always in 'some other's accent' (to employ a phrase of his), remained throughout his life, and subsequently, anachronistic, other to his times, and, still today in ways we have yet to fathom, to ours also?

These questions have much currency currently and in recent years amongst the more 'philosophically' inclined scholars of Hardy. They circulate especially amongst those with interests in interdisciplinary approaches to literature and for those who, through engagement with literary theory in the past couple of decades, have come to recognize that what were previously perceived as 'aesthetic flaws' in Hardy as a writer by earlier generations of critics are not flaws at all, but rather the signs of a writer whose practices cannot be gathered conveniently or comfortably under conventional categories of appreciation. Taking such questions as my cue, and coming to such points of interrogation from a number of philosophically and historically inflected perspectives anticipated by Hardy's text, I want to continue such work in the present volume.

However, it is not my intention here to address all of Hardy's work. I can do no more than sketch some possible directions for reading Hardy, and reading him differently – or let us say, reading the difference in Hardy. In reading this difference, I will seek to move in and out of a range of texts, primarily the novels, but also a poem or two. Taking up passages or motifs, recurrent figures and tropes, I will strive to read Hardyean difference with an eye to the writer's modernity. Hardy's modernity, irreducible to modernism, and so anachronistic to the futures of English literature as well as its pasts, is a modernity of ideas; through this, Hardy explores how the novel might become a poetic vehicle for exploring the abstract, the epistemological, even though this exploration is always grounded in materially recognized conditions of being, historicity, and subjectivity.

In order to gesture towards such an understanding, this book will be most appropriately apprehended as a preface of sorts, a preface to Hardy but always in his wake, not yet having caught up with Hardy, as well as an invention of the Hardyean text, an invention that does not create anything new so much as it finds what is already there – Hardy's 'secret', if you will. This introduction will suggest we apprehend Hardy's text as an archive, and a very peculiar archive at that. Hardy's text offers readers an archive of secrets, secrets concerned with who we are, what it means to exist as beings with self-conscious awareness of their own modernity, their historicity, but cut off from 'true histories' or 'true narratives' of collective, northern European and Anglo-Saxon identity. Hardy's writing is, then, the writing of 'mythic ... [or] poetic narrative belonging to the age of psychoanalysis' (Derrida 1986, xxxiii).

Reading Hardy presents us with more than the difficult apprehension that a writer may generate narratives inscribed out of different

times and different modes. The other 'problem' for the reader of Hardy is succinctly captured here:

> If individual close readings are unsatisfactory, so are attempts to survey the whole and organize it ... by noting similarities from poem to poem and generalizing on that basis. One of the themes of Hardy's poetry, as of his fiction, is the uniqueness of each moment of experience, as well as of each record in words of such a moment. Each moment, each text, is incommensurate with all the others. To ... begin to make grand interpretative patterns ... is to perform just the sort of falsifying simplification that the poems themselves repeatedly warn against. (Miller 1985, 270–1)

Accepting the logic of this statement concerning the poetry and fiction has ramifications for responding appropriately to Hardy's writing practices, his poetic and narrative performances. Given the unsatisfactory nature of close readings on the one hand, and the thematic or other holistic attempts to organize and so generalize on the other, I propose to proceed through a series of readings of moments of unique experience, without the assumption of grand interpretative patterns. Each of the following chapters will risk, nevertheless, the opening of such readings through commentaries on, if not themes, then iterable motifs or structural and epistemological recurrences in Hardy. In each case, I will read such moments as they operate in their singular fashion. I will explore how events and places in Hardy haunt because, whilst they are unique, they bring with them the recognition that this or that particular event has happened in different ways and will continue to take place. Places particularly are invested with impersonal memories, and without that possibility of recurrence and return, the unique or singular moment would not be understandable as an event, the sign of a crisis or irreparable transformation.

III. HARDY'S MANY RETURNS

Of the 14 (or 15) novels written by Hardy between 1871 and 1897, nine were published between 1871 and 1882. My equivocation is deliberate; it is not that I cannot count. The 'last' novel, *The Well-Beloved* (1897), though published after *Jude the Obscure* (1895), was first produced in a significantly different version as *The Pursuit of the Well-Beloved* (1892). Even such a revision of a work is suggestive. It indicates a restlessness within the author himself, a tireless and perhaps obsessive desire to work through a range of interrelated themes, images, tropes, narrative trajectories and interactions. After

1882, Hardy completed no more novels until 1886, when he published *The Mayor of Casterbridge*. This novel, produced at the end of Hardy's return to Dorset, to his home, and to both a new house and also a location in which the Hardys had dwelt for generations, appears to signal the 'return of the native': the return, on the one hand, of the native of Dorset to that county, and, on the other hand, the return of what is native *in* and *to* Hardy, so many remainders of the past dwell in him and, through him, in his writing. Hardy's novel writing career is marked in innumerable ways by such signs of recirculation, revision, supplement, and a desire to find the appropriate expression and appropriate frame for particular themes, motifs, and obsessions, if this is not too strong a word, which take on material form, and which become reiterated throughout his career. There is an incessant drive within Hardy's writing to return to that which is elusive, that which haunts the writer from the very start, and which comes back to push him to the revision of the same and the invention of what is found to be always already there.

Though not in any ostensible fashion concerning itself with the themes or interests of what is conventionally referred to as *fin de siècle* fiction, Hardy's fiction also remarks over three decades the sense of endings, of passage and passing away, of irreparable transformation, translation and an apprehension of *becoming-posthumous* intrinsic to the identities of many of his 'Victorian' readers, whether or not this was felt the part of some of his audience. Hardy's fiction, if it turns to the past and is haunted by the past, is also a fiction haunted by the anxiety of eschatological trauma. To give this another perspective, Hardy, in being at variance with the sociological or sensationalist preoccupations of his literary contemporaries in the last twenty years of the nineteenth century, manifests the ability to speak or, respond to certain deeper, older currents of Englishness, outside the urban, imperial mainstream. Such flows, as those already alluded to, belong to no one era or epoch, but shape the discontinuous narrative of national identity in numerous ways. And all flows tend towards the assumption that the present too will pass into obliteration, as is the inevitable and cyclical nature of human existence given social manifestation.

Despite the exigencies of reception and misperception, Hardy's novel writing career spanned a generation, the last thirty years, more or less, of the nineteenth century. But of Hardy's 'generation': how are we to locate Hardy, albeit in somewhat adumbrated manner, according to the idea of a 'generation'? Were we to speak with any confidence of 'Hardy's generation', it is worth observing in passing that, not least amongst those who comprise this generation include

Emmaline Pankhurst, Sigmund Freud, Friedrich Nietzsche, Gerard Manley Hopkins, Rhoda Broughton, Robert Louis Stevenson and Henry James. Historically, Hardy's generation witnesses the second and third Reform Acts (1867 and 1884), and the establishment of the Fabian Society, the Prime Meridian and Greenwich Mean Time (1884).

A list can give only the barest sense of a culture and generation, however. If anything, the identity of Hardy's generation, considered in the context of a reflexive modernity ill at ease with directions towards a future it could not control, became marked by an insistent sense of turning backwards, looking over its shoulder at a catastrophic rupture, by which the past was inheritable, knowable, only in ruins, if at all. As the nineteenth century 'progressed', so the signs of cultural anachronism intrinsic to a sense of modern identity were being registered in different ways, from the early modern influence on the Pre-Raphaelite Brotherhood, the fascination with all things medieval as expressed through the poetry of Tennyson, the Arts and Crafts movement of William Morris, to the neo-Gothic architecture of Pugin and his followers, and elsewhere. Cultural anachrony becomes that by which the Janus-face of Victorian modernity is recognized, and Hardy inherits to a great extent the representational economy of a generation haunted by the traces of the various pasts it seeks to aestheticize, dehistoricize and therefore master.

By virtue of generational logic, Hardy must therefore appear as the 'child' of this previous generation of cultures and authors. By the time that Hardy's career as a novelist began, Dickens was dead, as was Elizabeth Gaskell. Hardy's contemporaries experienced and interpreted the world in radically different ways from their predecessors, and while Hardy ploughed very much his own furrow, yet, at the same time, his experience of the difference between himself and others of his generation was haunted by traces of earlier experience informing his perceptions. This may sound paradoxical, but it is the spirit, if not the essence of late Victorian modernity, which in many ways Hardy embodies more intimately than many of his contemporaries. It is perhaps the reason why the reception of his work by his contemporaries is so fraught, so often misread, and why, conversely, so much of his fiction writing addresses past scenes and the traces of more distant pasts within any single narrative past, as haunting, disruptive forces.

The question of Hardy's generation is caught up with what Tim Armstrong has described as the Victorian subject's 'entry into history, the trauma of *becoming-historical* which is central to nineteenth-century conceptions of the historical' (2000, 2). Such

an entry, and the trauma that accompanies it, is for me the sign of an irreversible, epochal generational change. The trauma of material being as a becoming-historical is illustrated powerfully in *The Trumpet-Major* and *Under the Greenwood Tree*, two strikingly different, singular texts.

Hardy is, here, then, two novelists at least. Arguably, he is the last properly 'historical' novelist of the nineteenth century, whilst also being the first novelist of a phenomenologically inflected self-conscious apprehension of being's materiality and historicity. His works are central to our perceptions of a world in radical transition, as well as being testimonies to the ghosts of memory, as will be witnessed in the example of *The Trumpet-Major*. Much *fin de siècle* fiction might be read, arguably, as an escape from what James Joyce was to call the 'nightmare' of history. Hardy faces this nightmare, however, and presents us with narrative histories of a ghost-plagued culture. While the other novelists might speak, directly or obliquely, to aspects of national identity and subjectivity that are supposedly modern in the nineteenth century in a manner that obscures rather than foregrounds any self-consciousness about one's historicity and modernity (modernity being conceived as the tension between temporally distinct senses of self and other in contradistinction to the historical sense of organic continuity), Hardy, of all writers in the nineteenth century, engages most unflinchingly with 'the way in which the self is constituted by and writes itself into history', without any overt signs of the modernity of being (Armstrong 2000, 2). This is not to say his largely phenomenological interpretation of subjectivity and being is not thoroughly modern. It is. In Hardy's worlds, the modern experience of the self is not focussed through the desire to separate present and past, self and other, but to realize the self as a product of the irresolvable tensions that such binaries produce.

IV. KEEPING HOUSE

For Hardy, the past is always with us, however hidden its traces, however encrypted its signs. And concomitantly, any writer of the modern age must respond to such signs and address them through a language that suspends time for the reader in different ways, so as to call attention to matters of visualization, perspective, and focalization. This has less to do with a distance from past generations and the assumptions about modernity accompanying those perceived or desired acts of distancing, than with an apperception of the subject's

irreparably *being-riven, being-haunted.* In this condition Hardy places his characters, wherein, always already displaced from any genuine sense of self and repeating however differentially the actions of generations and cultures before them, they serve to symbolize that anachronic condition of being at the end of the nineteenth century, already noted.

Not a few of Hardy's novels situate their events at a generation's remove, or at a distance of a couple of decades at least from the time of their writing. Yet, somewhat discordantly and anachronically; as, we might say, reading so many signs of the times, the experience of reading them is markedly 'modern', self-conscious, their narratives not necessarily being *of* their time. A novel such as *The Return of the Native* (which indirectly dates its specific inaugural action as taking place on 5 November 1842, from the evidence of the first line of the first chapter, and another reference in Chapter Three) has been read in terms of its modernity, through its meshing of Darwinian and Arnoldian discourses. The very modish or evanescent temporality of such cultural and scientific discourses, themselves so markedly 'Victorian', is nonetheless subsumed within and offered a somewhat stark countersignature not only of the inhuman and initially ahistorical world of Egdon Heath; they are also juxtaposed ironically by the countersignature of older pre-rational or pre-modern cultures. In this, itself a reiterated and iterable structure with singular variations from novel to novel to greater or lesser extents, Hardy presents a world of simulacra and unstable identities, a world made up of numerous forms and manifestations of often thwarted or misdirected communication, and which present is rendered partly incoherent by the ghosts of the past. Whatever signals there are by which Hardy's characters attempt to communicate with one another in any given narrative present moment, such signals often go awry. They do so for two reasons: on the one hand, in a modern world everything appears to connect to everything else in a vast web of communication and information; on the other hand, such signals rarely connect or communicate unproblematically, and their delivery is hardly ever timely or on time. There is always in Hardy's writing an errancy in the destination of messages. The other reason for the breakdown in transmission is that, while certain types of signal are unreadable by virtue of their being anachronistically present, the signals are so many and so frequent, and the frequencies of transmission so variable and multiple, that there are interruptions in transmission and reception. Hardy's world is one troubled by a density of signs, and the interruption of signification as a result of the density of the flow.

Hardy's world is also one in which there is repeatedly a confrontation with anachronic spectres inhabiting the real. Hence, as a result of the tensions and gaps produced out of the spectral and material, the past and present, the anachronistic and the modern, we are given to read the signs of a 'particular kind of historicity ... [which] is opened up here, painful and elegiac, even as it is inevitable and progressive' (Armstrong 2000, 4). Such historicity finds itself insistently caught up in the communication of the inability to communicate, so densely insistent is the web of signs from out of which 'modern' society finds itself woven.

Hardy's Wessex, with its various 'worlds' and 'times', gives temporal and historical perspective on such moments of historical trauma. His worlds are as much haunting as haunted, and this is given particular expression in *The Mayor of Casterbridge*, but is registered forcefully in most of his novels. To approach the question of what haunts Hardy, and to supplement the sketch already given, I propose to pursue in this volume the relationship between historicity, reading and misreading, perception and the phenomenological self, which I take to be at the heart of Hardy's writing. At the same time, this will necessitate questions being raised in passing concerning discourses of sight, perspective, perception, and vision. The problems of perception and reading one's historically determined subjectivity through acts of reading the signs of past cultural moments that accumulate in the fiction of the self inform all Hardy's texts. In a different manner, this question of what haunts reading and reading as the haunt of the unreadable is also the problematic of generational position. Hardy does not belong to the previous generation, by virtue, obviously, of the accident of when he is born but also, more importantly, because of a pronounced epistemological difference between the way the previous generation's perceptions of being, historicity and representation are shaped and Hardy's own. However, this does not mean that Hardy belongs to his own generation. He, or at the very least, his text is other than those times. The misreading of cultural signs, the traces of the past, and the pulses of cultural memory, therefore inform the critical misreading of Hardy in both his own time, and in subsequent generations.

Returning briefly to the question of who we think Hardy is or was, then, it is perhaps best to turn to Hardy's poetry where the question of Hardy's historical or generational 'home' comes most acutely to the fore. From 1898 until his death, Hardy published poetry continuously throughout the first three decades of the twentieth century, editing the Wessex edition of his novels in 1912. In all, Hardy wrote and published eight volumes of poetry during his lifetime. It is a salutary point in any sketch of English literary and

cultural history to recall that, when Hardy died, many of the now canonical works of modernist literature – for example, Pound's *Hugh Selwyn Mauberley* (1920), Eliot's *The Waste Land* (1922), Joyce's *Ulysses* (1922), Woolf's *Mrs Dalloway* (1925) and *To the Lighthouse* (1927) – had already been published.

Even such a baldly factual statement alerts us to the problem of placing Hardy; and with that, the double-question of historicity and anachrony is raised once again. To rephrase this, does Hardy have a proper home? Where, in literature, might his texts be said to dwell? G. R. Elliott observes as early as 1928 how Hardy's publications belong to two different times simultaneously, one a forensic modernity of the 'laboratory', the other, the time of ghostly folklore and related, haunting atavistic traces (1928, 1185). Yet, surely one cannot dwell in two different times? The time that is absent for Elliott in the production of Hardy's clinically precise yet phantasmagorical world is that of overwrought nineteenth-century melodrama. Hardy's work, Elliott avers, 'is far from theatric', moving with a 'sincerity and simplicity' (1185) that, once more, is scientistic *and* fetishistic in its attestation. Scientistic *and* fetishistic: more modern than modern, and yet strangely superstitious, primitive. Like his near contemporary, Sigmund Freud (1856–1939), Hardy does not quite belong to any one epistemological or generational locus. Dwelling in the margins, as it were, Hardy, like Freud, cannot do away with ghosts even if he cannot quite believe whole-heartedly in their possibility, the possibility of the impossible. Hardy's 'secret' is this conjoined inability and desire. To put this another way, Hardy's 'modern' world of trains and telegraphs, the post, steam ships, astronomy, geology and photography exists uncomfortably alongside a collective and yet temporally heterogeneous and incommensurate field, as, in a 'decomposition' of the present moment, we come to read again and again of 'figures and tropes', which, belonging to times other than our own, 'cannot be subsumed by . . . a coherent configuration of meanings' (Plotnitsky 2001, 83). Such figures can be missed, or overlooked. But in every case, how Hardy considers and presents the world resists aesthetic formalization, and so disturbs our reading habits. It is for this reason that I turn to the reception of Hardy.

V. HISTORY AND MEMORY, MATERIAL AND IMMATERIAL

Hardy's sense of many subjects, but most especially time, historicity, temporality, and the role vision, narrative, representation and memory play in relation to the temporal and historical, is complex

and often apparently contradictory. It is as if there exist, as a coterminous mode of staging in most if not all Hardy's writings, two worlds, two times, each of which threatens the other, as an intimate and yet violent alterity. Concerning the function of memory in relation to the material world, 'Hardy's observations about the mental traces we leave upon the material world register a disparity between the fleeting nature of human consciousness and the comparative permanence of inanimate objects' (Vrettos 2007, 199). Between, that is, the material and the immaterial there is signalled the reflective experience of one's own being, neither one nor the other, and yet mediating both, as the *amaterial*. One's being is transitory, brief, and consciousness reminds us of that, even as it causes us to reflect on the material permanence of the world in which we exist. This leads to a question: what, exactly, 'does it mean for an object to be "saturated" with human memories? What kinds of traces might "thoughts and glances" actually leave on the material world?' (Vrettos 2007, 199). Such an interrogation is invaluable for expressing economically everything that takes place in Hardy. We can see those persistent obsessions in the first pairing of notes in Hardy's *'Facts' Notebook*. They may not answer the questions, but they do, undoubtedly, throw Vrettos' important commentary into sharp relief:

> The landlord leases land more & more frequently to capitalist farmers – the class of yeoman arise – Farmer dependent on his hay & straw for his winter keep. Cattle & sheep were fattened in summer & killed at its close, their flesh being salted for winter use – 'Summer is y-cumin in,' meant much more in those days than it does in ours on this account. Sheep farming takes the place of agriculture – vast enclosures are made from the common field, wh was the chief cause of Ket's rebellion in 1549 ...

> Families of the ancient Saxon & Norman race – either extinct or reduced to the lowest fortune – Could one of those illustrious shades return to earth he might behold one of his descendants dancing at the lathe – another tippling with his dark brethren of the apron ... a fifth poaching upon the very manors possessed by his ancestors. (*FN* 3–4)

Together, the passages can be read as opening onto the possibility of a mode of narrative that is at one and the same time visionary *and* historiographical, grounded by the remains of material cultures undergoing often irreparable transformation. These assume through translation a sufficient distance, as much epistemological as it is historical, so as to be either partially unreadable or wholly ignored by

many in the present (save Hardy, of course), However, their traces leave a certain resonance in play so as to inflect the present in such a manner that a decisive and disastrous effect is produced, a crisis or similar irreparable event, precisely because the subject or subjects in the present no longer know how to read. On the one hand, there is, in the first passage, above, a telegraphic précis of a review, taken from the *Spectator* in July 1883, of a book concerning the history of English agriculture. Specifically, Hardy has sketched a note concerning the effects of the Enclosures Acts, and the rise of 'capitalist farmers' (*FN* 3). On the other hand, the annotation in the second is a summary from John Fitzgerald Pennie's (a fellow countryman of Hardy's from East Lulworth, Dorset, but belonging to Hardy's grandparents' generation) *The Tale of a Modern Genius*. Pennie's *Britain's Historical Drama* may have been an influence on the writing of Hardy's *The Dynasts* by (Millgate 1994, 316). But whether or not this is so, Pennie provides Hardy with much information about 'families of the ancient Saxon & Norman race ... [who, by the 1880s are] either extinct or reduced to lowest fortune' (*FN* 3). We might also note how the 'enclosures' of the one note produces, historically, the poachers of the second.

However, as the note continues, another invention is expressed: 'Could one of those illustrious shades return to earth, he might behold one of his descendants dancing at the lathe – another tippling with his dark brethren of the apron ... a fifth poaching upon the very manors possessed by his ancestors' (*FN* 3–4). Between these two extracts from the *Notebook* a representation is to be read of Hardy's many narrative interests: rural political and social history; the effects of power and the transformation in the lives of people otherwise un- or under-represented historically, except as its subjects or victims; the imaginative sympathy with the chance, as well as systematic effects of historical and cultural change; and the apprehension of anachronic occasion in the possible communication or historical arrival at consciousness between the spectres of the past and the material circumstances of the present. Indeed, it might be risked that, between the two notes, we witness being woven and unravelled the matrix from which Hardy's fictive comprehension and presentation of modern English identity is generated. To go further, Hardy's presentation is performative. The crisis between self and world, self and other, habit and defamiliarization, modernity and the archaic are not simply observed, represented or otherwise commented on in some masterly control of mimetic delineation. Instead, figures and tropes, metaphors and inanimate objects play within consciousness, performing the very experience

of late Victorian consciousness, in a manner that bypasses individual consciousness of any given character, to become the movement of narrative itself, as dialect words, overly ornate Latinizations, and 'deformed' grammatical structures contend. There is thus enacted across Hardy's writing an iterable and mobile structure of presentation, which, though unfamiliar in one sense, nevertheless maps one's encounter with the world, in which relations between dissimilar and otherwise incommensurable tropes, images, languages, experiences and events become bodied forth in Hardy's modes of representation.

VI. TAKING BACK HARDY

While the internal logic of relation without direct or obvious connection or relation is, in some manner, unequivocally and forcefully *there* on nearly every page, Hardy's anachronistic intermixing of cultural traces must have made him appear to some of his own generation distinctly quirky, when compared with, say, a Wilde, a Gissing, or a James. As a result, Hardy was not well served by readers of his generation. A strange disjunction forms therefore around the reception of Hardy. On the one hand he was and has remained undeniably popular. He was and is much read, if not well read. On the other hand, critical voices have found themselves at pains to explain Hardy, often through their failed efforts at aesthetic formalization, becoming disquieted by what his work 'does' in the house of English literature, a *domicilium* if you will to which critics believe they hold the key, and with which they believe themselves to be familiar, which house it is their habit to guard.

For many years, during Hardy's lifetime and subsequently, after his death in 1928, there has been expressed repeatedly a sense that Hardy has been misread. For example, Terry Eagleton offers the following potted history of Hardy's reception:

> Not all that long ago, a standard account of Thomas Hardy might have run rather like this: Hardy was a self-educated author who struggled his way up from the ranks of the common people, and wrote gloomily fatalistic novels about an English peasant society whose traditional way of life was being undermined by external urban forces. (Eagleton 2005, 187)

He then proceeds: 'Not a word of that account is in fact true, except perhaps for [the definition of Hardy as an] 'author', and to inquire why not might lead us to a more accurate understanding of the man and his fiction' (Eagleton 2005, 187). While it is not my intention to

inquire 'why' exactly, yet it is necessary, nevertheless, to begin any critical engagement with Hardy's text with a consideration of the problem of 'Hardy' *qua* canonical literary figure, as this problem is articulated through criticism's misperceptions. Though I will not be examining many of the analyses that 'get Hardy wrong' to greater or lesser extents, I will offer a sketch of the failures and avoidances of reception in brief broad strokes, in order to indicate the silences and ellipses to which we ought to attend.

It might be asked why this should be worth our interest. Although Hardy criticism has done a great deal in the last two decades to counteract the hitherto prevailing tendencies in misreading Hardy that Eagleton outlines, *that* he can write this with any justification in 2004 hints at the extent of the work to be done with regard to reading Hardy aright. There is still much to be done to become the good reader that Hardy desired, if his own comments on the nature and purpose of fiction, or the reception of his works as he recounts this history in *The Life of Thomas Hardy* are anything to go by. Possible correctives to the 'avoidance' of reading and the history of misreading that Eagleton signals, which, in the author's own lifetime, caused Hardy to abandon novel writing, remain necessary and to come.

Of the tendency towards non-reception and as a sign also that Hardy was anachronistic to his own time, Donald Davidson has remarked that there 'was a real intellectual distance between [the author] . . . and almost three generations of critics' (Davidson 1940, 163). As Davidson continues, 'critics have not so much underrated – or overrated – Hardy as *missed* him' (163; emphasis added). This has come about, according to the critic, inasmuch as those generations of critics were misled, continuously and repeatedly, 'by the superficial resemblance between [Hardy's] work and the product current in their day'. Yet, as Davidson concludes, 'though Hardy was *in* [his] time, and was affected by its thought and art, he was not really *of* that time' (1940, 163). It is therefore clear from this commentary not only that there are the traces of anachrony in Hardy's writing, but Hardy himself was anachronistic, as it were, out of joint not exactly with the times in which he found himself but rather with the tenor, the dominant discourses of the day, and with that, at odds with the hegemonic cultural, aesthetic representational logics.

Beyond those three generations of critics (Davidson's article was published in 1940), Hardy continued to be 'missed', as it were, the delivery of his text deferred, gone astray, delivered to the wrong address. Eagleton identifies four 'distinct stages' in the development of Hardy criticism on which we have already touched (1981, 127).

The first two phases read the novelist as 'anthropologist of Wessex' and, subsequently, 'the melancholic purveyor of late nineteenth-century nihilism' (1981, 127). This particular assessment at least accords Hardy a certain comprehension on the part of the reader with the difficulties Hardy encountered in seeking to transcend what he called 'the analytical stage', which he felt novel writing had reached by the 1880s (*LTH* 183). Moving beyond this early assessment of Hardy, Eagleton describes the response to Hardy in the post-war years. Formalist criticism of the 1940s and 50s reads Hardy's work as 'irreparably violated by ideas'. At the same time, there begins a shift towards 'a more "sociological" reading of Hardy' (Eagleton 1981, 127). This latter phenomenon is not, however, unproblematically positive for Eagleton. For, as he argues, much of such criticism focused on what it took to a safe vision of a lost rural England, appealed to by Hardy in sentimental and mythological terms, while also criticising Hardy for the oddities of his language and style, a critical tendency persisting into the seventies (1981, 127–8). Peter Widdowson also similarly summarizes the 'problem of Thomas Hardy', alerting us to a selective critical reading of the novels aiming to discern a 'true' Hardy who can be made to belong comfortably to the literary canon, while leaving aside those novels which are read as 'exaggerat[ing]' perceived 'flaws' to be found throughout Hardy's narrative oeuvre. This involves detecting the '"improbable" use of chance and coincidence, "flat" and "stagey" characterization, melodrama, and an obtrusively over-elaborate style' in the 'critical fashioning of the "true" Hardy' (Widdowson 1998, 75–6).

We might say, then, that criticism of Hardy falls into two camps. On the one hand (to risk an overworked formula), it attempts either directly or indirectly to stay the complex and resistant texture of the novels through readings of them principally as character studies. On the other hand, there is also the reading, produced most frequently in the 1940s, 50s and 60s, though still in evidence in some more recent critical studies, which operates more or less thematically, isolating sociological, contextual, or tragic aspects. Reading Hardy's novels as social history or for the influences of Greek or Shakespearean tragedy provided a thematic path, which, in being thematically driven, tends, as with the readings of character, to avoid other aspects of the novels that problematize and dismantle undifferentiated ontologies of meaning. Academic criticism of the novel has thus conventionally stressed, imposed and returned to particular kinds of readings, and this critical legacy has been difficult to leave behind. Reading and its avoidance have been motivated

primarily through discussion of those harmonious elements identifiable as 'tragedy, character study', along with the reception of the texts as more or less 'realistic representation[s] of places, practices and "peasants"' (Keen 1998, 128). Such insistence has been pursued often in conjunction with that critical perception that aesthetically or ontologically Hardy's writing is, once more, awkward or deficient, that it is marked either by a lack or excess with regard to 'proper' modes of mimetic or realist novelistic representation.

Yet it is precisely in the affirmative resistance of Hardy's writing, in its fractured, heterogeneous nature, and its refusal to be read as a seamless, coherent, and unified form; *in* those narrative energies which insistently and repeatedly assert themselves, that the demand to be read aright is inscribed at and beyond the limits of critical aesthetic ideology. Allied to this, the anachrony of modern identity and its pervasive apprehension of being haunted by the traces of its past others is, itself, the mark of a historicity that no critical reading grounded in the search for harmonious elements can ever admit. As 'the archaic practices of an ancient environ erupt out of' (Keen 1998, 132) the contemporary present moment in Hardy's novels, so also do instances of discursive insurgence arrive to interrupt and deform accepted norms of realist fiction. Identity, meaning, and ontology are haunted by their own 'alienated image[s]'. Hardy's characters, Hardy's locations, Hardy's plots manifest repeatedly 'pattern[s] of self-undoing' (Eagleton 2005, 195, 197). This *just is* history: an ineluctable, violent force, distorting and deforming any placid surface of the present, in the present, thereby making it impossible to reflect or represent ourselves with any calm assurance; impossible, that is, if we are not to engage in fictions that disingenuously deny the presence of the past. In this aletheic rupture that marks Hardy's writing, there is a sign that Hardy anticipates a certain modernist interest in mark, sign, fragment, ruin, and the role of memory in the subjective generation of narrative flux between past and present.

VII. CULTURAL CONFRONTATIONS

Of course, that Hardy has been misread, poorly read, or not read at all, is suggestive of the estranging forces of historicity, historicality and anachronism within and on the form of English literature, so that certain readers remain blind to the codes and signs of their own cultures. That this *is* effected has, no doubt, to do with the belief that one can, in controlling the reception of the past, exorcise the more wayward phantoms from one's present. An element of critical negativity can be put down to contemporary cultural mores in

the face of Hardy's, at the time, frank exploration of desire and sexual relations. For example, *A Laodicean* was criticized in the *World* magazine for what was taken to be the novel's 'carnal suggestiveness' (Anon., 1882, 18). During editorial consideration of *The Woodlanders* at the time of serial publication, the final sentence ending Volume II, Chapter IV, was excised on the grounds that it was too sexually explicit. The scene leading up to this moment involves Edred Fitzpiers, the young doctor living near the village of Little Hintock, and Suke Damson. The night is that of Midsummer's Eve, a particular folk ritual concerning the divination of future husbands having taken place in which Suke and other young women from the village engage. Running through the woods, Suke is chased by Fitzpiers. Catching her, he begins to kiss her and, 'they sank down on the next hay-cock' (*W* II.IV.150). The sentence censored from the serial provides the punctuation to this nocturnal scene: 'It was daybreak before Fitzpiers and Suke Damson re-entered Little Hintock' (*W* II.IV.150).

There are many more such examples of moral censorship throughout Hardy's career as a novelist, being a result of both editorial intervention and negative critical reception after publication. Such misreading of Hardy's works in his lifetime, as injurious as they were to Hardy personally, is commonplace enough. Yet, there was that other aesthetic response to form and language, diction and construction, and the perception that Hardy was straining after originality or effect, thereby allowing his rhetoric to get in the way of telling the story. Contemporary reviews of *The Return of the Native* make just such assertions. *The Athenaeum* compared Hardy with 'a person who has a keen eye for the picturesque without having learnt to draw'. Furthermore, his observation was 'disfigured at times by forced allusions and images'. Eustacia Vye is singled out for critical opprobrium, belonging 'to the class of which Madame Bovary is the type' (*The Athenaeum*, 23 November 1878). This comparison with Flaubert is instructive, and *The Athenaeum* is not alone (presumably) in its cultural xenophobia. Going on to remark that 'English opinion' does not allow for the Bovary 'type' in the English novel, it anticipates a comment on the part of another reviewer, W. E. Henley, in *The Academy* a week later, who summarizes *The Return of the Native* as 'all very cruel, and very mournful, and very French' (having already spoken of Hardy's work as being contaminated by 'Hugoesque ... insincerity'). *The Saturday Review* (4 January 1879) also commented on the writers of the younger generation who 'scandalize traditional opinions'. Hardy is typical of this 'scandalous' behaviour in using 'eccentric forms of expression'

along with 'similes and metaphors [that] are often strained and far-fetched', while the story 'strikes us as intensely artificial'. 'We are in England all the time', continues the offended reviewer, 'but in a world of which we seem to be absolutely ignorant'. This might just be the point for Hardy.

Criticizing the sexual frankness or openness of a Hardy novel is, inevitably, only the most obvious way of signalling an inability to read what is taking place, as well as staging a resistance to and avoidance of reading. It is a sign of being unseated from what one assumes as one's habitual cultural positions. What is telling from the foregoing criticisms of *The Return of the Native* is the native anxiety in the face of identities that trouble Englishness in its supposedly assured stability. Sexuality taken too far is foreign, distasteful. The taking-place of domestic sexuality is an historical threat that serves to figure the threat of a foreign otherness erupting in one's own national home. If the rural is a site of fecundity, this in the 1870s is submerged within an economy of reproduction subservient to the production of foodstuff. Under the sign of an economic production, all reproduction in excess of such consumerist (or less commonly theological) narratives is radically disorientating. A second point, if we take the rural as either largely forgotten, or depoliticized and dehistoricized through the nostalgic and utopian idealization of Morris, Arnold, Tennyson and others, is that sexuality rehistoricizes and repoliticizes the rural.

Moreover, sexuality threatens the implicit Englishness of the novel as form and idea. It traces a return of the repressed, an irrepressible difference that affirms itself. Inasmuch as the reviews feel identity to be threatened, this threat is perceived as not only foreign, though. Hardy's very Anglo-Saxon 'heart of darkness' is much closer to home. The very ontology of Englishness is in crisis, perceiving itself however indirectly as under threat in these reviews, as already noted. For Hardy is repeatedly criticized for the strangeness of his domestic, yet not-quite-English rural inhabitants. The 'language of his peasants may be Elizabethan', remarks *The Athenaeum*, 'but it can hardly be Victorian' (23 November 1878). Having introduced the possibility of linguistic anachronism returning from some past to strike at modern identity, the review then goes on to remark on the artificial pitch of the dialogue: '[t]hese people all speak in a manner suggestive of high cultivation, and some of them intrigue almost like dwellers in Mayfair, while they live on nearly equal terms with the furze-cutting rustics'. Class and location (dwellers in Mayfair and furze-cutting rustics, city and country) are inextricably traced here, in a psychic topography of English selfhood and alterity. Critique of

dialogue makes the connection and, on Hardy's part, the 'confusion' of form and genre, clear between the ontologies of cultural and literary identity, signalling in this manner the site from which it is issued. It is as if Hardy contaminates the novel in the last decades. Equally, it is as if criticism issued from the urban centre of nation and empire, the capital, stages in encrypted form the trauma of Englishness in its secret confession that an older, rural England, having been sacrificed to modernity, to urban-centred capitalist modes of production, can neither be remembered as an other to the modern nor re-imagined as vital, surviving.

Identity is also troubled in the confusion of locations from which language appears to come, and to which it may be assigned, as the implicit metropolitan incomprehension of rural subjectivities seems to suggest. This is echoed in *The Saturday Review*. Commenting on the 'unreal and unlifelike' names of Hardy's characters, the reviewer surmises that 'we doubt whether nine out of ten of them are to be met with in the pages of the London Directory. It is true that they may possibly be local for all we know to the contrary'. *For all we know.* Hardy's rural England is so foreign, so untimely, so other than the world as it is apprehended by metropolitan and urban critics in the 1870s and 1880s that it baffles comprehension even as it assaults the supposed certainties of self from which location reading takes place. As the *Times* put it of *The Return of the Native* (5 December 1878), 'we are transported ... we feel rather *abroad* here, and can scarcely get up a satisfactory interest in people whose history and habits are so entirely *foreign* to our own' (emphases added).

The strange energy of Hardy's writing is such that it not only challenges critical mastery, but disturbs the critic to a degree that estranges the possibility of reading. More than this, though, the *Times'* commentary encapsulates a sense that the rural English are perceived as more wholly other than any more obviously 'foreign' culture. It is this strangeness of an English alterity tinged with anachronistic defamiliarization and, with that, the troubling depth of historical and temporal resonance, lost to the traumatic experience of modernity within Hardy's narratives of the English other, which amounts to an assault on Victorian self-reading from within the domestic space of literature. It is not that the rural English are simply at a remove geographically and therefore definable according to a set of paradigmatic models capable of incorporating difference within the self-same. Theirs is an otherness that will admit of no recuperation, and which, reciprocally, returns in

Hardy's fiction to usurp the calm assurance of self-reading seeking a reflection or inflection of the self. Hardy's fiction presents us with both a return of the repressed, a revenant reiteration of the forgotten, and additionally, as the many lost signs of pagan and folkloric alterity and archaic historicity attest, *the return(s) of the native*.

Pausing to reflect for a moment, a strong reading of the title in the manner just implied is justified, if only because this other reading indicates that which, arguably *in* the title, is precisely that which contemporary reviewers miss. For, while on the one hand the title may be read as signifying Clym Yeobright's return – he is after all the 'native' of Egdon Heath who returns to his home only to find it unhomely, himself a haunting stranger estranged from the familiar – on the other hand, the strong reading is there to be invented. In every being, however modern, there are always the anachronistic signs of some other, of something 'native'. If we pursue the etymology of *native*, we find buried beneath the more modern sense of someone belonging to a particular country, the older sense, equivalent to the Anglo-Norman *naïf*, signifying someone born in a state of bondage or serfdom. There is, in the resonance of this older sense, the signification of a mark made on someone, a legal inscription that ties someone to a place.

In the strong reading of Hardy's title, it is this invisible *trait*, the sign of being bound that 'returns' to the modern subject, as a revenant call of the other, and with that the demands of one's native historicity as the imprimatur, a counter-signature of one's being, however modern one believes oneself to be. There is that which is hetero-affective within being; the *native* returns in and to Clym, despite his cosmopolitan experience. While on the surface, the 'call' is a conscious one to which Clym responds, and so returns, my strong reading argues for this as an unconscious demand that Hardy reads at work everywhere in cultural identity. From such a micrological reading to the larger issues at stake, we return to the more general tension noted above. So disquieting is this confrontation that its effects are displaced in the act of reading onto literary form, or, it is arguable, the very ontology of the literary itself. Criticizing narrative on the grounds of form, the excess of its modes of articulation, and an inability or refusal to perceive that excess, exaggeration, and formal play may just be taking place for reasons beyond the comprehension of the reviewer, hints at a problem not with the identity of the novel but with those broader cultural and historical identities assumed by the critic.

VIII. DENSITIES & DETERRITORIALIZATION

Hardy's novels' intricacy and density, their patterns of doubling, 'and at times tripling and quadrupling', which structure the text and complicate the act of reading, thereby and in the process 'forming themselves into a dense web' (Hardy, ed. Wilson 1997, xxviii), result in 'the construction of ... narrative, [where] repetition and circularity are ... prominent features'. There emerges in Hardy, furthermore, 'a polyphony of different, even contrasting [narrative] voices' (Hardy, ed. Page 1997, 23). On the one hand, engaging in more than merely formal patterning, such narrative experiment results in the rejection of 'absolutist notions of identity' (Hardy, ed. Wilson 1997, 24) and a proto-modernist exploration of the fragmentation of the self. On the other hand, Hardy's structural networks perform a 'recovery of the past both spatially and temporally' (Hardy, ed. Page 1997, 27). Conventionally read by turns in the past as 'difficulty', 'thematic ambiguity' or 'stylistic awkwardness', Hardy's narrative, rhetorical and poetic play weaves matrices out of which is engendered and enacted anamnesiac recovery and a means to assemble alternative English identities, albeit identities in ruins. When one contemporary reviewer observed, '[Hardy] is most ingenious in devising problems, and bringing his people into situations of a complicated nature' (Anon, in Page 1997, 404), he was noting, albeit inadvertently a distortion of realist representation in order that the signs of the past might be found to trace themselves through the screen of the present. Moreover, Hardy's interlacing of countless aspects and facets that go to comprise his narratives finds its echoes in both the formal levels of the text and their archival and encrypted preservation of disparate, heterogeneous literary, cultural and historical traces. Every Hardy text, it might be said, offers a singular archaeological formation, albeit one offering no possibility of the location of an origin for its particular form. (It might therefore be better perceived as archival rather than archaeological.) Hardy's text displays repeatedly a rhizomic ingenuity, through a complex of endless interdependencies that are unavailable to any architectonic prioritization or ontological ordering. The patterns of tension and resistance to easy comprehension suggest that the more we seek a single narrative thread, the more we come to realize how each thread is interwoven into, shot through by, and generative of countless others.

To begin to glimpse the density of such generational weaving, consider another title, *The Mayor of Casterbridge*. Though an obvious point, it is a necessary to observe that the novel is *not* entitled

Michael Henchard. Clearly the title addresses immediately, even as it presents, a certain identity, which is public, official, and therefore impersonal; naming an office, it is constructed, historical, political, social. The title names and gives form to a social position, a structure within which any appropriate subject may be located, and thereby endowed with limited agency. Naming public office and specular role, the mayoral post is a locus of civil organization and power, to be filled by successive individuals. Henchard is merely a privileged agent of an already existing historical and cultural formation, occupying the position after countless others. Thus the title names simultaneously a social, a communal structuration, and a position which provides evidence of but one temporal thread, a continuum or stitch in the social and temporal weave of Casterbridge itself. The title is thus a site of contesting, and contested ideological and historical multiplicities, wherein are encoded iterable struggles.

Such staging of multiplicity reveals at the simplest level the intricacies of Hardy's text. What holds for the title is true also of the text in general. Indirectly, we can also understand, if not be in agreement with the reasons for, that critical desire to trace a single structure or ontology and thereby control the flows that inform, enunciate, and, it has to be said, *deform* the heterogeneous whole. A haunting excess irreducible to the very site from which such flows are glimpsed is read, as reading disrupts order and form. Yet, despite the complexities, there has existed a 'recurrent critical tendency' (Hardy, ed. Wilson 1997, xxv) to simplify textual relations. This act of simplification has demonstrated a propensity to reduce Hardy's significance as a novelist. Resisting such reductiveness, Terry Eagleton points to what we might describe as the 'problem of Thomas Hardy', the novelist's 'blunt disregard for formal consistency, ... his readiness to articulate form upon form – to mingle realist narration, classical tragedy, folk-fable, melodrama, "philosophical" discourse, social commentary' (1981, 126). This attempted taxonomy at once points to the difficulty that criticism, grounded on formalist and aesthetic criteria, has had in making Hardy conform to a single model.

At the same time, though, Hardy's text resists critical acts of recuperation precisely because of its discursive heterogeneity, and is understandable as an 'always protean *oeuvre*' (Page 1998, 75). In its 'blunt disregard for formal consistency, ...' is itself the material registration of historicity on the text through its formal openness to heterogeneity and resistance to ontological stabilization, as well as being a response to particular historical and cultural conditions. This response is double: on the one hand, it has to do with the history of the novel, and the forms it takes in its development

over the previous two centuries. Simultaneously and on the other hand, formal discursive, epistemological and ontological play (misread as 'fault' or 'failure') signals an equally material response to broader histories, beyond those of the novel, having to do with the mediation of cultural identity, the inheritance of the past, and a sense of destabilized, perhaps undecidable Englishness in Hardy's historical moment as a novelist.

IX. WHO'S AFRAID OF THOMAS HARDY?

In conclusion, I want to turn to the matter of anxiety. Anxiety is undeniably significant, whether it is found in Hardy's texts or as an implicit motivating force in much of the critical history of Hardy's reception. In her study of gender, subjectivity and corporeality, Marjorie Garson extends the critique of conventional critical methodology, suggesting that '"Hardy", the realist novelist of "character and environment", is himself a construction', a construction which has led to a distorted reading of the novels (Garson 1991, 1n.2). Connecting this misreading to anxiety, she argues that '[m]any of the instabilities, contradictions, and grotesqueries in the fiction ... make considerable sense' when the novels are read as the exploration and expression of a 'somatic' anxiety about the dissolution of bodily identity (Garson 1991, 1). This can be argued to be the case whether the body is the human body, on which Garson focuses, or the figurative 'bodies' of buildings, the structures of towns, or the very landscape, perhaps even the 'body' of the novel itself. Whichever we address, 'Hardy's fiction expresses certain anxieties about wholeness ... in ways which are fairly consistent, though never simple or predictable' (Garson 1991, 3). The 'problem' of Hardy is therefore not primarily aesthetic. Rather, the question concerns the ways in which the materiality of the letter can disturb, leading one to question the epistemological grounds of representation.

Take ghosts, for example – and phantoms, spectres, spooks, revenants, apparitions, spirits, and every other 'species' of manifestation. Neither there nor not there, how are they to be read in Hardy's work? Are we to take them literally as phantasms, and if so, do they belong to the mind or to an external supernatural world? Is their alterity internal or external? Or both, crossing somatic, material, and psychic boundaries, returning unbidden, and always hovering in waiting, waiting to return to remind us that memory, one aspect of one's being, is a haunted location? Memory, that which we think of as most personally ours, is nothing other than

this haunted house. I exist therefore I am haunted. Other questions obtrude, in the manner of unwelcome spirits: are we to take the ghosts in Hardy's texts literally or metaphorically, as prosopopoeic forms or figures of analogy (or all of the above?) Are we to see the work of haunting, conversely, in the interruption of the historical remnant? When, in a poem from *Poems of the Past and Present*, 'The Mother Mourns' (*CP* 111–4), the narrator, recollects, how when

> I fared Yell'ham-Firs way ... dimly [there]
> Came wheeling around me
> Those phantoms obscure and insistent
> That shadows unchain. (ll. 5–8)

The poem resists easy accommodation of its scene. The reader cannot say with any certainty what is taking place, initially. Place appears to conjure the phantoms from shadows. In this there is already a doubling, a slippage between the immaterial aspects of the material world, the possibility that place is haunted, and the not unreasonable sense that all effects of 'mid-autumn' wind and shadow merely serve to produce an uncanny experience for the superstitious mind. From this point, however, the poem stages a wholly unnatural voice; that of the title's mourning Mother: Nature. In 'aërie accents, / With dirge-like refrain', Nature bemoans how, having created human consciousness, she finds such consciousness distinctly 'unnatural'. In other words, humans exist inauthentically and have caused destruction, not being mindful of the true nature of dwelling. Nature is thus revealed as a phantom of sorts, but the anxiety of the 'mother's' complaint remains undecidable as to its origin or source. By the conclusion of the poem we are no closer to understanding whether this voice is that of the first narrator, 'externalized' as anthropomorphized Mother Nature, or whether there is a supernatural source for the voice; whether, in fact, the modern narrator has found himself somehow plunged into an atavistic pantheist universe. The strangeness of the poem does not desist, and there is no easy recuperation that reading can effect. In short, though, this destabilizing force is always at work in Hardy's writing, and hence the anxieties that plague his text and its reception.

Through addressing different, yet interrelated strands of the manifestation of anxiety in Hardy, criticism acknowledges Hardy's ability 'to sustain ... a multiplicity of causality' (Gatrell 1993, 3). Such multiplicity bespeaks submerged, 'partly concealed patterns'. Revealing submerged patterns suggests 'dangerous subversions of

mode and ideology ... which have been critically suppressed in favour of ... the production of an 'acceptable' Hardy' (Fisher 1992, 1). However, if Hardy is never 'single-minded or wholly consistent', this only serves to make 'the experience of reading his fiction both rich and contradictory' (Gatrell 1993, 6). There is, then, an aporetic experience in reading Hardy, an encounter with the undecidable, and a frankly incompatible or impossible confrontation of epistemologies that serve to produce the possibility of the impossible as the work of literature itself, which goes beyond notions of the 'contradictory'. Such experience is produced, if at all, in a reading that recognizes the relationship in Hardy's writing between the materiality of the event, the material force of vision, the mediating, haunting power of memory, and, weaving between these, that spectral insistence.

All such forces have little to do with realism and the common perception of the constitution of nineteenth-century or Victorian fictional modes. Hardy's own lack of interest in the constraints of mere realism stems from his rejection of 'realism' as art. Art should 'disproportion' the real in figuring, or rather disfiguring, 'distorting, throwing out of proportion ... [the representation of] realities, to show more clearly the features that matter in those realities' (*LTH* 229). What is empirically observable takes second place for Hardy to that higher, visionary mode of perception in the mind's eye: 'the seer should watch [one] pattern among general things which his idiosyncrasy moves him to observe ... the result is no photograph, but purely the product of the writer's own mind' (*LTH* 153). What the mind's eye is capable of decoding from the merely real or material is simultaneously a matter of reception *and* deciphering. Moreover, it is not a question merely of opening oneself to hidden patterns but also to the otherwise invisible echoes of the past, which vision distorts and disproportions the present of the gaze even as it opens the self to the arrival of some phantasmic arrival or, more accurately, the trace of an historical other, as we shall see. Hardy's novels speak not so much from a single, identifiable voice as from some form of phantom narrating machine capable of translating into narrative or poetic form site, topography, trace, history, and collective memory. Acknowledging this, if the only 'true', uncontested detail in the doxa surrounding Hardy's literary output and its biographical contexts is that Hardy is an 'author', then Hardy, it might be said, remains to be read; 'some other's accent' remains to be heard, to be received, and answered.

1

Apprehension, Suspension, Abstention: *Desperate Remedies* (1871)

I. HARDY'S PERFORMATIVE TEXT

Desperate Remedies, Hardy's first novel, is typically regarded as an apprentice work, as derivative. It is worthy of close reading, however, because it will teach us how to read Hardy if you pay close enough attention, and if your reading is directed especially to the unique manner in which it arrives as a series of epistemologically disconcerting textual events. *Desperate Remedies* is, in effect, a forceful, if crude, elaboration of transformations in the modern world brought about in perception, and how these mediate, and are mediated in turn by, narrative. At first glance, the novel appears to inhabit the sensation genre. On the surface it seems a merely imitative narration. Moreover, a surface reading might suggest that this is not really what Hardy does. At least, it does so if one reads the novel as if it were readable, and therefore capable of being subsumed, within the totality of Hardy's fiction. To put this differently, there is too great a readiness not to read and to ignore the singularity of *Desperate Remedies*. Such an avoidance of reading falls into a programmed assessment, however, which does not recognize Hardy's experiment with the 'machine', that narrative technic we know as the novel, which exposes the merely mechanical nature of much fiction. Even though Hardy draws on the sensational novel, which is 'already a subversive form, bringing the licensed margins of the gothic into daily life' (Goode 1988, 11), there is much that takes place in Hardy's 'parasitical' inhabitation of conventional

form. It haunts as much as it inhabits the genre in question, and in doing so subverts subversion, illuminating in the process through its phantasmal habitation the haunted condition of modernity.

Moreover, the parasite actively transforms the host; for Hardy's writing is marked by a 'formal break which [his] entry into the writing trade inaugurates' (Goode 1988, 11). *Desperate Remedies* announces this rupture in many ways, not least in the fact that it plays on its fictional status and its place in nineteenth-century fiction quite monstrously, quite knowingly. It disturbs, deforms, and destroys relentlessly any possible claim for organic unity in narrative, not simply that narrative which would promote a notion such as Hardyean themes, but also, internally, the very narrative structure of *Desperate Remedies* itself. It does so in a fashion that will not quite be resolved according to readings that attempt to domesticate its monstrosity according to the rules of pastiche or, for that matter, in gestures that seek to account for any apparent awkwardness or roughness of 'style' or 'composition' with reference to *Desperate Remedies*' status as a first or early work. What is read in aesthetic or organic terms is a misreading, inasmuch as there is little if any understanding that Hardy is 'already in the process of transforming narrative' (Goode 1988, 11).

Subversion of genre operates in *Desperate Remedies* in a number of ways. It takes place not least through the advertising and knowing foregrounding of the novel's narrative temporality, its arbitrary deployment and its temporal frames, the arbitrary condition of narrative motion, and a self-conscious revelation of the limits of mimetic and realist representation. In anticipation of many of his later more subtly 'haunted' or 'contaminated' texts, Hardy's first novel presents the reader with certain experiments both in fiction and the very language of representation, including significant reorientations and reformations of narrative handling of conventional motifs, themes, figures and plots, in addition to those other aspects of textual practice already mentioned.

One significant effect of such play or experiment is the production of narrative as having performative rather than merely constative powers, of which there will be more to be said. Additionally, there are moments when Hardy is either happy to express or else resigned to demonstrating the limits of narrative representation, and so, with that, the limits of fiction, especially concerning the 'true' – that is to say psychological and ontological – presentation of the subject as opposed to mere, mimetically faithful outward sketching of physical appearance. This he justifies through acknowledging a psychological associationism, which functions despite the absence

of any form of similarity or resemblance, the very conditions on which realist fiction[1] depends. 'Emotions', Hardy reflects, in the abstract and in present tense, itself a rhetorical ploy often used to present an apostrophe or instant of frame-breaking parabasis to the reader, 'will attach themselves to scenes that are simultaneous – however foreign in essence these scenes may be – as chemical waters will crystallize on twigs and wires' (*DR* I.I.15). This commentary, strangely dispassionate given that its context is the violent death of an architect through the fall from a church spire witnessed by his daughter, recognizes how trauma takes place, long before Freud theorizes the same. Thus it is, as a result, and at any subsequent time that 'sunlight streaming in shaft-like lines' brought 'mental agony' (*DR* I.I.15) to mind for the heroine of *Desperate Remedies*, Cytherea Graye, more than any other medium or phenomenon. Clearly, there is no direct mimetic correlation between shafts of sunlight and the figure of an architect plunging to his death. The association is phantasmic and analogical, for which Hardy owes much to Locke and Schopenhauer, amongst others like them. Hardy traces the connection between the inner and outer world through the indirection of analogy and the association of a 'relation without relation' that the mind perceives and memory enacts, in iterable fashion. It is as if Hardy wants to inform us of the ways in which literary narrative, its figures and structures, may be comprehended as working and not working. Representation is insufficient to the task of conjuring feeling, because it cannot show the inner workings of the subject. However, through the play of analogy literature can sidestep this aporetic experience for the reader to make the reader feel in a manner that, not necessarily traumatic, is nevertheless and by analogy similar in its mechanics to the subject's emotional response.

Literary form is in its most heightened or intensified manifestations when it bypasses the logic and economy of constative depiction in order to perform the sensation or effect it is describing, which performance takes place in the reader's registration of the same. Realist representation pretends to order, design and appropriate unity in design; there is the illusion of adequacy and efficacy in representation, which informs realist art. However, for Hardy such adequacy is found wanting when it comes to the presentation of subjectivity. Take Hardy's introduction to Cytherea Graye as an example:

> Indeed, motion was her speciality, whether shown on its most extended scale of bodily progression, or minutely, as in the uplifting of her eyelids, the bending of her fingers, the pouting of her lip. The carriage

of her head – motion within motion – a glide upon a glide – was as delicate as that of a magnetic needle. And this flexibility and elasticity had never been taught her by rule, nor even been acquired by observation, but, *nullo cultu*, had naturally developed itself with her years . . . At mixed Christmas parties, when she numbered but twelve or thirteen years, and was heartily despised on that account by lads who deemed themselves men, her apt lightness in the dance covered this incompleteness in her womanhood, and compelled the self-same youths in spite of resolutions to seize upon her childish figure as a partner whom they could not afford to contemn. And in later years, when the instincts of her sex had shown her this point as the best and rarest feature in her *external self*, she was not found wanting in attention to the cultivation of finish in its details.

Her hair rested gaily upon her shoulders in curls and was of a shining corn yellow in the high lights, deepening to a definite nut-brown as each curl wound round into the shade. She had eyes of a sapphire hue, though rather darker than the gem ordinarily appears; they possessed the affectionate and liquid sparkle of loyalty and good faith as distinguishable from that harder brightness which seems to express faithfulness only to the object confronting them.

But to attempt to gain a view of her . . . from a measured category, is as difficult as to appreciate the effect of a landscape by exploring it at night with a lantern – or of a full chord of music by piping the notes in succession. (*DR* I.I.12–13; emphasis added)

Like his subject, Hardy is not found wanting in attention to the cultivation of finish in the details. Indeed, there are so many details that, arguably, Cytherea is obscured as a 'whole'. However, such is the nature of a performative literary act: instead of merely describing, it 'does' the very thing it purports to represent – it performs the 'attention to the cultivation of finish in the details', yet without giving us a picture. The problem, if there is one, is not in Hardy's literary abilities. Nor does it reside in the subject, but instead in the very mode of representation, as that mimetic mode is assumed in realist terms to be adequate. The *external self* is all very well, and detail presents us with a picture, after a fashion. There is hair in curls, with corn coloured highlights, deepening to a nut-brown. The colour and light in the eyes is expressive of personality traits, moreover.

As to age, this is more problematic. Cytherea's 'lightness' in dance occludes what Hardy calls her womanly incompletion, suggesting that her motion is at odds with her physical age, and that this is as a result of that attention to detail which is also not typically that of someone twelve or thirteen years of age. It is as if Cytherea's is marked by a *contretemps*, that she is not of her time or 'on time', if I can put it like that, or that she in some manner appearance and

self are not synchronous. Such questions only anticipate the last paragraph, in which, having gone to such great lengths attempting to describe the fewest of details, Hardy admits that such representation will not do. Perception of the material circumstances will not give the reader access to the truth of Cytherea. Cytherea's outer form is approximated by motion and the play of light and shade. In short, her 'image' is produced as an effect of optical science, apprehended kinetic energy, and the physics of light, as far as the pen can capture this. With the reader's perception in mind, Hardy's text performs, therefore, to come back to the matter of the performative. It seeks to have language not merely describe but 'do' things. Representation is enacted for the reader, as if the reader were the one standing in the place which narrative appears to open to him or her.

However, all one can see is that one cannot 'see' Cytherea. She is irreducible to external traits, and the analogy of landscape is telling in the light of much of Hardy's later fictional and poetic attention to the idea of Wessex and all such historical or ghostly remains that such a name can be made to evoke. Such a narrative enactment becomes, in the event, indissociable from phenomenological translation. I read, I see, as does the character or narrator, over whose shoulder I am looking. I thus am put in the position of having to interpret, to be active in the deciphering of codes, whilst at the same time being confronted by the narrator's confession of, if not a personal failure, then at least the failure of the medium. That the analogy is necessary *and* incapable of being sustained – the landscape by lantern becomes a musical chord given in arpeggiated form – suggests a potentially endless series of substitutions. Everything is in the perception, but perception is partial, limited by the very powers it is capable of marshalling. The apprehended phenomena of another's being are incapable of being figured, except through the work of indirect literary devices, which substitute material and externalized tropes as ciphers of being. In effect, Hardy is subverting the efficacy of fiction, its modes and mastering or controlling devices, from the outset.

II. INSIGHT AND ILLUMINATION

To claim Hardy as a 'phenomenological' novelist, as I am implicitly doing, is not new (see Johnson [1970] and Miller [1970]). What is particularly interesting about such a perspective, though, is the extent to which Hardy can be read as drawing into his constitution of performative narrative modes matters of historicity,

identity, an ethics of memory, and the relation between the materiality of representational construction and the phenomenological involvement in the shaping of representation. Regarding Hardy's oeuvre, in most if not all of the novels' evident apprehension of the materiality and historicity of identity, and their exploration of being, subjectivity, and the temporal conditions of selfhood, they resist the seemingly organic unity required of conventional realist representation. With experiment comes knowledge that is simultaneously insight into the nature of existence. In their repeated, nuanced manifestation of an appreciation of the importance of personal memory and cultural anamnesis as an ineluctable ethical dimension to any narrative's responsibility to the past, the novels leave open a wound in the narrative representation of otherwise enclosed historical moments, to indicate how knowledge is always indelibly transformative.

Moreover, in Hardy's insistent interest in matters of the visible and invisible, perspective and lines of sight (what one can see of Cytherea, what remains hidden, how sunlight illuminates the traumatic process, whilst acting as the trope for the work of memory), one witnesses Hardy's struggle to suspend mere narrative representation in the implication of the reader in the event being represented through the time of reading, a temporality exceeding the moment described. With regard to the work of the narrative eye and the role of memory in the various forms of textual transmission and transport that arrive in Hardy's narratives often to interrupt them, we find the suspension of narrative movement, through a formal interruption of narrative that inevitably involves a distortion of perception. To return to the introduction of Cytherea, everything is motion, detail, substitution and impossibility. That Hardy does experiment with narrative modes of representation can hardly be overstated. Through such experiments there is readable a self-reflexive attentiveness to the epistemology of aesthetic perception and its subsequent phenomenal inscription.

The consideration of aesthetic perception in Hardy is not an end in itself. One is not presented with a mode of self-conscious reflection on art for art's sake. Instead, we read an author who questions the very means by which being is caused to reflect on its self-conscious location in a material and historical world. If 'the eye, the seeing subject, is antecedent to and formative of the I, or the speaking subject', as Judith Wittenberg remarks in an essay on Hardy's early novels of *Desperate Remedies* and *A Pair of Blue Eyes* (1983, 151–64), then that which strikes the eye with a pre-phenomenal immediacy, must, in the wake of that moment of revelation, translate what has been

seen. To this I would add, what goes for the eye, holds true also for the work of memory, which taken as a phantasmic camera or recorder, releases in Hardy's fiction at heightened moments of emotional and conscious awareness an image or memory, that interrupts the purely present instant and suspends character or occasionally reader and narration of principal acts.

The following moment in *Desperate Remedies* illuminates the observations just made:

> The direct blaze of the afternoon sun, partly refracted through the crimson curtains of the window, and heightened by reflections from the crimson-flock paper which covered the walls, and a carpet on the floor of the same tint, shone with a burning glow round the form of a lady standing close to Cytherea's front with the door in her hand. The stranger appeared to the maiden's eyes – fresh from the blue gloom, and assisted by an imagination fresh from nature – like a tall black figure standing in the midst of fire. It was the figure of a finely-built woman, of spare though not angular proportions. (*DR* I.IV.56)

As before, Hardy presents the reader with a performative event rather than a descriptive representation; or, more precisely, the performative is within description, and illuminates this in a such a manner that, once we attend, or are receptive, to the performative, we cannot return to a naive reading of the passage as 'heightened' or exaggerated representation. For what strikes the reader's eye is analogous with that which strikes Cytherea's: for both, though with that difference that is their respective perspectival positions, all that one can see is light, the direct blaze. We read and so see the form of a lady, a stranger, a tall black figure, as this appears 'to the maiden's eyes', and, as a result of that refraction through the crimson curtains, apparently in the midst of fire. Language here enacts the occlusion of more precise human detail through attention to light. In this, it illuminates how illumination can both define and obscure, can shed light and blind, albeit partially. What strikes the eye is, indeed, striking, whether the eye is that of Cytherea or the reader, but what the literary language also bears in it is the revelation – the illumination – of how it achieves its effects, for this is a reflective commentary on the work of literary language and its visionary force.

Thus, as the eye registers the effect of the visual on the mind, as if it were a wax tablet on which is left an impression before the mind can interpret the signal into something more meaningful, so Hardy's text interprets this pre-phenomenal registration in a phenomenal sleight of hand. As Judith Wittenberg observes: 'This

precept is relevant to Hardy's fiction, which linguistically enunciates the way in which knowledge is acquired and in which the I-world dialogue is carried on by means that are predominantly specular' (1983, 152). Hardy's process thus includes a recognition that all 'knowledge', that is to say all articulation of the world unveiled to the eye, is always belated. Moreover, as the detail of any moment of focalization in Hardy makes explicit, the eye, whether that of the character or the reader, is only a medium, a device for connecting between word and world. And the word, though arriving belatedly, takes place as a translation, which paradoxically, once placed on the page, is always temporally *before* the world, after which it seeks in effect to catch up with. There is, then, a disjunction, both spatial and temporal, in Hardy's constitution of the modern subject's powers of perception. This rupture between self-conscious location and the erstwhile belief in the immediacy of empirical experience is not to be closed up. Correspondence is displaced in the process of the subject's becoming aware that it is the work of what Jacques Derrida calls *différance* that makes possible the illusion of immediacy and presence. Beginning with the very idea of mimetic and representational framing and control, Hardy ruptures the frame within which representation is staged as visual form, and so invites the reader to become aware of the motions of the past not as distant representation but as flows and forces still reaching out, determining our responses in any given present.

To the end that Hardy wants to make the reader aware of one's mediating consciousness and mediated subjectivity, he suspends narrative movement in favour of painstakingly detailed and constructed instances of representation. Because of the time representation takes to stage, or due to the heightened attention to light, shade, colour, line, form, and so on, representation disorders realist time. What is graspable by the eye in a few seconds becomes, on the page, a matter of up to several minutes' reflection. For the moment, though, the point is that for Hardy's characters, or certain prominent protagonists at least, the world is no longer 'natural', whether or not they apprehend this. For the reader a suspension, or what Bruce Johnson, following Husserl, terms 'abstention' (1983, 2) is staged in the flow of narrative, in order to heighten the apprehension of apprehension, or to illuminate the fact that every perspective is always in some manner a perspective on perspective; the narrator frequently invites us to reflect on the fact that we are being shown a character in the act of looking and apprehending, of seeing but also of coming to consciousness about some event, thing or phenomena. More than this, the 'narrator' is also constructed as a perspectival form, so

that we in turn are invited to consider how we are being positioned through the act of visualization in writing and reading.

Consider what happens in the following example. When Cytherea stands before a particular landscape, she not only sees the scene in general but; her perception by-passes conscious, detached empirical appreciation as she loses herself and is lost in becoming the ocular medium or device for the reader's apperception of a strikingly *material* vision:

> She turned her face landward and strained her eyes to discern, if possible, some sign of Owen's return. Nothing was visible save the strikingly brilliant, still landscape. The wide concave which lay at the back of the hill in this direction was blazing with the western light, adding an orange tint to the vivid purple of the heather, now at the very climax of bloom, and free from the slightest touch of the invidious brown that so soon creeps into its shades. The light so intensified the colours that they seemed to stand above the surface of the earth and float in mid-air like an exhalation of red. In the minor valleys, between the hillocks and ridges which diversified the contour of the basin, but did not disturb its general sweep, she marked brakes of tall, heavy-stemmed ferns, five or six feet high, in a brilliant light-green dress – a broad riband of them with the path in their midst winding like a stream along the little ravine that reached to the foot of the hill, and delivered up the path to its grassy area. Among the ferns grew holly bushes deeper in tint than any shadow about them, whilst the whole surface of the scene was dimpled with small conical pits, and here and there were round ponds, now dry, and half overgrown with rushes. (*DR* I.II.29–30)

In effect, narrative motion is suspended. Apprehension is intensified through the event of abstention as the reader, seeing through Cytherea's eyes, discerns details of the coastline in so detailed a manner as to be impossibly proximate. The eye is 'strained', to use Hardy's word, but we see with such precision that it is *as if* we were there. Not simply in the boat, but with an impossible closeness, in that illuminated intensification that breaks apart the landscape as a whole, producing it as a series of spectral registrations that are 'strikingly brilliant'. Light and colour consume the subject here, so that in essence it is as if there were no subject, no mediation at all, merely an optical intensity verging on abstraction. Colour appears separated from form 'like an exhalation of red', and we register orange, purple and green, a vivid but restricted palette. How red can be an exhalation remains unanswered, but that is unimportant in this synesthesic event. Simultaneously, and complementary to Hardy's vibrant colouration, is a near abstract use of line and shape, striking the eye with equal force. Cones, dimples, rounds,

the verticals of the ferns, all are framed by the wide concave sweep which first impresses itself on the viewing subject. It is as if we read a sequence of brush marks, rather than mimetic prose sentences, in a sensuous apprehension that reveals how the 'aesthetic moment *is* that at which form reveals itself to be the clothing of an intuition (a true ingathering) of the world's order – its manifoldness, its belonging together in difference' (Clark 2001, 100). Hardy anticipates and oversteps impressionist modalities in order to illuminate for us how '[t]he relation of [literary] form and content is rooted in a relation of mind to world. The one relation analogizes the other. And the world', for Hardy at least, 'is unthinkable save as a texture and structure of phenomena, of sensate "experiences"' (Clark 2001, 101). Sensate experiences chained together within narrative form constitute Hardy's writing, thereby making available a transformation in our perception of the material and empirical world, providing we give attention to what takes place and do not read impatiently so as to hurry the narrative along.

III. THE DIVIDED SELF AND THE CONSTRUCTEDNESS OF TIME

Every Hardy novel involves moments of transmission, communication, and translation of one sort or another, and this is always a fraught process. This is illustrated in the very attempt to convey Cytherea's 'true nature' or the 'essence' of her character. Not every character has the same knowledge, and so not every communication communicates in the same way, if indeed at all. In this manner, Hardy produces a world composed of signs for which his subjects have no common access code, no 'universal translator', not even in their self-comprehension. What is at stake, then, for Hardy in his attempts to rework fiction and its function involves the very act of how one reads the world in the face of the constant possibility that communication is faulty. Additionally, inasmuch as the world can only be thought in Hardy as a texture and structure of phenomena, time is markedly perceived as an arbitrary construct, and the experience of its temporal motions is equally arbitrary in Hardy, as form and content are revealed once more as analogous to the relation of mind and world.

In *Desperate Remedies* Hardy makes us acutely aware of the constructedness of human time, and the ways in which perception of temporal movement fluctuates. The novel draws our attention to this in a particularly graphic manner, through the foregrounding of chronological and calendrical markers and divisions. Human

temporality therefore marks the times of narrative structure, through dates and times being given as chapter titles and sub-divisions. Such self-conscious artifice announces the times to which narrative draws our attention, the events in the world of the novel and the times of its characters' lives. Entering *Desperate Remedies*, we can harbour no illusion that we are any longer in the natural world. To this end, the tropes and effects of sensation fiction and related genres only serve to highlight artifice.

As just noted, Hardy calls narrative temporality and naive read-erly assumptions concerning narrative time into question through giving times, dates, hours as chapter and chapter sub-division titles. Temporality is thus merely a literary signpost, appearing to communicate but frustrating meaningful transmission beyond any 'factual' register. At any place in the text, one reads different expressions of time and duration, for example 'five to six, p.m.' (*DR* I.VIII.133), or 'from the third to the nineteenth of September' (*DR* I.VIII.115). The latter is a section of a chapter titled 'The Events of Eighteen Days' (*DR* I.VIII.115–43). Another chapter is titled 'The Events of Ten Months' (*DR* II.IV.216–40), with subheadings such as 'From the first to the twenty-seventh of August' (*DR* II.IV.226), while a third chapter covers just 'The Events of One Day' (*DR* II.V.240–80). This last chapter is broken up into various lengths, 'morning', 'noon', 'afternoon', but then there are smaller divisions yet, one section covering two and a half hours, yet another three hours and one given to the events of fifteen minutes, and titled 'A quarter past eight o'clock, p.m.' (*DR* II.V.270). Stepping from such examples to take a brief look at the contents of the novel, we find that chapter titles, such as they are, repeat themselves. There are four chapters entitled 'The Events of One Day' and two 'The Events of Eigh-teen Days'. Months, days, weeks, a night and a day, thirty years, and even three hours have their various chapters. Not one of the titles communicates to the reader any meaningful suggestion as to what each chapter or section might concern. A game is afoot, which demands we are aware of an intrusive and manipulative, appar-ently capricious mediator or *deus ex machina*. And what we are aware of, from the start, what is unveiled to us as the inaugural and iterable gambit, is the truth of fiction. Fiction involves us as if we were there, in the impossible scene. At the same time, however, it reminds us that while it takes us in (in whatever sense you choose to give that phrase), it maintains us in a passive location outside nar-rative action. We remain fiction's passive subjects, subject only to its capricious revelations, in whatever order or manner it chooses to make them.

In foregrounding narrative temporality in its multiple, differential moments, stretches and movements, Hardy displaces implicit assumptions and notions of stable presence, moment, or location. Additionally, he troubles our unthinking reliance on the novelist's power to make stable representation and the passage of time. In this manner he also foregrounds the experience of times, the times of reading constantly counterpoised against the times of action. The novel begins somewhat oddly with a recuperation of a past history, that of Ambrose Graye, and his thwarted plan to marry another Cytherea. The pages in question address thirty years (*DR* I.I.7-11), up to the moment when Graye eventually marries another, eight years after his disappointment, and has a daughter, whom he names Cytherea. In that the story, or what we might now call the 'backstory', of the previous generation is so starkly and perfunctorily presented, the 'remainder' of the novel is readable as an extended response and explanation. Moreover, it is as if the narrative constituting the majority of the novel is compelled to answer a telegraphic summons, required to do justice to the past. In this, it might be argued that the structure of the text is such that we are aware from the beginning how and to what extent the present is both generated and haunted by the past, or what Hardy in his first line calls 'the long and intricately inwrought chain of circumstances' (*DR* I.I.7).

Traversing a generation, then, but unable to leave that generation behind, the novel arrives at 'October the twelfth, 1863' (*DR* I.I.11), on which date Cytherea, 'now about eighteen' (*DR*, I.I12), is introduced. From this arrival, which is the locus of departure for the contemporary narrative, *Desperate Remedies* crosses almost another four years, until in the epilogue 'we are brought on to midsummer night, one thousand eight hundred and sixty-seven' (*DR*, 401), at which temporal and historical juncture, combining Christian calendar and pagan ritual, linear, dated progression and cyclical, seasonal recurrence, Hardy shifts the narrative from past to present tense. Such formal shifts, heterogeneous discursive and cultural in-mixings, arbitrary 'gear-changes' of register and rhythm, time and motion, are not simply formalist games for Hardy. They are integral to the ways in which Hardy seeks to disrupt the reader's relation to the text, whilst also striving to illuminate for the reader his or her modern, that is to say irregular or destabilized or disorientated subjectivity. Here is the perception or 'interruptive effect' (Weber 2008, 108) of the world for the modern subject, one who is at the centre of, and yet radically and repeatedly decentred or internally divided by, an age of print and related technological, or more accurately 'tele-technological' media – 'tele-technological' because

a medium or the media transmit across a distance, between a there and a here, a then and a now, time and space being 'out of joint'.

This is to be read on numerous occasions, as Hardy makes it clear that the rupture of the historical moment and the riven sense of the present is intimately bound up with the revealed historicity and mediated condition of one's being. To take an example, following the death of her father, and being left only with her brother Owen for support and friendship, Cytherea applies for a position as a 'lady's companion' by placing an advertisement. Hardy reproduces the advertisement on the page, utilizing typography typical of such advertisements of the time, and thereby reproducing the materiality of the word for the reader:

A YOUNG LADY is desirous of meeting with an ENGAGEMENT as GOVERNESS or COMPANION. She is competent to teach English, French, and Music. Satisfactory references.

    Address, C. G., Post Office, Creston. (*DR* I.II.22)

The advertisement appears here, reproduced from its implied proper context. Whilst notable for its brevity, the representation of Cytherea written by herself is different from that earlier representation of Cytherea already discussed only as a matter of degree rather than kind. One is clearly directed in the reading, through the use of small capital letters for key words. This telegraphic gesture produces its reading subject, and this is further enforced through the use of capitals for the subjects to be taught. All else is secondary, unnecessary, mere structural maintenance to aid transport and communication, whilst simultaneously and inadvertently admitting that such a 'translation' is only ever a crude approximation. In this gesture, the technology of printing is employed to reproduce and so draw attention to its own material and immaterial forces. A 'modern' technology given commercial manifestation, advertising becomes the sign of the self as an other self, a cipher reducible to initials ('C.G.'), as the accumulation of traits and signs, available for communication and therefore open to other times. One departs from oneself, one sends oneself away from oneself. In doing so, one admits that one's modern being, infinitely reproducible, legible, available for translation, is always already haunted by one's finite temporality. Through the agency of modern communication's tele-technology, the self is haunted by its own historicity.

Seeing herself, in her own words a 'YOUNG LADY' (*DR* I.II.22), Cytherea is caused to pause and reflect on this inscribed figure that

is uncannily double, both herself and not herself. Hers is less a representation than it is a cipher and projection, a subscription of the self under controlling economic factors: '[i]t seemed a more material existence than her own that she saw thus delineated on the paper. "That can't be myself; how odd I look," she said, and smiled' (*DR* I.II.23). There is a powerful sense of the modern, historicized and mediated self in this moment of doubling and division. Staged as a cipher of herself, Cytherea is made to feel the uncanniness of modernity, and the modernity of the uncanny. More than this, though, her sense of the uncanny is also a sensation of what Freud would term *unheimlichkeit*, literally unhomeliness, by virtue of the arrival of the 'dead' materiality of the hetero-affective trace of herself, of seeing herself, in short as externalized and a mediated other. And this Freudian *aperçu* haunts Cytherea in the modernity of her condition of being, quite literally, homeless as a result of the death of the father. Of course, one might equally read the scene as a singular example of the reification of the subject effected under Victorian capitalism, but this is not to deny the strangeness and estrangement at work here (which estrangement might in turn be connected to Marx's puzzled response to the commodity-fetishism). However, a strong reading might argue that the second generation of Victorians are imagined here through the figure of Cytherea Graye. For hers is a self-conscious knowledge of historical subjectivity expelled from the safe home of the past, on which so many novelists of the first generation gaze. This effect appears as a result of the becoming-conscious of the self as written, inscribed in some phantasmatic manner. As John Goode puts it, 'writing is at the very root of Hardy's self-consciousness', and this is clearly seen to be so in this particular instance, as is the truth of Goode's remark that 'the writing age is an age of dislocation' (Goode 1988, 2). In communication, correspondence breaks. Writing, relay, deferral and delay take over from the illusory immediacy of the mimetic form.

Tracing a path between Goode's remarks, we may read an understanding both of Hardy's formal experiment with phenomenological modes of self-reflexive perception and a response to the historicity of the text itself, whereby Hardy's transformative fictional process is itself understood as mediated by the age of technological reproducibility (to invoke Walter Benjamin) and the translation, difference and loss by which being, identity, subjectivity, are all marked (Koepnick 2002, 110). While Cytherea appears not to be dismayed by the deferral and differentiation of presence through the death of the self occasioned by appearance of the self's other through the technicity of writing and its technological reproduction,

the effect is disquieting, to say the least. As Maurice Blanchot has it, 'to write (of) oneself is to cease to be' (Blanchot 1986, 64). Hardy, we comprehend, anticipates just this material condition and experience. *Différance* gives to consciousness its belated reflexive cognition and apprehension of its being as always already different and deferred. And what resonates even today is that, for Hardy, in the 1860s of the novel, writing is more material, somehow more real, than the organic self. Cytherea writes, thereby producing herself as 'the other, a reader'. The subject only knows the self it is through a form of representation that is indirect, analogical rather than strictly or merely mimetic. Such disruptive apperception as the work of writing and reading is remarked on by Blanchot: 'Although read from my own book and articulated with the most present reality, it brings me to the feeling of the event that it signifies and to the act to be accomplished that will result from it, but without the knowledge it carries in itself being in any way expressed' (Blanchot 1995, 74). Charting the temporal and spatial *différance* of being, Blanchot discloses the emptiness at the heart of the experience of reading, within which being is intimately enfolded, and so gives expression to Hardy's implicit practice, as witnessed in Cytherea's coming to consciousness.

That Cytherea both writes and reads her other self, that she is involved actively in the doubling and dividing of her subjectivity, and that it travels back to her as a disembodied transmission, is quite startling. Commenting further on reading and the literary, Blanchot observes:

> This knowledge will normally remain that of an empty awareness that could be filled, but is not filled; as a reader aware of words that mean something, I have present in my mind neither the words that I read and that the meaning makes disappear, nor this meaning that no defined image presents, *but only an ensemble of connections and intentions, an opening onto a complexity yet to come* . . . to read and hear implies that language, far from giving us the fullness of things in which we live, is cut off from them, for it is a language of signs . . . (1995, 74; emphasis added).

An ensemble of connections and intentions, an opening onto a complexity yet to come: this in substance is what we have in that initial presentation of Cytherea. As we can see from her reading of the advertisement, Cytherea inhabits *Desperate Remedies* as a reader of signs, subordinate to and a supplement of those signs rather than being their originator, and, additionally, as that figure of difference that acknowledges the impossibility of a full or fulfilled awareness,

for which Blanchot argues so persuasively. Hardy's texts mark the always-adventitious opening of the present from within itself, not only by the returns of past *nows* but also by figuring in the opening, the *nows* to come. Without presence as such, memory is always the articulation of the past within the present that haunts presence. The novels deploy the past-in-the-present and that which is to come or which arrives unexpectedly as a disfiguration of full presence so as to indicate the text's revelation of being's always haunted, always untimely experience of its divided modernity. Cytherea's reading of signs, her active participation in history as a partial reader, an uncomprehending subject – uncomprehending, that is, except for the limitations imposed on her by the labyrinth of her successive moments, in which, and from which she has only ever a partial perspective – is maintained until her marriage, that stock romantic ending of the realist novel, is achieved. She is subsequently marked off in the text, no longer having agency, being merely a fixed character in a stable location.

IV. THE DEATH OF THE ARCHITECT

But how does Cytherea arrive at this pass, one which, in its readability and unreadability (she knows what it says but cannot take that in as a version or translation of herself), is also an impasse, the experience for the modern subject of an aporia at the heart of subjectivity? The death of the father expels Cytherea unwillingly into the modern world, and with that both Cytherea and the reader are propelled into the complexities and snares of 'modern' narrative convolution and the insoluble problems of being in the present, and what it means to be modern.

There is something violently symbolic to the conclusion of *Desperate Remedies*' 'opening'. Architect Ambrose Graye falls to his death from a church spire, as he is supervising repairs:

> The Town Hall, in which Cytherea sat, was a building of brown stone, and through one of the windows could be seen...the upper part of a neighbouring church spire, now in course of completion under the superintendence of Miss Graye's father, the architect to the work.
>
> That the top of this spire should be visible from her position in the room was a fact which Cytherea's idling eyes had discovered with some interest, and she was now engaged in watching the scene that was being enacted about its airy summit. Round the conical stonework rose a cage of scaffolding against the blue sky, and upon this stood five men – four in clothes as white as the new erection close beneath their hands, the fifth in the ordinary dark suit of a gentleman.

The four working-men in white were three masons and a mason's labourer. The fifth man was the architect, Mr. Graye. He had been giving directions as it seemed, and retiring as far as the narrow footway allowed, stood perfectly still.

The picture thus presented to a spectator in the Town Hall was curious and striking. It was an illuminated miniature, framed in by the dark margin of the window, the keen-edged shadiness of which emphasized by contrast the softness of the objects enclosed.

The height of the spire was about one hundred and twenty feet, and the five men engaged thereon seemed entirely removed from the sphere and experiences of ordinary human beings. They appeared little larger than pigeons, and made their tiny movements with a soft, spirit-like silentness. One idea above all others was conveyed to the mind of a person on the ground by their aspect, namely, concentration of purpose: that they were indifferent to – even unconscious of – the distracted world beneath them, and all that moved upon it. They never looked off the scaffolding.

Then one of them turned; it was Mr. Graye. Again he stood motionless, with attention to the operations of the others. He appeared to be lost in reflection, and had directed his face towards a new stone they were lifting.

'Why does he stand like that?' the young lady thought at length [. . .]

She moved herself uneasily. 'I wish he would come down', she whispered, still gazing at the skybacked picture. 'It is so dangerous to be absent-minded up there'.

When she had done murmuring the words her father indecisively laid hold of one of the scaffold-poles, as if to test its strength, then let it go and stepped back. In stepping, his foot slipped. An instant of doubling forward and sideways, and he reeled off into the air, immediately disappearing downwards. (*DR* I.I.14–15)

Prior to Ambrose Graye's death, it is remarked of Cytherea that 'it was the last hour of experience she ever enjoyed with a mind entirely free from a knowledge of that *labyrinth* into which she stepped immediately afterwards – to continue a perplexed course along its *mazes* for the greater portion of twenty-nine subsequent months' (*DR* I.I.13–14; emphasis added). Those figures of maze and labyrinth have a certain gallows humour in them, given Ambrose Graye's occupation. One cannot help but feel that Hardy is enacting the death, if not of the author, then certainly the architect as authority, as paternal figure, without which structure and meaning become random, subject to arbitrariness, chance and undecidability. Cytherea no longer has an authority to guide her; she loses universal perspective and gains entrance only to partial perspective and, therefore, equally partial knowledge.

This is made forcefully plain in that the scene builds to its violent conclusion in such carefully measured, proportioned and picturesque terms. The first paragraph presents a neatly delineated

town scene, before moving vertically upwards to the spire, and its surround. Line and form present pictorial harmony, and this is echoed in the restricted tonal palette of blue, white and black, all of which is described as an 'illuminated miniature, framed in the dark margin of the window, the keen-edged shadiness of which emphasized by contrast the softness of the objects enclosed'. In what appears an amalgam of medieval sketch and photographic vignette, Hardy presents the carefully composed, organized still world to the 'mind of a person on the ground', that is to say Cytherea, anyone chancing to look up and, importantly, the reader. Cytherea's consciousness comes into play in a prescient moment, immediately prior to the 'skybacked picture' breaking into violent motion, the frame, and scaffold broken simultaneously.

Most interesting in this scene is the reader's own partial positioning and implicit involvement, to which I have already alluded. Narrative gives no greater access to events for the reader than it does to Cytherea. Hardy places Cytherea, seated at a window, framed and looking through the same frame, and he allows the reader to watch not only the fall but also Cytherea watching the fall. In this scene, the gaze is doubled, divided. There is no single eye-line to the moment, no simple perspective on this event. With the death of the architect – and do not forget that Hardy's architectural metaphors for Cytherea's own 'fall' from innocence are the labyrinth and maze – Hardy's inaugural gesture marks itself as signalling a forceful and irrevocable rupture from the heightened perspectival control of realism and omniscience. Being plunged into a labyrinth proscribes one from taking a properly architectonic view of things. The subject becomes enmeshed, and so must decipher the partial signs available to her, without access to an overview. Such vision belongs to the past, to the 'innocence' of realist fiction in the previous generation.

V. VISIONARY MOMENTS, PARTIAL PERCEPTIONS

All Hardy's subjects, and we as his readers, experience or suffer alterations in perspective and perception. We receive events and the past as we might an unanticipated postal delivery: in this telemediatic posting, we become the addressee of a message never destined for us necessarily. We become implicated in the message, written as the subjects of that posting, inscribed in and as the provisional subjects of a postal relay, one which never arrives at a final destination because it never ceases in its being sent. We thus, in response, act

according to the way in which we have been addressed. In perceiving our reception of an event or message, we may 'ascribe to the mind the faculty of experience...even though the mind does not possess any obvious equivalent to our eyes or ears for registering what is given to us' (Ankersmit 2005, 8). This faculty of experience is clearly of a different order than that which is purely physical or material. It is phantasmic in nature, and yet bears directly on material and historical realities and events.

Arthur Schopenhauer, with whom Hardy had more than a passing familiarity, provides us with an interesting insight into this matter. 'Every incident', he writes, 'even if very insignificant, which stirs a disagreeable emotion, will leave in our mind an after-effect which, as long as it lasts, obstructs a clear and objective view of things and circumstances. In fact, it tinges all our thoughts, just as a very small object, brought close to our eyes, limits and distorts our field of vision' (Schopenhauer 1974, 592). Whether one sees one's father fall from a church spire, or whether one receives a Valentine Card sent as a joke, as does Farmer Boldwood in *Far from the Madding Crowd*, the postal effect takes place, translating us even as our field of vision, to use Schopenhauer's phrase, is transformed. Beginning with the material event Schopenhauer's commentary registers the phenomenological effect-as-reception of what he terms the incident as it returns, thereby haunting memory, and perceived as those 'after-effect[s]' which, 'in our mind' produce a colouration and distortion related to the figure of sight as *in*sight, memory as *re*vision. The double moment is then redoubled, spaced temporally, and thus 'historically', and simultaneously dispersed, in that *re*vision names both the return of a vision, a phantasm, to the mind's eye, as that trace of the other, and the 'sight' by which we see what once had been invisible.

Hardy's text mediates such apprehension endlessly in the mental recollection or moments of insight endured by his characters. Memory recalls the past encounter between self and other, as in the moment when in *Desperate Remedies* Cytherea Graye, who provides us with yet another example, is disorientated by the 'wet shining road', which in turn, in the illumination's penetration of the eye and the mind, calls into being the oscillating phantasms of Edward Springrove and Aeneas Manston: 'The wet shining road threw the western glare into her eyes with an invidious lustre which rendered the restlessness of her mood more wearying'.

> Her thoughts flew from idea to idea without asking for the slightest link of connection...One moment she was full of the wild music and stirring

scene with Manston – the next, Edward's image rose before her like a shadowy ghost. Then Manston's eyes seemed piercing her again ... (*DR* I.VIII.141).

Such experience is mediated by a 'movement comprising at the same time the *discovery* and *recovery* of the past' (Ankersmit 2005, 8). Discovery is there in the unveiling of the trace left by an event. Recovery is the process by which one seeks to give significance to that trace or otherwise acts in response to that which remains as phantom inscription. In Cytherea's case, the chain of signifiers – idea to idea – is put into play with such rapidity that significance between the links is unavailable. What can be said here is that, whether Cytherea has available to her ultimately that which brings about the analogy, Hardy's language expresses the relation without relation as phantasmic, and in a double fashion, for not only are the two men iterable images, the one for the other, but music is itself a phantom figure, available to perception but having no immediate representable material form. Music, in this moment, analogous to some shadowy ghost, operates as if it were a figure for the work of literary discourse, conjuring and offering indirect relation.

Subjective encounter or experience is therefore most intimately engaged through the attempts to read the texts that are placed before one, whether these are letters, paintings, telegrams, or the forms of architecture, archaeology, the landscape, or topography, even as each of these operates equally through displacement, deferral, misdirection and what Derrida calls *destinerrance*: the possibility of errancy in any destined posting or direction. As disparate as these forms and their discourses may be (they each serve as analogies for one another, in endless substitution), in Hardy's world there is always present someone for whom these are visual forms primarily, waiting to be decoded, to be read. Reading therefore produces another form of vision, a visualization or envisioning beyond the merely visible, material and empirical world. It produces knowledge of vision's partiality, the limits of a single perspective. Hardy reminds us, or introduces his readers to the notion, that no one can claim to see everything. There is no omniscient location and with that, absolute knowledge, whether one is a novelist or God.

The obverse possibility of partial perspective and limited perception is that one might come to know one's placement in the universe. One can glimpse creatures existing in a world of their own, having no knowledge that they are being watched. The inference is that one might be equally unaware of a consciousness other, if not greater than, one's own, observing one's motions. In later novels, Hardy

will repeat this motif of human existence, but gives it first form in the image of Aeneas Manston, contemplating the insects on the water's surface in a rain-water-butt:

> Turning aside, he leant his arms upon the edge of the rain-water-butt standing in the corner, and looked into it. The reflection from the smooth stagnant surface tinged his face with the greenish shades of Correggio's nudes. Staves of sunlight slanted down through the still pool, lighting it up with wonderful distinctness. Hundreds of thousands of minute living creatures sported and tumbled in its depth with every contortion that gaiety could suggest; perfectly happy, though consisting only of a head, or a tail, or at most a head and a tail, and all doomed to die within the twenty-four hours. (*DR* II.IV.221–2)

Consciousness, artifice, composition and aesthetics touch on one another in this remarkable momentary hiatus in the narrative flow. The reader is at once at a remove from Manston, as great a remove as he himself is from those 'hundreds of thousands of minute living creatures'. Narrative motion suspended for this moment of reflection, the formal structure and, with it, the artificiality of conscious perception, is foregrounded on the one hand by the comparison of Manston's reflection with the colouring of Correggio's nudes, and on the other by the reference to those 'staves of sunlight', a stave being a vertical wooden plank in a building or another structure, such as the very barrel into which Manston is looking in a reflective manner. The shafts of light recall very similar, yet distinct, 'staves' as those by which Cytherea has called to mind the death of her father. However, obviously, the shafts or staves do not hold the same significance for Manston: it is only the reader's comprehension that allows for the concatenation of otherwise dissimilar scenes. In effect, the reader is invited to reflect on similarity and dissimilarity, to reflect in a manner both similar and dissimilar to Manston's own mode of reflection, even as his reflection in the pool is a cause for our reflection on perception, consciousness and composition.

It might be asked, is it Manston's reflection that the seemingly 'happy' creatures are 'doomed to die' or is it the narrator's? Whose is the mediating consciousness here? Strictly speaking, whilst Hardy is the author of the passage, the location of conscious reflection on the condition of existence – what goes for the creatures in the water goes for both characters in a novel or the novel's readers, albeit in different ways – remains unlocatable. Perception has its limitations. If Hardy's characters share anything, it is that which escapes their knowledge, and thus some at least come to this knowledge of their own conscious and epistemological limit. There is no universal

perspective. While one person may have an empirical or epistemological advantage over an other or others, there is no transcendent
location in Hardy's novels, unless it be such momentary insight into
consciousness of the limits of perception as is given to the good
reader of Hardy who observes his characters observing one another
whilst remaining unaware that they are, themselves, observed.

A humorous image of this comes from a scene that somewhat
parodically illustrates the impossibility of absolute knowledge in
Hardy's world, whilst also introducing the significance and limit of
perspectival vision and lines of sight into his text. Anne, Manston's
wife, follows her husband out of the house, on an evening when
'Night herself seemed to have become a watcher' (*DR* III.VI.373).
She perceives an 'other watcher' (*DR* III.VI.372). This shadowy figure follows Manston. Manston does not know he is being watched,
either by Anne or the anonymous figure. The anonymous watcher
is unaware that anyone is looking at him. Then, as a fourth in
this comic proceedings, there is an 'unknown woman' who watches
also the unknown watcher who watches Manston. It is hardly any
wonder that Ann was 'impressed . . . with the sensation of people in
hiding . . . [and that] Nobody was visible' (*DR* III.VI.372). So, the
'four persons preceded across the glade, and into the park plantation, at equi-distances of about seventy yards' (*DR* III.VI.373).
Only the 'Night herself' witnesses the strangely comic, strangely odd
parade. And there still remains some consciousness to observe and
reflect on the Night, personified as a watcher but unaware that she
is watched. It is as if we are watching a chase sequence from a silent
movie, but with the added, unnerving reflection that we might be
observed equally. Hardy constructs consciousness as spatially and
relationally, albeit partially, embodied. Such embodiment, constituted through the formal iterability of planes, lines, reflections, and
illumination, illustrates for the reader how one's identity is both
similar and different from another's. With that, and with the notion
that as one watches one might also be watched, one gains insight
into identities being simultaneously congruent and incongruent, the
difference remarked here being that of the historicity of one's being
and the historical narrative to which one belongs and to which one
is consigned.

VI. CULTURAL REVENANCE AND FUTURITY

If the narrative fact that there are two Cythereas and so two stories
to be told teaches us anything, it is that narratives change, history,
though repetitious, is not fixed, and that there is no repetition which

is not, in its revenance, haunted by transformations which are the signs of a narrative or character's historicity. The first Cytherea's history, and the novel properly belonging to her history, is already accounted for, done away with, by Hardy in the first chapter. Such a storyline is consigned to the past, even as Hardy's novel belongs to a later generation than those of Dickens, Collins, Eliot and others of the 'first' Victorian generation. However, this is not to say that the second Cytherea who both replaces and substitutes for the first is not also written into narrative fiction as a figure already consigned to a fictive past and its representation waiting to arrive. This is something Hardy desires to make clear in his Epilogue.

While the novel begins with (the second, supplementary) Cytherea's story on a Midsummer's Eve and returns in conclusion to another in its Epilogue, it also doubles beginning and ending in another sense, narrative adventure getting underway with a church spire and coming to the belfry of another church. Whilst Ambrose Graye's death is the symbol of an end of one form of institutional authority, the novel concludes with its figure of organic community echoing over several hundred years, the bell-ringers inside another church tower, responding to arcane signs drawn on the floor, and bringing a voice to the structure. The voices of the bells, the shadows of the ringers, returning generation after generation, figure an auratic, spectral return, for the spirit of the church is in its community, not in its structure or institution. The lone figure of the architect makes way for a community haunted by its own past and continuance. At the same time, the silent, highly visible exterior of the spire from which Graye falls, gives way to the imagined aural world inside the belfry, invisible but audible to those outside.

In the Epilogue, which takes place on Midsummer's Eve 1867, we find ourselves in a belfry, with a group of bell ringers (*DR* 401–7). No longer outside, looking up at the church spire as Cytherea had done, we are inside the tower of the church, amongst a group of equals. We are witness to the scene of the eight bell-ringers and one stranger (*DR* 401), by the illumination of a single candle. In this scene, the ancient and the modern cohabit, in the same space, for it is remarked that the bell-ringing had taken place here for four hundred years (*DR* 401). In that remark the reader is invited to 'hear' the sound of the bells ringing not only in 1867 but also down through the centuries, one event from an iterable series of events that take place now and now, and now. Of interest in relation to this is Hardy's use of present tense in the opening paragraphs. It functions to maintain an always ghostly present, a 'now' without present. For every time you read, the bells toll in the instant of reading, they

are no longer consigned to the past of narrative history. The event is both dated and undated, even as the unrepresentable sonority is both more and less than the visible scene. More than that, it is a double event in another manner, being marked by both the Christian calendar, and taking place in a church, but taking place on Midsummer's Eve, a pagan calendrical marker, the temporality of which is circular and recurrent rather than progressive and linear. That shift to present tense dislodges the historical record of dating and fixing in place to which the previous narrative history is now consigned. An other history is thus ghosted here in this collective, visionary moment and its experience, which, with its contrapuntal pagan revenance, figures the scene with a vigorous instance of iterable alterity.

Of course, as already implied it is impossible to hear the bells as such. They are irreducible to any but the most indirect narrative representation. If figured at all, their sound registers, perhaps, only apophatically. They may be imagined as heard through a visual analogy in the moving, spectral image of 'ever changing shadows [that] mingle on the wall in an endless variety of kaleidoscopic forms' (DR 401). From the shadows, our attention is drawn to another image: 'the eyes of all the nine are religiously fixed on a diagram like a large addition sum, which is chalked on the floor' (DR 401). We read the following movement in this scene: from abstraction to abstraction; from spectrality to geometry; from the dissolution of the image and fixed representation to the indirect figuring of an encrypted semiotic trace that is simultaneously already translated by the bell ringers and yet to be read by the reader. That symbol on the floor is though as unavailable as the sound of the bells. The narrator does direct us, however, to the possibility of a reading. We are invited to 'read' that the eyes read the diagram and so 'translate' the otherwise mute marks into corporeal, rhythmic and contrapuntal movement, which in turn becomes the peal, the changes being rung.

But we can never hear this. Everything remains irreducibly phantasmic. Indeed, the peals are themselves significant. They are encrypted messages, to the meaning of which we have no unmediated access, unless we are campanologists. This makes me ask, why there is no detailed footnote in the edition cited for the triple-bob-major (DR 402), a phrase that is, arguably, amongst the least comprehensible in the entire novel, for many readers at least. Perhaps the editor feels this is not as significant as Shakespeare, or any of the other sources that are annotated. Yet, it might be asked: is the ringing of changes not as significant to particular histories of Englishness as a given author? Arguably, as that figure of '400

years' (by which the time, the few decades of *Desperate Remedies* is quite paltry) attests, change-ringing, the ringing of tuned bells in mathematical patterns, is important to the life of a community, to the survival of the spirit of community, its living on across centuries, beyond the mere life of individuals. Yet Hardy presents us with this reference to a knowledge, leaving it undeciphered, to be read in the moment or not, to remain unread and so to delivered over to a chance reading, when it may arrive at some future date, however adventitiously.

The ringing of the changes might be read as Hardy's signal that one order, a different generation, supplants its predecessor. Hardy, we might say, rings the changes on generations and modes of narrative. In this acknowledgement of ritual practice, the narrative thereby signals a new direction for the novel, with the arrival of a different generation (Hardy himself). In this fashion, the narrative reminds us again of different, historically grounded epistemological models of knowledge and different modes of consciousness. Yet, if we turn away from the bell-ringing, there remains in the bell-tower the odd figure of the ninth bell-ringer, a stranger, 'who has appeared from nobody knows where' (*DR* 401), and who, we find out, is a journalist. To understand his presence, we should turn to the final paragraphs of the Epilogue. The peal concluded, Clerk Crickett and the stranger walk away, the journalist having to catch a train. As they walk, Crickett relates the remaining events of Cytherea's life, thereby introducing a spaced, spacing perspective on that narrative, and shaping it as a displaced, no longer central narrative presented as if it were the only version, and so embedded in Crickett's recounting of events. In the course of their walk, they pause on one side of a lake to take a view of Knapwater House, the inherited country home of Cytherea and Edward, who are now married. Hardy remarks on the fact that the two men halt to observe Cytherea and her husband, at a distance, figures in a framed, suspended landscape, on which one is offered momentary perspective. In the image of the house, and in 'two contrasting figures', Cytherea and Edward Springrove, who stand motionless in front of it, we are presented with figures belonging to the most artificial and conventional of narrative endings, the happily married couple, in a moment of closure that could only happen in novels. It is as if we are witnessing at a distance artifice as cliché, and with that the limits of realist construction. This stale predictability is authorized by the instant of static, framed representation, as the house is described: 'a magnificent *picture* of the English country-house' (*DR* 406; emphasis added). Against the oscillations and echoes of an aural, communal

culture figured by the bells, there is presented the convention of English country house representation, with its associations of secular, lone authority. Even as the implicit frame suggests artificiality and recalls the framing, to Cytherea, of Ambrose Graye's death by the window of the Elizabethan Town Hall, it is as if Hardy is consigning the conventions of realist fiction to a frame, leaving it to stand as something at which to look from a distance, and on which to take a suitably disinterested perspective.

Far more important, arguably, is the motion and conversation between the journalist and Crickett. In their animated image one may read Hardy's persistent interests. Clerk Crickett is the representative of archaic communal culture. A 'bowdlerized rake', he is the bearer of doxa and carrier of the oral tradition. He 'translates' legal documents into hearsay and provides plot outline and recapitulation, offering self-reflexive comments such as, '[a]nd so the romance has ended well' (DR 405), or, 'I've illustrated my story with rale liven specimens' (DR 406). Then there is the figure of modernity, the reporter, a writer without a name, generating mass-produced text, perhaps anonymously, in the form of dated, documentary writing, machinic, inscribed memory, communicated across distances impossible for the older, oral community to traverse.

So we are given the choice, on the one hand a static, illusory closure, typical of the previous literary generation's 'realism'. Or, we have the ancient and modern dialogically juxtaposed. The reader is presented not with a monolithic narrative authority and voice, but the division of communication between the oral and the printed. The novel thus speaks to the necessity of an interanimation of cultural anamnesis, through personal and impersonal memory. It speaks of the need for remembering, recording, and archiving, in the face of the inescapable acceleration of dissemination and fragmentation. These are the forms for Hardy by which being is always caught up in a becoming-conscious of its historicity. In coming to this partial perspective, we may move forward beyond the confines of realism, and beyond conventional closure also. We assign our narratives to other modes of transmission, from oral 'illustration' to tele-technological 'posting'. Traces of ourselves are sent out as that which remains to come, remaining to be read; and as that which is given over to chance, transmitted, however precariously, from culture to culture, generation to generation, perspective to perspective. In Hardy's worlds, apprehension risks everything not on representation, which forecloses on knowledge, but on legibility and illegibility, translation and loss.

2

Distortions and Transformations: *Under the Greenwood Tree* (1872), *A Pair of Blue Eyes* (1873)

I. PASSING GENERATIONS

That we are vouchsafed visions of Midsummer's Day, such as the one on which the bell-ringing occurs at the close of *Desperate Remedies* – *Under the Greenwood Tree* and *The Return of the Native* also close on the same day – is indication of Hardy's insistence that the world is comprehended as moving to at least two times within the same time: Christian, calendrical and progressive, linear temporality and *at the same time*, within and yet other than the time of the modern, a cyclical pagan calendar. A generation may pass but given moments in time return, the same and yet not the same. In this, there is the idea that a previous generation is not departed entirely, but leaves its traces in subsequent generations, such remains being the spectral signature of the past in the present. Thus there will be read in Hardy an irreducible tension between the spectral and material, which tension is often put to work in Hardy through, on the one hand, aural and auratic experience, perceptions of the pagan, and so on, and the heightened or intensified visual experience that Hardy inscribes through the emphasis on line, shape, and colour field. In this, Wessex becomes the imaginary site which bears the burden

of all history and memory, in a dialectic challenge to modernity understood as urbanism, as the presencing of the present, in the face of the increasingly absent – because forgotten – 'organic' home of the rural.

The generation of Dickens, Gaskell and Eliot came to maturity in the years of the Corn Laws (not repealed until 1846). Concomitantly, they would have been privy to news at least of agitation by the Anti-Corn Law League. Though all were born too late to have had direct knowledge of the Luddite movement, the generation of their parents could have heard of the social movement and its radical acts of industrial sabotage. They, along with their parents and their parents' parents, belonged to the generations affected directly or indirectly by the imposition of successive 'Inclosure Acts', laws by which common grazing rights were denied throughout the country through the enclosure of land previously understood to be common land. Though having a long history, the Inclosure Acts were systematized first in 1801 through the Inclosure Consolidation Act, which gave formal consistency to all previous acts extending back to the twelfth century and extending well into the nineteenth century. The General Inclosure Act of 1845 made provision for the employment of commissioners, whose powers extended to effecting autonomous enclosure, without recourse to parliamentary permission. The 'first' generation of Victorian writers were, then, the last generation during which and for whom what I would like to refer to as the English diaspora imposed its effects: the transformation from a predominantly rural to urban modes of existence, the transition from largely feudal to capitalist economic and social relations, the shift decisively to a distinctively modern bourgeois hegemony.

The context I have sketched insists on legislation directly affecting the rural and farming communities of England, even though the nineteenth century is commonly thought of as the age of industry, of 'steam' (to use a now somewhat quaint and phantasmagorical metonymy for all too material effects), and of empire. This is deliberate. For, what should be reflected upon is that most of the canonical writers of the first Victorian generation have little to say about rural life. With the exception of George Eliot, the other writers mentioned in question are by and large urban, metropolitan authors, along with many other authors of their generation. The reasons for what one might call Eliot's 'exceptionalism' or 'ex-centricity' is considered in the pertinent chapter. But briefly, it is as if Romanticism offers the last literary gasp, so to speak, the final act of attestation to the irrevocable transformation of English culture produced by the complex

of events known as the industrial revolution. Where the countryside does intrude in many of the 'first' generation of Victorian writers, it is, if not as an afterthought, then certainly as an incidental for the most part. It may well be that the rural and pastoral became phantomized by the historical trauma of the first decades of the nineteenth century, serving only in semi-visible and encrypted ways to motivate literary sensibilities and modes of representation. This in turn serves to mark a distance in acts of self-reading for those early Victorians who saw themselves as modern, distinct from and quite other than the previous generations. Where the rural does appear in the novels of the nineteenth century it is arguably primarily as backdrop, stage- or scene-setting device, a literary trompe-l'oeil only in the service of character-grounded, psychologically motivated realist story-telling. That is, until the novels of Thomas Hardy.

When Hardy brings back to the reader's vision the rural world, it is with particular transformations very much in mind; not merely those transformations effected by industrialization and its side-effects, but transformations having to do with how, from the 1870s onwards, one might 'see' a world now largely occluded, a world from which one's being is in the process of being estranged. There is a sense in which Hardy's interest in the landscape of England is not merely a matter of biography, but has to do with the rural places of Wessex 'as arenas in which lives are lived ... [and] as images of how private and communal life could be conducted' (Davie 1998, 243).

Arguably, in this philosophical reflection on one's emplacement in the world as the register of one's being Hardy transforms the cultural staging of the rural significantly, making the articulation of other identities possible. Occasionally, a dissenting English alterity emerges, given representation through its indelible impress on the landscape. It is not to be thought that Hardy simply poses a dialectics of hegemonic modernity and a dissident opposition. Rather, that which passes leaves its traces to be read by future generations, and its 'dissent' remains to be read in Hardy's textual memory work as the gathering of the signs and voices of some other in danger of occlusion or obliteration. The dissent is, at its most neutral, simply the affirmation that 'I do not belong'; 'I no longer belong' in the historical and cultural transformation of social and cultural determinations of identity. Hardy gives early expression to this in *Under the Greenwood Tree*, his second novel published in 1872, which perception is expressed most directly in the words of Michael Mail, who delivers the opinion that ' "times have changed from the times they used to be"' (*UGT* I.IV.22).

Generally, irreversible generational transformation of parochial culture is indicated as one more inevitable change allied to seasonal cycles in *Under the Greenwood Tree*, the story of which is set at the time of initial composition in the early 1870s as being 'less than a generation ago' (*UGT* I.I.7). As Tim Dolin notes in his edition, from 1872 to 1896 in his revisions Hardy changed the temporal distance between reader and events from less than thirty to more than fifty years (*UGT* 191–2n2). Hardy widens the gap in his act of revision even as that moment retreats from Hardy's present. In the novel, a close affiliation or bond is traced implicitly between the 'natural' and 'cultural' worlds inhabited by the people of Mellstock, and, particularly, their choir, the group of musicians most personally affected by a cultural sea change. That affiliation is marked by Hardy in his choice of titles for the volume divisions of the novel: winter; spring; summer; and autumn. This chronological progression and cycle is abruptly interrupted, as the novelist reminds us that a mode of presentation structures, mediates, and informs our perception of this seemingly natural world and its 'realist' representation. That Hardy chooses to implicate the natural and cultural conceptually in one another is perhaps itself a sign of the material moment of cultural and historical transformation. The reader is suspended between differing modes of perception, between the assumption of an empirically governed worldview and a perspective that is conscious of itself as interpretative perception.

Specifically, the ineluctable change occasioned in the generational shift is marked by the advent of an organ in the church, with which the vicar, Mr Maybold, wishes to replace the Mellstock choir, who provide the music in church on violins, serpents, clarinets and other instruments. The transformation is both generational, an innovation signalling a change in cultural practice, and technical, the organ signifying changes in ecclesiastical attitudes to liturgical practice in the Church of England, as a sign of modernization at some point in the 1840s, the decade in which the narrative is set. One aspect of this historical upheaval is that it removes the village from church, so to speak. While, obviously, a congregation will remain, the boundary between church and congregation, institution and parishioners, and therefore between ecclesiastical institutional organization and secular life, is erected, a hierarchy made manifest. The overlapping cycles of natural, cultural and historical change are reinforced further, because the organ is introduced in the second volume, 'Spring'. (It is worth noting that Maybold's name symbolizes the force or vitality of spring, of new beginnings. In his name, however, are two signatures: on the one hand, there is the natural seasonal cycle

from given identity by language. On the other hand, there is the countersignature of the energy of cultural, social and historical transformation.) As Mail's uncannily prescient remark cited before testifies, the past inevitably gives way to the arrival of the future. But the members of the choir feel an injustice in the peremptory manner of Maybold's decision.

Visiting Maybold, the choir request that their services not be dispensed with till the following Christmas (*UGT* II.IV.65), the time of year at which the novel began. Tranter Dewy's appeal notes the correspondence between liturgical and seasonal cycles in its teleological anticipation, and thus expresses a perception of temporality and historicity that is cyclical. Additionally, it marks the anticipated departure with a respect for symbolic ritual, in what Dewy calls a 'glorious' fall 'with a bit of a flourish' and a 'respectable end' (*UGT* II.IV.66). For the new generation given face in Mr Maybold, however, modernity has to take place with what amounts to impetuosity, if not urgency: '"there is no reason for longer delay"' (*UGT* II.IV.65). For Maybold organ music is the 'most proper' medium for the musical translation of spiritual feeling, the implication being that the older generation's form of music is less proper, or even improper (*UGT* II.IV.66). Propriety for the younger generation has everything to do with form and the observation, while for the older generation in the body of the choir the question is one of emotion, expressed by the tranter as 'feeling' (*UGT* II.IV.67). Feeling or sensibility is, moreover, revealed through Dewy's remarks to be communal, while clearly, as Hardy stages the scene between Vicar Maybold and the choir *in toto*, modernity's cultural transformation of practice implicates both mechanisation, efficiency and economy, and individualism. This is staged in the novel in spatial terms: for, while traditionally, the choir play in the gallery, elevated above the congregation and out of immediate sight (the sense being that music, in being invisible, is more truly spiritual), the organ, and therefore the organist, are foci of attention, in plain view. It is almost as if, without wishing to be overly paradoxical, there is a secularization of liturgical practice to be read in generational modernization, and its usurpation of the practices of the past on the part of an ecclesiastical institution seeking to escape cultural anachrony. The choir doesn't argue against generational revolution; it merely wants to observe its passing by its last performance taking place on an ecclesiastically significant day. And so, it comes to be agreed between choir and vicar that the change will take place 'about' Michaelmas. ' "And then"', says Tranter Dewy, ' "we make room for the next generation"' (*UGT* II.IV.69).

The scene is neither sentimental nor nostalgic, though an over-hasty reading might assume so. The choir accepts its fate as a sign of that eschatological inevitability that befalls '"martel men"' (*UGT* II.IV.69). It is a marking of generational and historical process in its constantly dialectical processes and registrations. Were there only this scene, one might be tempted to read Hardy as expressing a longing for the older ways, so to speak, rather than recognizing that his sense of the historical, of the past, is more neutral. It concerns itself in maintaining the traces of the past, his novels readable as so many instances of archiving and memory work, if not mnemotechnic machines. In effect, his texts exemplify the ways in which 'nineteenth-century fiction is a site of interrogation and dramatisation [of the status and meaning of "history"]' (Reilly 1993, 11). Hardy's generational, temporal and historical explorations ask the question 'where does [history] take place?' (Reilly 1993, 11) One answer is that history takes place to the transformation of literature's modes of representation, from empirically governed to phenomenologically orientated modes of narration for example. Or, another answer might be that Hardy traces the taking place of the historical in the transition from framed image, with its controlled predominantly visual, mimetic representation, to the destabilizations of a mobile text 'so that material reality is displaced as the goal of representation by shadowy and spectral anti-realities' (Reilly 1993, 65). Such 'anti-realities' or anachronistic scenes haunting the real in Hardy also acknowledge and resist, it might be argued, the historical and ideologically driven 'framing' of the countryside through the legislation of successive inclosure acts.

II. FRAMING AND OPENNESS

Hardy demonstrates generational displacement from earlier novelistic modes of production in the contest of representation itself: between framing and openness, closure and motion. This occurs throughout his novels, especially in the representation of landscape, and not least in the opening passages of *Under the Greenwood Tree*.

The full title of Hardy's second novel is *Under the Greenwood Tree: A Rural Painting of the Dutch School*. The subtitle situates a particular mode of genre painting and realist representation which is highly formalized in its mimetic verisimilitude, and which relies for its aesthetic force on withdrawing the very means by which it causes the stationary image to appear. Painters assigned by critics and art historians to the 'Dutch School' of Hardy's subtitle

include Rembrandt, Jan Steen, De Koninck, Teniers, Adriaen van Ostade, who painted Flemish peasant scenes, Gerard Terborch the Younger, the first painter of what have subsequently come to be recognized as characteristic Dutch interiors, Jakob van Ruisdael, who specialized in landscapes, Pieter de Hooch, and Jan Vermeer. Such painters deliver depictions of landscape, peasant life, domestic interiors, and generally everyday scenes combined with psychological insight. Certainly, it is arguable that in large part these are also the abiding interests in Hardy's fiction. But there is an irony to this. Hardy's writing has to do with, and seeks to convey, the interior sensate apprehension of such a world, those fleeting impressions, movements, and perceptions belonging to the inhabitants of such a world, in such a manner that the reader receives what is perceived *as if* s/he were within, as well as observing, the representation. Hardy thus breaks the frame, exceeding even the naturalistic style of Dutch genre painting, first developed in seventeenth century, in response to the more overtly stylized mannerism. In this, by analogy we might say, there is a sense in which Hardy is leaving behind, reacting against, the representational modes of the earlier generation of Victorian novelists.

If we wish for examples of writerly representations that translate as they mimic paintings belonging to the Dutch School, we can consider the beginning of volume two of *Under the Greenwood Tree*. Hardy offers the reader the writerly approximation of just such images: 'The chief members of Mellstock parish choir were standing in a group in front of Mr. Penny's workshop in the lower village. They were all brightly illuminated, and each was backed up by a shadow as long as a steeple, the lowness of the source of light rendering the brims of their hats of no use at all as a protection to the eyes' (*UGT* II.I.53). Tim Dolin highlights this image in its 'painstaking composition' suggestive of 'Dutch and English genre painting'. However, as he continues, 'the dramatic chiaroscuro denotes ... an intensification and abstraction' that is excessive when compared with English artists, though typical perhaps of 'seventeenth-century Dutch landscape painters' (*UGT* 204n2). Accepting this, it has to be said that the mode of representation is already anachronistic, at odds with the period of the narrative and the time of writing. There is thus a distortion of vision in the translation not only from the visual arts to fictional discourse, but also between the different generational contexts.

However, taking this further, it is interesting that Hardy seeks both to intensify and abstract, as Dolin has it. In this manner, Hardy produces an image or representation the energy or, if you will, the

somewhat spectral 'vitality' of which resonates in excess of what is being represented. There is a vibrancy irreducible to representation. Hardy's writing overflows the frame. Recalling the subtitle of the novel, we might see how representation contains that which cannot be contained. Hardy pushes at the boundaries of representation, threatening to break the frame in a particularly vivid if not visionary manner, having to do with the articulation of the spirit of Englishness, the ghostly afterlife of rural national identity that, caught in *Desperate Remedies* through the change-ringing scene (and here the commonplace of 'ringing the changes' takes on a specific, ironic resonance), and elsewhere in those scenes of Midsummer's Day, or the Barn raising scene in *Far from the Madding Crowd*, lives on generation after generation, despite efforts at historical eradication, transformation, or containment.

Such phantasmatic vigour is a performative aspect of Hardy's writing. More than this, his writing is capable of conveying that which visual representation and faithful mimesis in the pictorial arts may suppress, albeit inadvertently, or which they fail to convey. Take the very opening of the novel:

> To dwellers in a wood, *almost every species of tree has a voice as well as its feature.* At the passing of the breeze, the fir-trees sob and moan no less distinctly than they rock; the holly whistles as it battles with itself; the ash hisses amid its quiverings; the beech rustles while its flat boughs rise and fall. And winter, which modifies the note of such trees as shed their leaves, does not destroy its individuality. (*UGT* I.I.7; emphasis added)

The inaugural paragraph gives the lie, or at the very least supplements Hardy's subtitle. It emphasizes sound. It does so furthermore as part of an indirect inscription of the echoes of mythic, archaic and pagan England, in the knowledge of the increasing aesthetic hegemony of various scopic regimes. More than this, it bespeaks the singularity of voice of every tree, providing one knows how to receive, to hear, and so tell the difference. Here, Hardy admits us to a knowledge not necessarily ours, and from which we are excluded, not being 'dwellers in a wood'. Additionally, through this Hardy admits us, albeit at a distance, to a world in which animism is no mere metaphorical or symbolic device but epistemological framing. The reader gains access, however indirectly, to that which is otherwise unavailable. Painting cannot convey this sense with the immediacy of sound, and sound, gestured toward in writing, is only ever available apophatically. But sound is only significant if we know how to hear, and so translate it.

Sound is maintained in the second paragraph of the novel, as the 'natural' world informs human intelligence and so is seen to give meaning to the rural subject:

> On a cold and starry Christmas-eve less than a generation ago, a man was passing along a lane in the darkness of a plantation that whispered thus distinctively to his intelligence. All the evidences of his nature were those afforded by the spirit of his footsteps, which succeeded each other lightly and quickly, and by the liveliness of his voice as he sang in a rural cadence:

> > 'With the rose and the lily
> > And the daffodowndilly,
> > The lads and the lasses a-sheep-shearing go.' (*UGT* I.I.7)

Taken back a number of years, given a specific temporal marker (24 December), the reader encounters the figure of the rural subject who apprehends the singularity and difference of the floral voices. His identity is not immediately revealed, this being less important than the representation of the fact that he belongs, he is of this world, he dwells in it and with it. Hardy maintains the link between human nature and the natural world by giving aural rather than visual representation to this singular example of the wood dwellers (who, we find out, shortly after, is Dick Dewy), first through his footsteps, their implied sound and motion – 'lightly and quickly' are interpretations of sound, if you know how to translate such terms – and, subsequently, through his voice, which sings a folk song, commonly known by the title 'Rosebud in June'. The song, a kind of cultural *souvenir*, is maintained through generations and passed as part of a predominantly oral culture. There are variations to the words in the English tradition, but the earliest printed version of 'Rosebud', a sheep-shearing song largely found in the South-West of England, comes from 1715, when it was inserted in a play by Charles Johnson (1679–1748), *The Country Lasses or, The Custom of the Manor*.[1] Another printed version appeared in 1877, in *Nursery Rhymes and Country Songs*, collected by Marianne H. Mason. Both Hardy and Dewy, of course, would have learned the song by aural transmission, from other Dorset / Wessex farmers and shepherds.[2] Hardy does not give the title, but the image of sheep-shearing should alert the reader to the fact that there is something at odds here, in that a song celebrating fecundity and recurrent cyclical rural practices, with just a hint in the chorus of sexual activity between the 'lads and the lasses', should be sung on Christmas Eve. Once more, time is out of joint, and so too are different cultural registers.

Not only is this scene germane to many of Hardy's fictional practices and cultural concerns, it also serves to highlight the relative neglect by Hardy scholars of Hardy's rural, oral and folkloric, often pagan influences. Most scholarly editions in the present day fail to give the kind of attention to annotating 'Rosebud in June' that they do to say, classical, Shakespearean or literary references and allusions. Whether deliberately or out of lack of recognition, alternative English cultures, already well on the way to being marginalized in Hardy's time, remain at a distance culturally and temporally.

Coming back to the matter of representation, and amplifying a little on what has just been remarked, what one should also observe in Hardy's opening is that we cannot see Dick Dewy. If his voice is allied to those of the trees, then he, too, is part of a world that, existing in the dark, nonetheless emerges out of that dark, through the indirect representation of sound. Writing thus exceeds representation. Literature overcomes painting, succeeding it as it supplements the hegemonic dominance of the earlier historical form, in a mode of representation responding to its rural scene. Hardy produces such effects from the very start of the novel, in its opening scene. Beginning with a response to what cannot be seen, the multiplicity of non-human 'voices' heard in the motion of trees in a wood undoes the calm illusory representation implied in the subtitle, a 'rural painting of the Dutch school'. Hardy establishes frames and contexts, only to open them from within. The rural image is further solicited through the recording of the sound of footsteps in the darkness, already mentioned, the 'spirit' of which, unavailable to any painterly depiction, attests to the anonymous figure's 'nature' (*UGT* I.I.7). The text of the song (an anonymous textual production) arrives, and the reader is left to imagine the tune, if she or he does not know it, or otherwise to imagine its sound in concert with the 'natural' sounds of the various trees and bushes making their distinct sounds (*UGT* I.I.7). The words' arrival relies on text, on writing, on a mode of *sending*, which cannot be accommodated by painting, and which also cannot be anticipated or guaranteed in their delivery. What the seasonal 'round' of song and date suggest is a cyclical revenance to an anonymous yet memorialized Englishness. Countless generations are implicated here in what marks the scene and moment with its historically iterable condition. This could be December 24th, 1848 or, it could be 1648. We cannot fix the moment, any more than the image remains static. In a vision of rural timelessness and anachrony, and in the virtual absence of any visible landscape, Hardy transmits a cultural memory to which the always 'still-life' of painting is unable to bear witness.

III. SILENCES, SOUNDS AND VOICES

'He can keep silence well. That man's silence is wonderful to listen to.'
   'There's so much sense in it. Every moment of it is brimming over with sound understanding.'
   ''A can keep a very clever silence…'A looks at me as if 'a could see my thoughts running round like the works of a clock'. (*UGT* II.V.71)

This comic dialogue between members of the Mellstock Choir offers a quite eloquent commentary on imagination, the limits of representation (whether visual or aural), and what might be projected beyond mere pictorial skill or reportage. The commentary on Geoffrey Day, Fancy's father, is made all the more acute in that the speakers recognize their view of Day as but one perspective, given that "'any one o' these up-country London ink-bottle fellers would call Geoffrey a fool' (*UGT* II.V.71). The counterpoint between an urban, cosmopolitan writing culture and a rural, oral one is telling, and not least in that ironic pun, which remarks on silence as the expression of *sound* understanding. What the Choir have implicit faith in is that there is always the possibility of imaginative apprehension, and that silence marks the break or hiatus in the construction of meaning, sense, and representational modes, in order to open onto a quite other space of thought. That there is a self-conscious awareness here is registered in that last observation concerning Day's silence and its connection to his gaze, which apparently has the force, if not the actual ability, to suggest that it sees beyond the material world, and into one's thoughts. Silence is, unequivocally, preternatural. Tied to vision, it presents the imaginative subject with the uncanny image of himself as an automaton.

   Such quirky, visionary and impressionistic aspects of rural England that we find in Hardy, which tap into and draw upon folklore, rural history and prehistory, superstition and the supernatural, there are to be read anticipations of E. M. Forster's moments of visionary oddness in *Howards End*. Additionally, and more generally, Hardy's representation and understanding of the English landscape and all that resonates invisibly and across time in that landscape, irreducible to any merely objective representation, may be found in the novels of D. H. Lawrence, Stanley Spencer's apocalyptic paintings, and the poetry of Ted Hughes. Hardy effectively transforms the language of rural representation, and with that the modes of perception of rural people and topography as the former are haunted by, and the latter relate to cultural memory and to the trace of the other apropos enduring and recurrent manifestations of rural Englishness. In doing so, he figures a poetics

of rural Englishness that always haunts any reader of Hardy. Hardy opens representation to countless traces of difference that distort and transform, through a singularity of voice responsive to the perception of the equally singular quirkiness of vision.

When Hardy describes the perception of 'thickly-leaded diamond glazing' on Fancy's part as 'circular knots or eyes [which] distorted everything seen through them from the outside ... lifting shoulders from bodies ... and bending the straight fir-trunks into semi-circles' (*UGT* II.V.73), his description is a faithful reproduction of what might be seen through such glass. What Fancy sees is what we are invited to see. And yet, there is a disquieting quality here, which will not be calmed by rational commentary. That the windowpanes become eyes gives life of sorts to the house, suggesting one more dimension to perception in the passage. As the distorted visions attest eloquently, how one sees and what one sees lends itself, or is possessed by an older, anachronistic, folk-fetishism in the rural scene.

Moreover, regarding the complex and encrypted traces in a given scene, landscape or representation, Hardy stages a series of singular interrogations concerning the very ontology of the historical and inquiry into it, as event and discourse in the final decades of the nineteenth century. As Dick's song reminds us, the present is never sealed off from the past, and the past can always return out of the dark, in a fragment, an impersonal cultural memory, or in the ruin of hitherto daily practices and snatches, which in returning with apparitional force ruin the present by opening it onto a future, which cannot be foretold. In this, Dick's song anticipates the end of Hardy's novel. Though *Under the Greenwood Tree* is divided into four parts, named after the seasons, there is an epilogue of two chapters. These give details of Dick and Fancy's wedding, the very last concluding with the sound of the nightingale 'from a neighbouring thicket', which suggests to Fancy, now Dick's wife, a 'secret she should never tell' (*UGT* V.II.159). There is a quiet echo here of the myth of Philomela, who, raped, her tongue cut out, can never tell her secret. In this violent allusion, *Under the Greenwood Tree* concludes with the formal violence of realist fiction in the wedding and the sacrifice that closure demands. Marriage in its violence and institutionalised violation is offered as a marked contrast to the playful pastoral sexuality of Dick's song, 'Rosebud in June'. At the same time, though, in moving beyond the cycle of seasons, the novel breaks the tension between cyclical and linear temporality. It thus implies that the moment of modernity is complicit in acts of silencing, and that the future cannot be narrated.

Under the Greenwood Tree begins and ends, then, with 'voices', with song, and the silencing of a female voice, even though that voice had initially been given an 'organ', itself is a replacement, an historical updating, of earlier forms of music. This ephemeral trace of the living, transcribed and recorded as the silent trace of an oral trace signifying the temporality of existence, works in concert, yet from tension also, with the title and its implicit framing and temporal suspension. All life in painting is a 'still life'. Indeed, in that it is suspended, animation gone, there is nothing of life there, arguably. One reads merely a simulacrum, from which one strives to read, and so respond to, what we might call a 'still death'. The moment of the trace of the voice has its own temporal moment. That it is present at all suggests the possibility that the singer is dead. The iterable trace remains beyond presence. In this, silent and yet implying music, it is a purely graphic gesture, and so accords with the brush stroke of the painting. Yet, inasmuch as the trace is registered as unheard music and emanating from the human voice, the registration implies more than can be shown: an invisible resonance that communicates more nearly, with greater immediacy, than a purely visual image or sign.

If I know the music, that is. Otherwise it remains on the page, as silent as the grave, with an intimate proximity that is also an unbridgeable distance. I cannot envision that which I cannot receive or perceive. Hardy's text thus disrupts and distorts the visual aspect of its representational modes from within by the work of sound, which work serves multiple purposes. Sound is not narrative, at least not necessarily, or immediately. It arrives in the narrative but not, I would argue, wholly consonant with the narrative movement or trajectory. Sound draws our attention in different directions. It serves other purposes. Sound, whether of the natural world or that made by those who live in the world, intimates both singularity – as in the distinctness of a voice in the dark – and community, as with the music produced by the Mellstock Choir. Music also belongs to revelry, where community comes together in ritual gatherings in the first part of *Under the Greenwood Tree*, 'The Tranter's Party' and 'They Dance More Wildly' (*UGT* I.VII-VIII.35–48). The party begins on Christmas Day but dancing is not allowed until midnight, in deference, as Mrs Penny observes, to the Church of England (*UGT* I.VII.37). Thus, the tuning of the instruments is put off till five minutes before midnight (*UGT* I.VII.38), as sound intrudes upon the scene. The dancing soon moves on at such a pace that the men's sweat – a 'ghastly dew' (*UGT* I.VII.40) – leaves a film on the women's faces, whilst waistcoats become unbuttoned and a general air of dissipation is observed (*UGT* I.VII.40), before all moves on to

a 'further phase of rural revelry ... disclosed itself' (*UGT* I.VIII.42). The dancers, in turn, continue in a 'cadaverous phase', accompanied by music which leaves the fiddlers, those 'far-gone musicians' (*UGT* I.VIII.43), unable to sit down, their faces glowing red as they 'saw madly at the strings ... eyes closed, regardless of the visible world' (*UGT* I.VIII.42). All such wildness intensifies until the room appears, to Dick at least, 'like a picture in a dream' (*UGT* I.VIII.43).

Everything we see in this scene tends to excess, distortion, impropriety, and an almost daemonic transgression. If 'Hardy's use of musical allusion becomes the central metaphor through which he explores the underlying themes of community and sexuality' (Asquith 2005, 24), it is also that which brings about dissolution and the possibility of impropriety. The scene is, to the readers' and Dick's eyes alike, unreal, conjured as images within phantasmic image. The matter of perspective is not merely one of simultaneous perception; 'the reader's perspective is transformed into the observing consciousness of Dick' (Asquith 2005, 25), and with this, through Dick, we seem 'to be looking past tradition to a single unifying power governing the "steps" of all mankind' (Asquith 2005, 25). To intensify the unheard and its effect, to translate music into the writer's medium, Hardy shifts from past to present tense, as if to keep time with the motion of the dancers and the music of the fiddlers. Indeed, while we are witness to a surreal scene, the details of which touch on the spectral and grotesque, a dance of death as well as one of transgressive life force, it is the music, the imagined sound, which causes this to take place, as an uncanny counterpoint to the Christian occasion of celebration.

And it is disquieting because music 'introduces' in the novel – regardless of Christianity, part of that and yet frequently interrupting Christian discourse as its other-within – the 'idea of a community in which each man has his allotted role, fulfilling a traditional ritual' (Asquith 2005, 24). Yet, there is no sound as such, only the signs of sounds, none of which are ever capable of direct representation. Music arrives indirectly, to be apprehended analogically through the signs, the traces, that remain in the writer's frantic effort to contain the activity through literary representation. It is as if the music is Hardy's dark matter to the materiality of the rural universe: imperceptible as such, yet leaving its effects on the world. Between the intuition or perception of the reader and the sign on the page and the concept, object or event for which that sign stands, there is an unbridgeable gap; this space is marked most acutely, most materially, in the text by the sign that stands in for the sound, whether that sound is that of the bees in *Under the Greenwood Tree*, the

'baa' of the sheep in *Far From the Madding Crowd*, the waterfall in *Desperate Remedies,* or the frying fish inside William Worm's head, in *A Pair of Blue Eyes* (*PBE* I.IV.27).

This last example might strike some as odd, to say the least, or simply inappropriate. After all, the sound can never be heard, because it is an imaginary sound, a neurological disorder perhaps, an aural phantasm of Worm's mind. But, then, it has to be asked, what sound is not imaginary, spectral, strictly speaking? Are not all sounds, as distinct from those organs or phenomena responsible for producing them, both material and immaterial? Sound reminds us that there is that in the material world which cannot be represented directly, that a certain presentation takes place in the gap between the subject and the sign, but that presentation is only ever, always, appresentative. When Hardy cites the well-known lines from *Macbeth* in *Far From the Madding Crowd* – 'full of sound and fury, signifying nothing' – he is perhaps indicating the nature of textuality itself, as so many signals, so much interference which we, as readers, channel, mix, and produce in so many meaningful ways, whereby we invent meaning, we mark the brute and otherwise mute materiality of the world with a significance that, since Hardy at least, it has been implicitly understood as lacking intrinsically. Where meaning is absent, the page is blank; it remains to be written – and to be read. If Hardy's principal characters fail to understand this, it is perhaps a sign that they are both caught up in, and themselves marked by, the material signs of their own historicity, those material traces that come to articulate their being, often to such devastating effect. Hardy's characters, it might be said, are caught in historically anachronistic modes of self-reading, where the act of reading the self is already an afterthought, too late or just late enough. In glimpsing indirectly the ways in which they have come to be written, they no longer read how they write themselves and write the moment, the event, in which they are engaged. Perhaps this is an appropriate definition of Hardyean tragedy. Hardy's protagonists are neither Victorian nor Modern. Caught in some liminal place of transition between discernibly reassuring self-readings, they are post(humously) modern.

IV. IMAGE AND IMPRESSION

Of course, it would not be accurate to say that there is no visual representation in *Under the Greenwood Tree*. It is simply the case that frequently there is a visual, as well as an aural impressionism, which exceeds the calm order and stability of Dutch genre painting,

bringing such a mode of representation into the present day, intimating temporal and historical instability, anachrony or impermanence. In order to perceive this further, I ask the reader to follow me, in the rest of this section, through a difficult, but necessary engagement with some challenging philosophical ideas relating to the limits of representation and visuality. To begin with an example: take the details from descriptions of Geoffrey Day's house. In what to Fancy is a familiar scene, every piece of furniture is duplicated: 'There was a repetition upon inanimate objects ... consisting for the most part of two articles of every sort' (*UGT* II.VI.73). Everything is duplicated because Geoffrey is storing up items for Fancy's house in the future. The future is destined to be a repetition of the past; at least, this is a strong reading of Geoffrey's desire. Yet, in that there are two eight-day clocks, these tick alternately, one striking the hour in 'two and half minutes', the other in 'three minutes' (*UGT* II.VI.73). Hardy brings to this quaint order a disjointing, a dissymmetry or dissy-chrony, which temporally takes up the 'double vision' that haunts the room. I say 'haunts' deliberately, for it seems that there is something not a little uncanny in the repetition of furniture. Hardy creates an estranging image within the homely and familiar scene through this doubling, as though the eyepieces of a nineteenth-century optical toy were slightly out of alignment. This distortion of vision not only disturbs from within both the home and realist representation, but also finds its aural echo in the timepieces' polyrhythmia. A little further on in this representation of Geoffrey Day's house, Hardy observes of the 'window-board' that it 'was curiously stamped with black circles burnt thereon by the heated bottoms of drinking-cups, ... the result giving to the ledge the look of an envelope which has passed through innumerable post-offices' (*UGT* II.VI.74). Two distinct and markedly different 'worlds' come together in the single place and single representation, thereby transforming how we see in drawing our attention to what would otherwise go unremarked through the strangeness of the somewhat catachrestic analogy.

The question of vision, of how one views the world and how one's being is viewed as of the world, is taken up repeatedly throughout *Under the Greenwood Tree*. In the novel, vision of the landscape is all but obliterated in a rainstorm, as the wind whips the branches of trees back and forth, up and down, in innumerable violent movements, which neither the eye nor the reading can fully comprehend in a single reading:

A single vast gray cloud covered all the country, from which the small rain and mist had just begun to blow down in wavy sheets, alternately

thick and thin. The trees of the old brown plantation writhed like miserable men as the air wended its way swiftly among them: the lowest portions of their trunks, that had hardly ever been known to move, were visibly rocked by the fiercer gusts, *distressing the mind* by its painful unwontedness, as when a strong man is seen to shed tears. Low-hanging boughs went up and down; high and erect bows went to and fro; the blasts being so irregular, and divided into so many cross-currents, that neighbouring branches of the same tree swept the skies in independent motions, crossed each other, passed, or became entangled. Across the open spaces flew flocks of green and yellowish leaves, which, after travelling a long distance from their parent trees, reached the ground, and lay there with their undersides upwards. (*UGT* IV.III.124; emphasis added)

An aesthetic and phenomenal after-effect is produced as a result of the reader being placed before a scene which is, because of its formal, material occlusion of vision, and because of its mimetic ruination, impossible to see as such but only as so many graphic marks, visual signals all the more disquieting because in their performativity they resist any coalescence or recuperation into a meaningful or organic whole. And more than this, the windswept, storm-torn trees of *Under the Greenwood Tree* offer us form which impresses itself upon us as at once at an uncloseable distance and yet also impossibly near to us. (Indeed, as I have implied in discussion of *Under the Greenwood Tree*, Hardy's text travels from the stable location of the reader as viewer before what he calls in his subtitle 'A Painting of the Dutch School', with all its implications of control, order, architectonic harmony, mimetic propriety and readability in some humanist vision of a knowable world, to the final chapter, where we are placed, impossibly, *under* the greenwood tree, in the midst of fecundity and dissonance, motion and fragmentation.)

What Hardy demands that we should seek to recognize and respond to is the apparent fact that, in the words of Schopenhauer,[3] 'a book can never be more than the image and impression' (Schopenhauer 2000, 509). This remark finds a number of echoes, not only in Hardy's novels, but also in his personal writings, whether he is reflecting on the nature of the novel or that of poetry. A novel is, for example, an 'impression, not an argument'. It is also a 'series of seemings', a phrase hinting simultaneously at the limits of accurate representation and the analogical or apparitional force by which writing may communicate, if at all. Similarly, poems should be 'a series of feelings and fancies ... possess[ing] little cohesion of thought'. Hardy argues that one should 'catch the vision which the writer has in his eye ... even while it half eludes him'. Elsewhere, comparing his interest tellingly – for us, at least – with 'the

much decried, mad, late-Turner' (*LTH* 185) with his acts of writing, Hardy avers that 'my own interest lies largely in non-rationalist subjects since non-rationality seems, so far as one can perceive, to be the principle of the Universe' (*LTH* 309).

While Schopenhauer acknowledges the event as traumatic in its distortion of vision, whether inner or outer, metaphorical or literal, Hardy, it would appear, sees distortion as the necessarily inescapable condition of response, of reading and writing, and of memory's re-vision. The poem, being the registration of the traces of aesthetic and sensuous apperception cannot cohere, while the novel comprises fleeting phantasms and simulacra. While Schopenhauer privileges the disagreeable, Hardy appears to assert that analogical apperception is the only access to what we call 'reality' which is available through reading and memory, and which then becomes differentially refigured through the relay we call writing. Indeed, it would seem that Hardy sees reading, writing, and memory (which, I would like to propose, are non-synonymous cognates) as so many encrypted manifestations of *just this distorted vision*. In order to produce the vision, in order to *see*, that is to say to form language as meaningful structure, 'the human must already be constituted by affects and percepts' (Bourassa 2002, 64), which are in turn so many instances of the inescapable translation of incident or event, and not simply the result of that which is disagreeable. However, despite this small, albeit significant divergence between Schopenhauer's text and that of Hardy, what the novelist reveals, I think, is that what is necessary in any reading of an author is to understand '*how* he has thought' and that access to this *how* is through attention to '*style* [which] is an exact impression of this *how* . . . . a man's style shows the *formal* nature of all his ideas' (Schopenhauer 2000, 516).

But how are we to understand the question of style with regard to Hardy, while not assuming, of course, that style is ever a single style, but that this term is, it has to be stated, a figure by which we provisionally gather various oscillations and resonances without any otherwise justifiable organizing principle? And what might the figure of style have to do with the necessary matter of sight, of vision in all its senses as these pertain to Hardy's 'vision' of the novel or the poem? It is important to assert that sight, along with its cognates, as these pertain to memory and understanding, is to be considered not as a simple figure, a metaphor that dominates Hardy's text. Rather, we should see sight and vision as the material signs, the marks on the page, of an immaterial troping flux, mediating spectral resonances travelling between the visible and the invisible, between the now of the reader, the now of the narratorial articulation, and the absent

moment, never available as such that memory and writing call to mind. And style, it might be said, is another name for this fluctuating irrythmia.

The problem of seeing, of vision, is, however precisely *a problem* because of the manner in which it can come to tyrannize, whether one turns to another of Hardy's influences, Coleridge (himself under the influence of Kant). Take, for instance, the following remark:

> Under that despotism of the eye ... under this strong sensuous influence, we are restless because invisible things are not the objects of vision; and metaphysical systems, for the most part, become popular, not for their truth, but in proportion as they attribute to causes as susceptibility of being seen, if only our visual organs were sufficiently powerful. (Coleridge 1984, 107)

Hardy comprehends this problem and, ironically, it seems to have been his curse that so few of his critics, relatively speaking, do not. In his text, Hardy militates against this ocular despotism through a self-conscious textuality that is always reliant on the work of memory as having a visual power greater than mere visual representation. At the same time, Hardy's text works tirelessly to impose a material vision on the reader that is material to the extent that it produces and performs its effects through a resistance to slippage into the facile vision of a merely mimetic narrative art, from which a certain kind of critical reader can, by virtue of his or her ocular mastery, translate the singularity of the text into a representation of the metaphysical and universal. Hardy's *style* as this distortion of one aspect of sight and vision, and as the bringing to perception, those 'impressions' which 'catch the vision ... even while [they] half elude him', the barely visible oscillations of the spectral flux. Hardy's style as endlessly modulating observation is the ineluctable registration of 'an imprint, an indentation, a stamp' (Berger 1990, 3) as, on the one hand, the response to the impossibility of full presentation or representation, and on the other, the acknowledgement of the necessary and irreversible translation of observation into 'sensory experience', returning in turn as memory, as narrative, as *apparitioning*. We can observe style as spectral in the following:

> The writer uses words, but by creating a syntax that makes them pass into sensation that makes the standard language stammer, tremble, cry, or even sing: this is the style, the 'tone', the language of sensation .... The writer twists language, makes it vibrate, seizes hold of it, and rends it in order to wrest the percepts from perceptions, the affect from affections, the sensation from opinion. (Deleuze and Guattari 1994, 176)

The figure of vision, always coloured, always a translation, is the figure by which Hardy eludes its problem as the assumed conveyer or vehicle of truth. Vision as trope thus translates the materiality of history into the apparently 'prosaic materiality of the letter' (de Man 1996, 90); it is simultaneously vehicle and inscription, both constative and performative. More than this, however – and this is the difficult thing to grasp in the de Manian thought – the materiality of the letter corresponds to, is the linguistic approximation of a materialism of vision. There is a dynamic dislocation from that which appears self-evident to vision as the empirical guarantor of a meaning seemingly inherent, to a breaking up of organic inherence into the disarticulation of language; or as de Man would have it, meaning breaks down into sentences constituted through tropes, propositions into words, words into syllables, syllables into letters (de Man 1996, 89).

Vision as despotism of the eye, transplanted into the blind modalities of memory and narrative, becomes other than itself, showing what it cannot show *through the linguistic medium* and, in Hardy's case, through a hyperattentive, rigorous and detailed *metarealism*, thereby unveiling the impression, the memory, the sensuous apperception as the intensity we call singularity: as singular moment, singular event, singular, material individual, each, once translated via vision to language into numerous fragments become estranged in their being foregrounded. The singularity is, we might say, the drawing of focus, as well as being '[t]urning points and points of inflection' (Deleuze 1990, 52). And vision is what brings us into singular proximity with that which is nothing, strictly speaking, in the instant of envisioning, in the event of the revenant's arrival as trace. Sight and vision as the signs of style thus show us, indirectly, the occluding illusion harboured by mimesis in the service of metaphysics. And in revealing the limits of what can be seen and the limit of vision as a privileged figure, they also give us to 'see' – thereby unveiling irreversibly vision's countersignature or countertext, its hypogram – in another sense; that sense where 'seeing' means 'apprehension' (as in the phrase 'I see what you mean').

This apprehension, which is also apperception (indirect perception), apperception of the appresentative other (that which never presents itself directly), perceived through that analogical *poiesis* by which all texts may be understood as singular instances of mnemotechnicity, where all literary making is a 'making-appear' (in the full sense of *poiesis*), functions through the proximity which the figure of sight makes possible. The tropes of sight and vision, as these are inflected through notions of memory and recall, allows

for what otherwise cannot be articulated: '[w]hen there are unrecognized or barely recognized perceptions, when there is language that only gestures to something that it cannot name, when there are effects that seem unrelated to any discernible causes – there the force of the singularity is at work' (Bourassa 2002, 70).

V. HARDYEAN SINGULARITY: 'NEUTRAL TONES'

One place in which this 'force of singularity' might be understood to be at work is through the conjunction of event and landscape, as memory gathers them together only to leave them as the ruins of vision. Memory brings back the event with a force that erases the distance in time between the moment of the event and its phantasmic appearance in the materialization of memory that appears in the form of the text. The poem, 'Neutral Tones', written before Hardy's novels in 1867, though not published until a generation later in *Wessex Poems and Other Verses* (1898), exemplifies this:

> We stood by a pond that winter day,
> And the sun was white, as though chidden of God,
> And a few leaves lay on the starving sod,
>   – They had fallen from an ash, and were gray.
>
> Your eyes on me were as eyes that rove   5
> Over tedious riddles solved years ago;
> And some words played between us to and fro –
>   On which lost the more by our love.
>
> The smile on your mouth was the deadest thing
> Alive enough to have strength to die;   10
> And a grin of bitterness swept thereby
>   Like an ominous bird a-wing. . . .
>
> Since then, keen lessons that love deceives,
> And wrings with wrong, have shaped to me
> Your face, and the God-curst sun, and a tree,   15
>   And a pond edged with grayish leaves. (*CP* 12)

Tom Paulin reads the poem in the following way, speaking of the poem's narrator: '[t]he lesson that time and experience have taught him is presented visually, not conceptually . . . Because both their scenes are so starkly delineated and so sternly expressed it would be wrong to dismiss them as pathetic fallacies. It's *as though* the scene and the perceiver have become fused, instead of remaining separate like a landscape and a pair of spectacles' (Paulin 1975, 31; emphasis added). Paulin's *as though* registers the work of analogical relay in the poem. Sight returns with every reading of the poem, for

every reader, and in the narrator's memory of what was seen, and what comes to be seen without being present to the reader, there is a process of disordering, displacing the promise of presence even as the intimacy of the scene implies its possibility. The materiality of vision returns as those ruins we refer to as the materiality of the letter.

What is 'fused' is the proximity of distance and intimacy. What we 'see' through indirection is nothing other than the fact that the relationship between distance and intimacy, as a gap which can never be closed, nonetheless produces repeatedly what Walter Benjamin terms an 'auratic' experience. This is dependent on the phenomenological response to what is seen, whether one is speaking, as Benjamin does, of the work of art or the landscape. In that memory re-calls the response, there is about the experience of the auratic the shadow of a constant, ineluctable separability of that which is the aura from the event, as Samuel Weber makes clear: 'the aura would ... be something like ... the emanation of an object [landscape, or event] from which it removes itself' (Weber 1996, 88). As the memory of the other comes back in relation to the self – the poem is, after all, nothing other than this spectral interplay between the 'me' and 'you' by which these otherwise anonymous 'locations', locations as locutions, come into being – so the apparition of the moment also returns, with a vengeance. Identity cannot take place unless there is relay, whether communicated spatially or temporally, whether as an act of mapping spatial co-ordinates or through the folding of time back on itself through the quasi-teleological retrospect that is memory.

So, we are there and not there, almost simultaneously, almost witness to the encounter, but distanced by the fact that memory occasions reencounter. 'In this strange weave of time and space' (Benjamin 1979, 250) that is reading, 'the singular appearance of a distance, which may be near, propels us to think the simultaneity of presence and absence' (Richter 2000, 223). When I read 'Neutral Tones', the poem approximates, in the literalist sense: it marks a distance in the presentation of the singular. The moment of reading the poem endows the inanimate text with an afterlife, where the subject is nothing more than the fleeting instance of pronominal displacement, figuring the re-vision of the past in the doubled present tense, that of memory, and that of reading. The experience of the auratic is the experience of this spectral oscillation, caught by the analogical work of the text: when I read this it is *as though* this memory were mine, it is *as though* I stood in the place of the poem's narrator, it is *as though* I were remembering *you*; and it is all the more uncannily resonant inasmuch as, in reading, it is *as though*

the *you* were *me*. The subject disappears in the auratic authenticity experienced through reading, the force derived from the spectral continuity of the text in its bearing witness to the past. In this, Hardy's text – not merely the poem 'Neutral Tones' but by extension each of his texts in markedly singular ways – is involved in a becoming-political. The text's anachronic disarray enacted through the revenance of memory brings about what David Ferris, with reference to the notion of the auratic, calls the 'advent of a present, a now that disarticulates the continuity of the past' (Ferris 1996, 19).

With that disarticulation comes a revelation of the mystification that is effected in monumentalizing the past as the past through acts of dating and historical sequence, which cannot account for revenance or overdetermination. While many of Hardy's poems mark the always-adventitious opening of the present from within itself, not only by the returns of past *nows* but also by figuring in the opening, the *nows* to come (without presence, memory is always the articulation of the past within the present), the novels deploy the past-in-the-present as a disfiguration, the distorted vision and transformation, of full presence so as to indicate the text's untimely modernity, as a modernity where the archaic and the modern are necessary mobile. In this, they open realist modes of representation from within to conjure the transcendental force of an auratic gaze that touches us most nearly in the intimation of humankind's iterable experience.

Hardy invokes just such an auratic gaze, and in this gathers the individual and the community, the singular experience and that which is shared through time, encouraging in the reader, through sensate apprehension, 'contemplative identification and communal integration'. The experience of the auratic thus promises to articulate 'forgotten bonds' (Koepnick 2002, 110). This is the experience traced in 'Neutral Tones', in the otherwise unconnected analogy between landscape and human encounter, or in 'The Photograph' (*CP* 465), between the inanimate portrait, and the uncontrollable memories that it conjures. As we see in the opening of *Greenwood Tree*, the auratic is grounded in 'cyclical and revenant time', the apperception it encourages reminding us 'of the human in nature, the natural in humanity' (Koepnick 2002, 110). We witness this in those places where trees are anthropomorphized and men emerge from the trees or disappear into them, as though they belonged to the forest, and elsewhere throughout Hardy's fiction, where the cultural rituals of society reiterate themselves according to the seasonal-cultural cycle. Hardy distorts vision in order to enable us to experience the auratic from within the merely real.

VI. PERMANENT IMPRESSIONS

A Pair of Blue Eyes gives further insight into the nature of personal and historical or transcendent vision. As its title suggests sight, the gaze, and vision are all significant. What the title does not quite reveal is that a pair of blue eyes that have to be observed, there is another position from which those eyes are seen; equally, those blue eyes can return the gaze. Hardy's concern with the historicity of identity is orientated 'less in terms of "how [the] work reflect[s] historical trends and events" ... than in terms of the way in which the self [and the text] is constituted by and writes itself into history' (Armstrong 2000, 2). Perspective and perception, visual orientation and comprehension gained through vision constitute one aspect of the subject's self-constitution and composition. Yet looking and seeing do not give immediate access to the meaning of the world: there is always mediation, and so distortion in transformation or translation. In Hardy, writing the self through self-reflection and reflection on others occasions reflection both on one's identity or ontology as this has come to be transmitted, and also, as it may come to be received. When Dick Dewy looks beyond the immediate conditions of the dance he receives a vision of other worlds and that which flows through time so as to make connection between discrete temporal moments. Whether Dick understands fully is not the question; that the reader has such vision opened from within the material frame of the narrative is.

Hardy is aware of this somewhat uncanny apperceptive self-reading from very early on in his career. In *A Pair of Blue Eyes*, Elfride Swancourt asks Henry Knight, one of her two lovers:

> 'You are familiar of course, as everybody is, with those strange sensations we sometimes have, that our life for a moment exists in duplicate.'
> 'That we have lived through that moment before?'
> 'Or shall again.' (*PBE* II.V.166)

In a moment of what we familiarly term for our experience of the unfamiliar introjection concerning a memory that is never ours, *déjà vu*, Elfride draws attention to the way in which the self is shot through by other selves, other times. Of an older generation, if not precisely that of her father's, Knight is led through his somewhat geological and archaeological understanding of the world to translate Elfride's remark purely in terms of retrospective temporal revenance. His version concedes that we only experience an intimation of the past, clutching after its memory traces. However, what

dislocates and estranges is Elfride's suggestive self-consciousness concerning how the self, in writing itself into history, becomes its own supplement, transmitted into the future that it will come to haunt. Indeed, what haunts Elfride's words is the sense that haunting comes from the future as well as the past. Not to over-emphasize the matter, it is this question of self-inscription as a self-reading of the grounds of being that has been misperceived, if noticed at all in Hardy's text.

Elfride Swancourt's reading of temporality affords her a privileged place within the novel named for her most distinctive and representable feature. As the narrator observes of Elfride, 'There seemed to be a special facility offered her by a power external to herself ...' (*PBE* I.XI.104). In her apprehension of the haunted nature of sensate temporal experience she escapes fixity within any mere temporal location. Her two lovers, Knight and Stephen Smith, have access only to particular forms of information and knowledge that are culturally and temporally bound. Smith, an autodidact educated through correspondence courses, is, in effect, a modern man in Hardy's world. As he responds to Swancourt, his teacher, Knight, fears that ' "the speaking age is passing away, to make room for the writing age"' (*PBE* I.VII.53). Stephen is thus a figure produced by the post, a subject inscribed by the transmission of others' writings. Knight, on the other hand, fearing a future that has already arrived in the form of Stephen and contributing to that very future he anticipates with anxiety, is a geologist, a subject who, produced by his readings of a material past, has little access either to the modern, or to that which is not immediately comprehensible in terms of materiality. Elfride, so difficult, if not impossible, to describe for Hardy – 'the height of her figure, the turn of her head. These things may never be learnt to the very last page of the commentary' (*PBE* 8) – verges on the ineffable, and her eyes bespeak this intensely. Yet even this feature, 'blue as autumn distance – blue as the blue we see between the retreating mouldings of hills and woody slopes on a sunny September morning. A misty and shady blue, that has no beginning or surface, and was looked *into* rather than *at*' (*PBE* 8), escapes depiction. Note how Hardy attempts to approximate that which, though partaking of impermanence, nevertheless makes 'a permanent impression', which is 'afterwards recalled to [the] mind's eye'

as she appeared in one particular scene, which seems ordained to be her special medium of manifestation throughout the pages of his memory. As the patron Saint has her attitude and accessories in mediaeval illumination, so the Sweetheart may be said to have hers upon the table of her

true love's fancy.... Miss Elfride's image chose the form in which she was beheld during these minutes of singing from her permanent attitude of visitation to Stephen's eyes during his sleeping and waking hours in after days. (*PBE* I.III.22)

Hardy's analogical approximation of the eyes – he strives through a chain of commentaries concerning the colour blue to hit on that analogy or impression nearest the colour it is impossible to describe – only serves to defer precise representation, concluding in the conscious deliberation over propositions, to hint that in Elfride there is nothing there: there is no *there* there. Though obviously a living woman, 'who' Elfride is remains inaccessible and is irreducible to the 'what'. This is intimated when Hardy remarks that Elfride 'lived' in her eyes, and that in her eyes one might see 'the sublimation of all of her' (*PBE* I.I.8). The nearest one might come to representing the 'who' is either through brief reference to a works of art (*PBE* I.I.8), all of which only approximate by analogy or through the chance that one may gain a sense of the singularity of aura, or through the vague impression of pellucid and diaphanous atmospheric tint, which in some strange manner ties Elfride to the landscape of Wessex more intimately than any more material relation. The eyes thus give us to see everything and nothing, unless in the most indirect manner.

As we see from the passage that follows the longer quotation above, in which Hardy admits the reader to Stephen Smith's perception of Elfride, perception is not general, but specific, singular. Moreover, what one person sees and how that person is affected by vision is always tied to a specific event. There is, inescapably, historicity in the registration that sight imprints on memory. Perspective is partial, subjective, impressionistic, and as much imbued by the trace that Elfride leaves on Stephen's senses – the sight of her is allied to her singing – and thereafter on his memory. Hardy's prose marks this phenomenal register even as it remarks the imperceptible shift from the event of inscription into the iterable resonance in the subject's memory. That the 'who' of Elfride is particularly evanescent, uncanny in its force even, may be caught in Hardy's description of Elfride's ghost-like power, her 'special medium of manifestation'. At the same time, it must also be acknowledged that for all this spectral capacity, Elfride's projection is received as an inscription on Stephen, for she leaves her mark on the pages of his memory, on the 'table' or tablet of his 'fancy' or imagination. Stephen, in response to Elfride, is nothing more than a wax tablet onto which marks are inscribed. The temporal and subjective

slippage already acknowledged is signalled more clearly as the passage develops and Hardy effectively suspends narrative time, breaking the realist frame, by shifting into present tense:

> The profile is seen of a young woman in a pale gray silk dress with trimmings in swan's-down, and opening up from a point in front ... the cool colour contrasting admirably with the warm bloom of her neck and face. The furthermost candle on the piano comes immediately in a line with her head, and half invisible surrounding her crown like an aureola. Her hands are in their place on the keys, her lips parted, and trilling forth, in a tender *diminuendo*, the closing words of the sad apostrophe:
>
> > 'O Love, who bewailest
> > The frailty of all things here,
> > Why choose you the frailest
> > For your cradle, your home, and your bier!'
>
> Her head is forward a little, and her eyes directed keenly upward to the top of the page of music confronting her. Then comes a rapid look into Stephen's face, and a still more rapid look back again to her business ... (*PBE* I.III.22-23)

The shift to present tense suspends the conventional narrative time, demanding or encouraging the reader to see the vision as if it were a spectral presence manifesting itself before the reader's mind's eye, as a memory that is not his or hers. Stephen is described as 'pausing motionless' (*PBE* I.III.23), and this, as a result of a shift in position on his part, enacts the shift and suspension produced by Hardy in the narration for the reader. This, as the opening sentences make clear, is Stephen's afterthought; this is the event that produces the *après-coup*, which, in coming before Stephen's memory as an apparition, appears also directly to the reader; or rather say, directly, indirectly, because writing as representation is as indirect as memory itself; it is the structure of traces and not the event, obviously enough. But Hardy is alluding to the oscillation between graphic and visual, between two distinct temporal occurrences, one of which is endlessly iterable in its recall of the singularity of the past moment. The shift to present tense might be read as serving to signal that singularity, in bringing back both the intimate immediacy of the moment and also, in that immediacy, the very fact of that moment's inaccessibility.

There is a further act of doubling operating here, for we witness both the trace of memory, as it reappears for Stephen, and, at a remove from that also, that remove which allows the reader

to experience a memory which can never be his, we witness the textual intervention, to which Hardy directly points our attention, with the self-conscious reference to historically distinct modes of textual representation, in a binocular instant connecting the artifice of mediaeval illumination with the equally artificial form of nineteenth-century fiction. And this condition of artifice and text is further given force through that image of Elfride's lips permanently parted in song, given with the very words of that song printed on the page in verse form. However, more takes place still: for inasmuch as this moment suspends narrative, drawing attention to both the doubleness and artifice, and with that all necessary acts of self-conscious and irreversible translation that comes to be foregrounded – so that, arguably, as readers, our experience of the vision and memory of Elfride is as 'real' as Stephen's own moment of anamnesiac hiatus (the event gives pause which memory causes to be reiterated) – there is nonetheless a gradual temporal progression in the passage. Thus, we witness in the very suspension the ineluctable motion of time, recorded in the reciprocal action of eyes. In that present tense, we become aware that we are watching someone watching someone else, who for the briefest of moments looks up to gaze at the observer.

Though significant in what it shows us and gives us to see about the work of vision, this scene and the opening commentary on Elfride's eyes are not the only passages in *A Pair of Blue Eyes* which address sight. We read, elsewhere, that 'it was a time when mere seeing is meditation, and meditation peace' (*PBE* I.X.94). Sight sees past the material world, hinting at insight or inner vision. Such vision, already associated with Elfride and imagination, is announced elsewhere. Elfride 'had an inner and private world apart from the visible one about her' (*PBE* I.XI.105), while, of her eyes, it is observed that they 'seemed to look at you, and past you, as you were then, into you future; and past your future into your eternity – not reading it, but gazing in an unused, unconscious way' (*PBE* 161). It is also a quality of Elfride's that in 'looking at things with an inward vision, she lost consciousness of the flight of time' (*PBE* I.VIII.71). To return to the opening chapters of the novel, we are reminded that there is a 'great contrast between the reality [Elfride] held before her ... and [that which] ... lurked in her imagination ...' (*PBE* I.II.15) when she first meets Stephen. This is hardly surprising, but the disjunction between the mind's eye's projected vision and reality is more generally important in Hardy's text as an expression of the interplay between visible and invisible, the real and the imagined. As the narrator reflects later in the novel,

[w]hen ... our different fractions of consciousness are reduced to their lowest terms, rain or no rain is ... found to be the *primum mobile* of mood ... and mental conclusions affecting our humours at such times, which seem drawn from independent incidents, are really but extreme corollaries of one of those atmospheric conditions (*PBE* I.V.34).

Vision and emotion are closely connected, narrative presenting a border or limit to visualization even as it strives to give an impression of the inner consciousness. Clearly, Hardy follows Schopenhauer's assertion that, of the senses, sight's 'sphere is the most far-reaching, and its receptivity and susceptibility the keenest ... due to the fact that what stimulates it is an *imponderable*, ... *something* hardly corporeal, *something* quasi-spiritual' (Schopenhauer 1966, II. 27; emphases added). That indefinable aspect towards which Schopenhauer gestures resides at the heart of vision for Hardy. Additionally, seeing and perception, comprehension and interpretation belong to one another in a close-knit network that structures the act of reading. The text is thus a surface, *into*, rather than *at* which we gaze, hoping that from this boundary, an invisible gaze might be returned, affecting consciousness as if it were addressing us directly. Like those *Blue Eyes* of the title, we remain at a threshold, straining to see into, and so be touched by, the invisible. Yet, if what we see marks a border across which we cannot cross, there remains also a phantom trace to be 'remembered ... as an indelible mark in ... history' (*PBE* II.XIV.260).

VII.   MARGINS, BOUNDARIES, BORDERS, LIMITS, THRESHOLDS (AND SO ON ...)

Shortly after his first meeting with Elfride, Stephen Smith looks out of his room's window 'a short time after dawn', to see 'two bold escarpments sloping down like the letter V' (*PBE* 24). As soon as there is light, there is sight. Importantly, this is specifically for some one, from whose vision we receive the mediated world. What we, as readers, are given to see, is not merely an objective rendition of the world but a view which is always already an interpretation, a translation, which requires reading. With that comes a perception of perception. Hardy foregrounds this through drawing attention to the constructedness of the image, tracing, and directing us toward the limits of the visible, in the form of topographical lines, limits and horizons. These materially re-enforce and frame vision as someone's vision, and, with that, the visuality of the visible as this, in its simplest elements, touch the eye and imprint themselves on the mind.

Through foregrounding of plane and line, utilizing terms that map and delineate the landscape as a series of visible phenomena, Hardy effectively presents the world and doubles the impression on the eye and the subject, through the transformation of the seen into the lines on the page. Escarpments, slopes or ridges most commonly associated with plateaux, are especial geological borders, but also marks on the page that give shape to the otherwise invisible. In this particular moment of vision, the lines of the land form a letter, illustrating a vertical descent: V – for verticality, for vision, or, indeed, for vanishing point, to risk a strong reading here. The land is inscribed, incised in a perpendicular, precipitous manner, and the eye transforms the land into meaningful form, which the reader is invited to replicate.

Prior to any meaningful transformation or secondary interpretation, however, we may observe and acknowledge that the scene is composed of frames and borders. There is the window and the limit that the escarpments mark. There is also that temporal liminal marker of dawn, separating dark from light, the invisible from the visible. The motion of time effects its own temporal inscription on the seen, as if the world were in a process of 'becoming visible', or 'becoming-there' for a first time of our reading. Frames and lines divide the moment, even as the passage of time is divided. We are invited in turn to look through the window at the escarpments forming the letter V. (This raises an unanswerable question: is this Stephen's perception or that of the narrator?). At the same time, though, we are also looking at Stephen as he looks through the window. Representation is thus revealed through and as a series of lines of sight, through displacements and reiterations of the act of looking, as invisible lines intimated through the divisions and lines, and the various sectors, lines, planes and spaces that constitute the scene.

As with many of Hardy's novels, *A Pair of Blue Eyes* repeatedly and continuously draws our attention towards such liminal sites and the work of boundaries, borders or thresholds. Such structural, formal and geometric division effectively produces the text as a network of surfaces, which the eye translates into a vision of a real world. This is what takes place, of course, in any act of reading, and in any novel. In Hardy's case however, there is a foregrounding of surface and line, such structural marking often accompanied by stark or brilliant lighting effects, with sharp juxtapositions of light and shadow. Amongst the boundaries which come to be traced, there are: doors; archways; windows; eyes themselves; the horizon; walls; graves and gravestones; gateways; hill-ridges; the edges of cliffs against the sky.

There are too many such references to be able to reproduce here or to discuss at any length, but a few examples and allusions should suffice. One chapter title (and titles are themselves forms of boundary) ' "'Twas on the Evening of a Winter's Day"' (*PBE* I.II.11), an apparently unidentified quotation, introduces a liminal temporal moment, which is then reproduced on the first page of that chapter, when 'two or three additional hours had merged afternoon in evening' and 'some moving outlines might have been observed against the sky on the summit of a wild lone hill in this district. They circumscribed two men, having at present the aspect of silhouettes . . .' (*PBE* I.II.11). The temporal passage and diminution of illumination serves as the preface to the adumbrated iteration of various outlines and borders, human and natural, all of which are qualified by conditional sight ('might have been observed'). Time moves with an almost imperceptible transition, as the world is divided and reduced to summits, outlines and silhouettes. All light being gone, 'the outline and surface of [a] mansion gradually disappeared', but in place, 'windows' appear, 'illuminated', and so 'transfigured into squares of light on the general body of the night landscape as it absorbed the outlines of the edifice into its gloomy monochrome' (*PBE* I.II.13). Shortly thereafter the reader's attention is drawn to 'an additional mile of plateau . . . reposing on the horizon' (*PBE* I.II.13). Later in the novel, the church wall, dividing foreground from middleground, is observed (*PBE* I.IV.24). Such division also marks off the living from the dead, for description of the graveyard is given, which itself is 'a mere profile against the sky, serrated with the outlines of graves and a very few memorial stones' (*PBE* I.IV.24–25). As the eye is taken up the hill towards the background via the line of a path, itself 'bounded on each side by a little stone wall' (*PBE* I.IV.28; the movement of the eye is conducted in a manner that replicates the division of seeing and the passage of vision from foreground to background in the poem '*Domicilium*'), so the eye is drawn to gleaming 'fragments of quartz and blood-red marbles' (*PBE* I.IV.28). A further boundary in the form of a stone stile is acknowledged (*PBE* I.IV.28), though the 'within' of the graveyard is 'not . . . so divided from the without as to obliterate the sense of open freedom' of the wild hill (*PBE* I.IV.28).

To move on from this moment, the sea is subsequently observed, 'visible to a width of half the horizon, and meeting the eye with the effect of a vast concave', while a 'collar of foam' marks the place where land and sea meet, which foam repeats 'in its whiteness the plumage of a countless multitude of gulls' (*PBE* I.IV.28). Line and

limit repeat themselves, from one to another, one in another. There is a further echo of the sea as margin and limit later in the novel:

> Two or three degrees above that melancholy and eternally level line, the ocean horizon, hung a sun of brass, with no visible rays, in a sky of ashen hue. It was a sky the sun did not illuminate or enkindle.... The sheet of sky was met by a salt mass of gray water, flecked here and there with white. (*PBE* III.IV.308)

Hardy's geometry of representation, broken down into degrees, becomes oppressive. The self is not only oppressed, though. Simultaneously, he or she is enclosed *and* displaced, externalized, as the 'melancholy' of the horizon is intensified by the association of line with muted tonal range: ashen, grey, white. Everywhere the eye looks, it finds itself enclosed, *by and at* the very limits of vision. The subject is nothing more in this moment than a seeing eye, on the surface of which the world impresses itself. The paucity of illumination illuminates only the enclosure of the self in the ubiquity of the finite, which is all the more oppressive perhaps because it stretches to the furthermost limits of sight.

Other significant manifestations of threshold or limit appear: 'an ancient gateway...spanned by the high-shouldered Tudor arch' (*PBE* I.V.39) places in the present moment the architecture of the past as a material remainder and memorial, a representation of architectural form that is echoed near the end of the novel in '[t]he heavy arch spanning the junction of tower and nave' (*PBE* III.V.315). The tracing of such a boundary is intensified further in being described as a 'black frame' to the 'distant misty view'. This complements 'the wide and convex sea behind', all of which is defined as a '*coup-d'oeil*' (*PBE* III.V.315). This phenomenal effect – rendered aesthetically as *coup d'oeil*, literally that which strikes the eye – is read as an effect of medieval origin. Thus it is that the past leaves on landscape, architecture and any representation of the two a trace that is indelibly that of historicity, which strikes the eye in the present. This is also the effect described in the first passage cited. In the description of the ancient gateway already mentioned, there is added 'the faint outline of...ditch and mound', the merest trace of fourteenth-century origin and survival (*PBE* I.V.39). There is an aesthetic apprehension here that is closely tied to cultural anamnesis, an impersonal memory, which, again breaks into, and suspends narrative, through the historical detail: law (the decree issued by Edward II), architecture, and the intermixing of languages notably disturb the passage, and arguably such a gesture is indicative of the polyglot layers of location and the signs of temporal event, all that

is invisible but which serves in the production of the identity and memory of Wessex. The act of representation is both architectural and historical, structural and temporal, and thus its act of tracing plays on the visible and invisible, the invisible within the visible, in excess of any merely mimetic representation or realism. Landscape, spatiality itself, is a form of inscription, on which are the signs of the writing of temporal event. And it is this revenance of the ruins of historical event that disturbs from within the present, in an effective de-sedimentation of the aesthetic act of representation. Realism is suspended in favour of phenomenal reality, aesthetic apprehension, and appearing, or apparitioning, if you will. That which informs structure is that which makes possible the (temporal, historical, memorial) other within structure to overflow representation.

All such temporal traces thus deconstruct any simple notion of presence and the present or the adequate representation of the present, informing the reader of that which, in producing present meaning, remains, nevertheless, irreducible to received meaning reassembled as aesthetic whole in the form of aesthetic representation. They are thus also signs of a limit, across which we may or may not pass, but which interrupt vision through the divisions and repetitions that they impose upon the surface of sight and text otherwise undifferentiated in a geometry of more or less stark representation. They mark sites, loci in and of architecture, topography, the world, the self. Each is a point to which the eye is drawn, and against which one places oneself in the world. All are spatial, but there are also those liminal temporal moments, margins such as twilight, dawn, sunset. Even Elfride's underclothing, soaked by the rain and backlit suggestively presents itself as a boundary – between the proper and improper, the seen and the imagined, the visible and invisible. It is not merely between; it is also that double boundary between outer clothing and the naked body. In its revealed state and illuminated for Knight, and therefore the reader, from behind, it also presents a frame against which is projected the silhouette of the body.

What, though, might we read from the frequency of borders, thresholds, frames, boundaries or limits? Elaine Scarry has explored how plot and meaning are generated out of the interaction between corporeal boundaries and the material world through work (1994, 49–90 *passim*; see also Robson 2004, 495–503). However, as just remarked, the forms that the limit or border takes are manifold in Hardy's textual world, and closely related to questions of vision and sight. I reiterate this point in order that we do not lose sight of it. There are two paragraphs that begin the first three-volume

edition of *A Pair of Blue Eyes*, published in 1873, which Hardy subsequently removed when the novel was published in 1895 as Volume Four of the Osgood, McIlvaine Wessex Novels edition. These paragraphs, reintroduced in the Penguin Classics edition by editor Pamela Dalziel, draw the reader's attention to the list of characters. In beginning in this fashion, and asking:

> who shall put limits to the possible extent of good, bad, or indifferent circumstance that, in connection with these few agents and this narrow scene, may have arisen, declined, and been finally deposited in the Past as valuable matter for inspection by eyes who know or care where to find it? (*PBE* I.I.7)

Hardy not only stresses the arbitrariness, if not the impossibility, of assigning a limit, but also introduces his narrative as a series of sedimented deposits in the past, which chance to have been embedded, only to become subject to the gaze of someone who may happen to locate the remains. The opening two paragraphs of the first edition of *A Pair of Blue Eyes* are, then, nothing less than a boundary, to which the reader has her attention drawn, constructed with a degree of self-referential artifice. Hardy's opening forms a threshold, which turns back to both the preceding page, a text that, strictly speaking is already a margin, not part of the narrative-proper, and to a past 'narrow scene'. It is as if the margin of the past were expressing itself from within the framing of the present, breaking that frame but also reminding us of vision's constructedness. The paragraphs immediately suspend the narrative they are intended to introduce in this gesture, calling a halt to proceedings before we are even underway. In this, the paragraphs situate themselves as yet one more framing device or border. In doing so they complicate the very idea of an introduction through the acknowledgement of retrospective and self-reflective consideration of that which takes place, apropos the past, anamnesis, and narration, and how one, unjustifiably, shapes that material. We are not allowed for a moment to forget that this is what Hardy calls a 'record', a choice of word which is disruptive because it records both the idea of a record and the process of recording; it signals both process and structure.

Such doubleness is the very sign of the motion between the materiality of history and that of the letter, and therefore affirms the silent, graphic and irreversible shift that is, in effect, translation of what Hardy is pleased to describe in his introductory gesture as a 'congeries of significant phenomena' (*PBE* I.I.7). This phrase identifies precisely the mode of representation by which Hardy brings

the world to the mind's eye. Hardy 'heaps' or 'piles' up objects that impose themselves on the mind's eye, demanding that the subject's perception determine their significance, as they appear to view. In this manner, through particular attention to the visible, the inner and outer worlds of sight and insight, through the various liminal and marginal lines that give place to vision inviting interpretation, Hardy foregrounds how the human ability to encounter reality is both aesthetic and phenomenal. Hardy's narratives come to a halt, temporarily suspending their motion in order that, in paying attention to the divisions within the visible field, we might perceive event and object in a sensate apprehension that is peculiarly ours, and which enfolds us in the world, as beings in that world, and for whom the world has a more than merely material existence. Such enfolding and emplacement – expressed in *A Pair of Blue Eyes* most insistently in the focus on optical powers and their relation to narration and consciousness – grounds human consciousness through place and time. It does so, moreover, through that intense metarealism, which, in foregrounding its surface play – in the direction of the gaze, in the differentiation between inner and outer vision, in the continuous reminder of frames and borders by which the realist image of the world is divided – gives me to apprehend that 'I see something in something that I do not see as that which I see in it' (Seel 2005, 179). Hardy's text thus affords 'glimpses' of that which can never be seen as such, through the traces of the past, that which is other than a present moment, whilst in doing so intimates how, in the act of reading, a phantom world is made to appear, as if it were momentarily present, and as if I were capable of, if not entering that world, then made phantom, dematerialized and so transported across a temporal border, which is also the spatial interstices of word and page. Hardy wants me to understand my vision as a revelation concerning vision itself, my mode of perception affording me knowledge of my groundedness and historicity as a being, a being capable of reflecting on myself 'in the given' that is the historical, temporal world. He also gives to the reader an intimation of the visionary transformation that it is in the power of the literary to effect, or cause to take place.

VIII.   BEING-IN-THE-GIVEN

The ramification is that certain of Hardy's characters are therefore disconcertingly 'modern'. They are self-consciously 'historicized' subjects 'in the given' (Deleuze 1991, 87), even if they cannot always

apprehend this, as would seem to be the case with Elfride. Hardy's writing makes available to his readers an awareness of the extent to which the mind is world, although the world, for the reason that is it perceived by the limitations of a single mind, is not a totality. Moreover, that which Hardy understands as 'character', 'mind', or 'subject' is 'a particular set or a particular collection' of experiences, and begins from 'an animated succession of distinct perceptions' (Deleuze 1991, 87). Experience, in Hardy's world 'is succession, or the movement of separable ideas, insofar as they are different, and different, insofar as they are separable' (Deleuze 1991, 87–88). To the extent that Hardy can figure this as formal quality of representation he does so through the endless division of representation through border, boundary, threshold, margin, frame, and so on, in a thinking of being 'as fundamentally linked with time and history' (Schmidt 1988, 29).

That differentiation and separation are called into question, at least in part, is not to doubt their validity but to call attention to the limits of consciousness of apprehending in experience difference, singularity and separation. The affirmation of the limit in Hardy's world is borne witness to in the fact that so many of his characters act out repeatedly similar mistakes. Mistakes are made, misapprehensions hold sway, because the limits of consciousness prohibit or at the very least make problematic for his characters the possibility of thinking '*at the right moment*, of a harmony between the unknown powers on which the given appearances depend and the transcendent principles which determine the constitution of a subject within the given' (emphasis added). *At the right moment*, indeed, for no such moment is ever seen to arrive in Hardy's world. The 'real problem' in Hardy's world 'would be to think of a harmony between the powers of nature and the subject' (Deleuze 1991, 89). It is precisely the contingency of being-modern that makes such harmony impossible.

Hardy's narrators afford scant glimpses of such a harmony. For the novelist's creatures the problem remains even more insoluble because, in being suspended in the given they are, of course, caught in mortal time. Henry Knight recognizes this when hanging from a cliff-edge in *A Pair of Blue Eyes*. A novel that 'revolves entirely around secrets' (Dalzeil *PBE*, xvii), *A Pair of Blue Eyes* addresses the question of self-reading, identity and knowledge in a scene that offers the Hardy reader an exemplary figure for perceiving the relationship between one's being and one's historicity. Archetypal Victorian male that Henry Knight is, heir to Lyell and Darwin and

a generation of close readers and translators, he observes embedded into the cliff face a fossilized trilobite, eye to dead 'eye' with him:

> Knight was a geologist . . . his mind found time to take in, by a momentary sweep, the varied scenes that had had their day between this creature's epoch and his own. There is no place like a cleft landscape for bringing home such imaginings as these.
>
> Time closed up like a fan before him. He saw himself at one extremity of the years, face to face with the beginning and all the intermediate centuries simultaneously. (*PBE* II.IX.214)

Geology and palaeontology aside, this 'face to face' with the other leads Knight into a self-reflective consideration of temporality and mortality, and the place of the self in the universe perceived historically. Clinging to the margin between sea and land, life and death, Knight is also pressed up against the threshold between present consciousness and the material traces of the past, to which he is connected in being given consciousness of his own mortality, and the anticipation of himself as just one more future trace, unveiled to another and possibly greater, though certainly different consciousness.

Here is the trauma of becoming-conscious of one's historicity up close, being revealed to itself as a vision of being-in-the-given. Knight's experience of a radical, destabilizing anachrony, with its simultaneous phantasmagoria of past moments in which he apprehends his own as just one more in a temporal sequence, takes place precisely because he is written into history at his moment. The historicity of his being is traumatically unveiled to his consciousness, because his apprehension involves the phenomenological reflection – and anticipation – of his moment of modernity as being imminent in its own passing away. Despite his theoretical knowledge of geology, he cannot anticipate the sudden apocalypse of 'sensuously accessible *phainomena*' (Seel 2005, 22) that project themselves 'in the ephemerality of this . . . presence of appearing', which is the result not only of his personal education but also as the historical result of much scientific research in the nineteenth century (Seel 2005, 20). Knight's training in geology has not prepared him for the aesthetic and phenomenal mode of sensuous apprehension by which self-reading comes to takes place. In this scene, we might suggest, is a motif or metaphor for the untimeliness of all reading, and with that the perception of one's own modernity. The world in all its times is to be read, if only we know how; but knowing how is by no

means guaranteed, and the risk is that if we become the addresses for whom historicity's postal relay is destined, we might come into uncomfortable knowledge concerning our identities. As is remarked in *Two on a Tower*:

> the knowledge that scarce any other human vision was travelling within a hundred million miles of their own gave them such a sense of the isolation of that faculty as almost to be a sense of isolation in respect of their whole personality, causing a shudder at its absoluteness. (*TT* I.VIII.57)

Here, as in so many moments of reflection in Hardy, the singular perspective outweighs scientific knowledge. In a performative manner, perspective gives to the narrative observation an apprehension for the reader of that isolation. That shudder, along with Knight's 'face-to-face' and the reflexivity it engenders, intimates all that mere knowledge cannot prepare one for, and for which one cannot be prepared. In the singularity of perception, no 'unified epistemological center whose all-too-powerful gravitational force' (Benjamin 1996b, 93–94) can hold.

3

Being and Dwelling: *Far from the Madding Crowd* (1874), *The Return of the Native* (1878), *Two on a Tower* (1882)

I. WORLDS WITH, IN WORLDS

In *Tess of the D'Urbervilles*, Mr Crick tells the story of an ' "old aged man" ' who tricked a bull by playing a Nativity Hymn on his fiddle when it wasn't Christmas, in order to escape a violent altercation with the animal (*TD'U* III.XVII.110-111). The old man's name was William Dewy who, at the time of telling, ' "is a-lying in Mellstock Churchyard at this very moment" ' (*TD'U* III.XVII.111). A ' "curious story" ' that ' "carries us back to medieval times" ' (*TD'U* III.XVII.111), the tale not only invokes a distant world recovered through narrative, it also reintroduces the figure of Dick Dewy's grandfather. In *The Mayor of Casterbridge*, Michael Henchard's bankruptcy case is heard. In addition to his assets, Henchard offers his gold watch and purse, which are turned down in the following manner:

> The creditors, farmers almost to a man, looked at the watch, and at the money, and into the street; when Farmer James Everdene of Weatherbury spoke.
> 'No, no, Henchard,' he said warmly. 'We don't want that. 'Tis honourable in ye; but keep it. What do you say, neighbours – do ye agree?'

'Ay, sure: we don't wish it at all,' said Grower, another creditor.

'Let him keep it, of course,' murmured another in the background – a silent, reserved young man named Boldwood; and the rest responded unanimously. (*MC* 217)

The Everdene mentioned here, James, is the uncle of Bathsheba Everdene, the heroine of *Far from the Madding Crowd*, published twelve years before *Casterbridge*. Everdene also appears in the later novel as one of the names painted on a stall in the corn-market room of Casterbridge (*MC* XXXI.113). The young Boldwood, who joins with Everdene and others in assenting to Henchard's retention of his personal property, also 'returns' as his more mature self in the earlier of the two novels, his name apparently having appeared alongside Everdene's on one of the corn stalls in the manuscript of *The Mayor of Casterbridge*, but taken out by Hardy (*MC* 324 n.7).

This near correspondence between fictional worlds is more than mere intertextual reference. I say *near* because a number of years separate the narratives. *Tess* and *Under the Greenwood Tree* are separated by a generation approximately, *Mayor*, beginning in late summer, 1829 (*MC* I.3), and moving forward by almost eighteen years in Chapter III to the mid-1840s. At the time of *Madding Crowd*, Boldwood is forty (*FMC* XVI.103) and so approximately fifteen to twenty years older than in *Mayor*. This would put *Crowd*'s setting as being some time in the late 1860s. It is impossible to be more precise though for, although Hardy 'describes this novel as contemporary', in the 1912 edition he had removed references to war 'to avoid too close an historical specificity' (*MC* 359n.4). Such matters of dating aside, the question of this correspondence, with its suggestion that a character, appearing briefly in one novel, disappears from that only to turn up, or to have his relatives arrive in another, nearly a generation on in another novel is suggestive of partly overlapping or commensurate worlds. It also offers a perspective from one novel to the other, or more exactly, a perspective on the work of perspective. The authority for such a reflection does not reside in the chance recurrence of Everdene or Boldwood, but is given us by Hardy, who chooses the name 'Wessex' for a somewhat vague conglomeration of English counties. In his Preface to the 1912 Wessex Edition, Hardy reflects on his use of the name 'Wessex', which he calls, in a phrase now familiar to Hardy scholars, a 'partly real, partly dream-country' (*FMC* 393). Insisting, not unreasonably, that the name Wessex 'had never been heard of in fiction and current speech' before his usage in *Far from the Madding Crowd*, Hardy observes that were the term associated with any place

or time, it would 'theretofore have been taken to refer to nothing later in date than the Norman Conquest'. Wessex was, therefore, for Hardy presented to his reading public as an 'anachronism' of 'railways, the penny post, mowing and reaping machines, union work-houses, lucifer matches, labourers who could read and write, and National school children' (*FMC* 392).

The idea of an imaginary topography, recognizable in part, is today redolent either of virtual realities or parallel universes. All literature produces these, of course, and Wessex clearly names such an idea, and it does so, what is more, in a consciously foreground-ing manner. While George Eliot may create a midlands town called Middlemarch, Hardy invents a world, worlds within worlds, which has in certain aspects, historical and cultural identity and precedent. Wessex names more than just a landscape. It identifies more than a map-palimpsest, a simulacrum which may – more or less – be super-imposed over a map of England, being predominantly Dorset but incorporating also parts of Cornwall, Devon, Somerset, Hampshire, Wiltshire, and extending as far east as Aldershot and as far north as Oxford, or Christminster as it is known in *Jude the Obscure*. As Hardy's remark concerning the Norman Conquest makes plain, Wessex also names alternative times, in which ancient and modern are, if not coeval, then enfolded in one another.

Hardy gives vision to this interanimation quite specifically in *Far from the Madding Crowd*. Writing of the sheep-shearing barn, of which there will be more to say, he makes the avowal that:

> [t]his picture of to-day in its frame of four hundred years ago did not produce that marked contrast between Ancient and Modern which is implied by the contrast of date. In comparison with cities, Weatherbury was immutable. The citizen's *Then* is the rustic's *Now*. In London, twenty or thirty years ago are old times: In Paris ten years or five. In Weatherbury three- or four-score years were included in the mere present, and nothing less than a century set a mark on its face or tone. Five decades hardly modified the cut of a gaiter, the embroidery of a smock-frock, by the breadth of a hair. Ten generations failed to alter the turn of a single phrase. In these Wessex nooks the busy outsider's ancient times are only old; his old times are still new; his present is futurity.
>
> So the barn was natural to the shearers, and the shearers were in harmony with the barn. (*FMC* XXI.127)

Contrast is erased as two worlds inform one another. Possibility and actuality dissolve as discrete conceptual frameworks are traced within the fictional representation, and fictional time is caused to question both the subjective experience and objective understanding

of real time. Temporal motion is markedly different in Wessex, that difference sustaining custom, behaviour, dress, and language, this last maintained in its idiocultural locutions by ten generations, or approximately somewhere between 200 and 300 years. Whilst our 'notion of the temporal existence of things in the world often attempt[s] to grasp the reality of time through its mental appearances' (Ronen 1994, 203), Hardy's narrative perception of time destabilizes that grasp through its power to imply the apparitional and visionary event, whereby the physical world shimmers as though seen through a heat haze and an alternative reality is projected. Wessex as temporal world disorders consciousness and perception of time for those who do not belong, whilst sixty to eighty years are recorded as the 'present' in Wessex. When Eric Lorentzen remarks of the same passage that this illustrates a 'continuity [that] offers a communal frame of reference that brings solidity to everyday life', he is in part correct (Lorentzen 2006, 5). What this misses, importantly however, is that it is not a question of continuity or solidity solely, if it is even that.

What Lorentzen fails to take into account is that Wessex is, as Hardy remarks, an anachronistic place, and that anachronism determines being through the apparently coeval, but often dissonant interaction between different times. The sheep-shearing barn is a figure in miniature of all Wessex, and of the ways in which very different worlds occasionally manifest themselves in visionary fashion, suspending time through the registration of the iterability of material acts. But in that iterability is also the trace of a difference, which cannot be covered over by a family resemblance. Thus, Hardy's Wessex, a 'multiverse' if you will and also a 'polytemporal' site, is never the place of undifferentiated rural permanence. It is, as I shall go on to explore, a double place where the same and difference become visible in their interplay. It is where Hardy's characters, or some of them at least, come to a consciousness of their world as disordered, discomposed, out of joint, haunted. Consciousness in Hardy's novels is consciousness of the world's difference and in-difference, as material object indifferent to their sufferings, outlasting them. Consciousness, then, is also a 'world' in that it never exists in isolation, and comes to consciousness of itself as always already expelled in its being from a lost dwelling that remains irrecuperable.

II. 'FRAGILE LINES OF SIGHT'

Terms such as 'multiverse' and 'polytemporal' do not adequately define Hardy's Wessex, its fold of worlds in worlds, its layering of

worlds with worlds, or Hardy's exploration of the ways in which uncommon events are produced when worlds of markedly different orders and their different times come into contact with, or are exposed to (and, indeed, *through*) one another. When Hardy offers us apprehensions of one's relative location in a universe, he produces the event as the individual perception in all its dawning force, after the realization of which one can never return to a condition of ignorance of such knowledge. *Two on a Tower* presents one such perception in a particularly radical manner, which echoes, but takes to extreme, those in *Far from the Madding Crowd* and *Desperate Remedies*. In the former Hardy provides a perspective on, and for, Gabriel Oak in his relation to a lamb he tends, and his emplacement in relation to an indifferent universe (*FMC* II.12). In a different context, Aeneas Manston in *Desperate Remedies* is offered a model of perspectival reflection when looking at the miniscule creatures skimming across the surface of water in a rain-butt (*DR* II.IV.221–2).

With its stark historical and cultural juxtapositions of eighteenth-century towers built in imitation of Tuscan classical style, ancient burial sites, the origins of which cannot be known but which are variously speculated on as either Saxon or Roman (*TT* I.I.5), and the technological modernity of telescopes, telegrams and, of course, the postal system, *Two on a Tower* reminds us that we live with the past, that the past informs our identities, and the modern moment is always rent, divided within itself. Different worlds of different times have access to our comprehension, in much the way that memories can manifest themselves without our conscious effort. Such devices and images demonstrate the existence of an impossibly fraught, anachronic world, in which the traces of cultures exist together in the same sites, in a manner at once all too possible and yet impossible. One is thus offered simultaneously the apprehension *and* the impossibility of communication between worlds or any absolute understanding of one's place in modernity when touched by both the archaic and the modern. How is one to perceive one's identity in the face of the contest of signs? What does one receive in this intricate web, and how does one read? The infinitesimal breadth of the universe, its abyssal space and time opened to view through a telescope, places Swithin St Cleave, the astronomer, and Viviette, Lady Constantine in a location of unbearable self-conscious awareness concerning the condition of being (*TT* I.IV.28–9).

Such moments illustrate that even the intimation of absolute knowledge in touching the subject threatens to annihilate the self, as Lady Constantine comments (*TT* I.IV.29). The 'ghastly chasm

which' one bridges 'by a fragile line of sight' only forces on one the weight of one's modernity through the reflexion of consciousness (*TT* I.IV.29). However, what may be available as knowledge for one, is not for another. Time can cause significance to be erased, whether materially or through the loss of witness and the degradation of memory:

> Over the door [of the tower] was a stone tablet, bearing apparently, letters or words; but the inscription, whatever it was, had been smoothed over with a plaster of lichen. . . . Here stood this aspiring piece of masonry, erected as the most conspicuous and ineffaceable reminder of a man that could be thought of; and yet the whole aspect of the memorial betokened forgetfulness. Probably not a dozen people within the district knew the name of the person commemorated, while perhaps not a soul remembered whether the column were hollow or solid, whether with or without a tablet explaining its date and purpose. (*TT* I.I.6)

Here, at the tower to which the title of the novel refers, not only has the meaning of the inscription been occluded, so also is that of the tower itself, intended originally as visible memorial, but now a reminder of nothing other than the loss of significance. We read that there, materially, is that which is intended to communicate, but all that we can read is that we cannot decipher what is irretrievably lost, forgotten, expunged. Alternatively, one sees that 'here and there shade-loving insects had engraved on the mortar patterns of no human style or meaning; but curious and suggestive' (*TT* I.I5). Vision gives to one patterns, traces and signs, and the human desire is to transform what the 'fragile line of sight' presents to one into meaningful content, but the desire is frustrated, knowledge withheld. Significance and the possibility of communication invests *Two on a Tower* throughout, especially when whatever may be conveyed or transmitted remains incapable of reproduction, as in the moment when Swithin's grandmother is seen 'gazing into the flames' of her fire, and, supposedly, 'quietly re-enacting in her brain certain of the long chain of episodes, pathetic, tragical, and humorous, which had constituted the parish history for the last sixty years' (*TT* I.I13). While the flames become the evanescent traces, *aides de mémoire*, for Mrs Martin, other marks and signs remain encrypted, secretive. Pointing to charcoal sketches on the wall, she observes, ' "Here's all his equinoctial lines, and his tropics of Capricorn, and I don't know what besides, . . . I shall never rub 'em out; no, though 'tis such untidiness as I was never brought up to, I shall never rub 'em out." ' (*TT* III.IX.232) Perspective and perception always reach limits, beyond which another world remains tantalizingly close, but

impossibly far regarding the possibility or impossibility of comprehension. Thus, whether by the naked eye or through the most precise technology that modernity can imagine, certain phenomena remain beyond knowledge and interpretation; even the motion of a fixed star cannot be revealed, for 'moving with inconceivable velocity ... no magnifying will show that velocity as anything but rest' (*TT* I.IV.27–8). Or, to see the difficulty from another viewpoint, as Swithin puts it, ' "no person can see exactly what and where another's horizon is" ' (*TT* I.VI.42).

Even God's perspective is not absolute, if we pause from considering Hardy's novels to reflect on a poem from 1906. Because Hardy's characters are embedded, like the trilobite, in radically material conditions, they cannot become, nor are they given access to the possibility of becoming transcendent figures. Stepping back from *Two on a Tower*, in one of the poems from *Time's Laughingstocks*, 'New Year's Eve', God is interrogated by the poet. The narrator asks 'what good' is creation, for what purpose and why has it taken place again? As the second stanza querulously demands in its search for the reason for existence, why is there something rather than nothing, a query that anticipates Martin Heidegger's interrogation into fundamental ontology. God can only reply ' "My labours – logicless – / You may explain; not I:/... without a guess/... I evolved a Consciousness/To ask for questions why" ' (*CP*, 277–8; ll.16–20) And God continues:

> 'Strange that ephemeral creatures who
>   By my own ordering are,
> Should see the shortness of my view,
>   Use ethic tests I never knew,
> Or made provision for!' (*CP*, 277–8; ll. 21–5)

God acts, then, not only without reason or purpose but also without either consciousness or conscience; certainly his actions take place with no foresight or apprehension as to the ramifications of his 'ordering' (suggestive both of 'arrangement' and 'commands'). Thus, God is brought by the demand of the human to reflect in a moment of belated consciousness on the limits of his own knowledge. The exclamation used as end-stopping for the final line increases in intensity God's perplexity, his being taken unawares, and the sense, for God, that knowledge arrives as a somewhat forceful, but still perplexing *après-coup*. If Hardy's characters, his minute life-forms thrown into topographical and historical relief by the landscape, its structures, and its pasts, are frequently unequal to the task of apprehending in any full or meaningful way the

experience or event that they are in, then no comfort is to be found in the thought of a higher, divine power having any greater wisdom or insight. As the example of the divine limit attests, no being, no consciousness is capable or demonstrates capability of reflecting on and digesting the details or phenomena of that experience in any greater perspective.

The world is thus structured and rendered, by partial, fragmented, occasionally incoherent or failed, transmission and comprehension. It is also represented through the events produced by the interanimation of different worlds, the temporal locations those worlds imply or manifest, and the tension produced out of the incommensurability between epistemological models that pertain to those worlds. One of the difficulties regarding the interpretation of what remains of past worlds is that knowledge cannot be verified absolutely. Hardy alerts us to this throughout *Two on a Tower*, and certainly in its opening chapter, if we come back to the tower itself. Having shown us the copse thicket from a distinct viewpoint, and, in the midst of that a column, which 'had been erected in the last century' (*TT* I.I4) in imitation of the 'Tuscan order of classic architecture' (*TT* I.I.5), the reader is then informed, not very helpfully, that:

> The fir-shrouded hill-top turned out to be (as some antiquaries said) an old Roman camp, – if it were not (as some insisted) an old British castle, or (as others swore) an old Saxon field of Witenagemote, – with remains of an outer and an inner vallum, a winding path leading up between their overlapping ends by an easy ascent. (*TT* I.I.5)

Different worlds are juxtaposed, if only in supposition. Narrative circulates, or perhaps engenders speculation and hypothesis. It circulates, getting no nearer fact, and only distances *in fact* through the unfamiliarity of the term *Witenagemote*. The materiality of the hill is supplemented by the materiality of the letter, while the one reproduces the relative epistemological inaccessibility of the other. All that narrative can affirm is that the mound is a 'prehistoric earthwork' (*TT* I.VIII.54).

If *Two on a Tower* develops a 'meditation on human significance', therefore, this meditation is recorded through the mapping of distinct worlds and their different times. Present-day mid-May time is noted in passing, in that it is not 'quite so blooming as that assumed to be natural to the month by the joyous poets of three hundred years ago' (*TT* II.X.143). In a wholly different context, two tuning forks are commented on, one being seventy years or so older than the other, and so 'wrought before piano-forte builders had sent up the pitch to make their instruments brilliant', the elder was

'nearly a note flatter' (*TT* I.II.20). Elsewhere in *Tower*, other signs of the past and the difference between worlds and times assert themselves. There is the 'wardrobe of some member of the [Constantine] family ... when muslin reigned supreme, when waists were close to arm-pits, and muffs as large as smugglers' tubs' (*TT* II.VII. 131). Again, when Lady Constantine settles temporarily in the city of Pumpminster (Bath) lamp-posts are noted, which were 'still those that had done duty with oil lights; and rheumatic old coachmen and postillions' are human reminders of a past in the process of passing away (*TT* II.III.106). (In this passage one might read the 'world' of Jane Austen's fictions momentarily reverberating from within the representation of Hardy's Wessex.)

Science and geographical exploration, two bulwarks of Victorian modernity, confront archaic and atavistic worlds, which do not acknowledge or accommodate the modern in *Two on a Tower*. While the place of humanity in a virtually unfathomable universe as brought into view through the science of astronomy is indicated, Hardy also gives us to read the minutiae of the rural world of Wessex, of the natural and the human worlds He also gives access through those details, and through the fragile lines of sight they afford, to past epochs, only barely discernible, hardly interpretable at all. And even as the light from the stars is understood as being always already extinguished by the time the eye receives it, so individual perspective allows apprehension of mortal time, as in that moment when Swithin, looking around the church, notes the 'heavy, angular, and massive' frames of the 'young men and boys' who work the land, that they will return at some future moment 'to that mouldy nave for the last time' (*TT* II.X144). In this, Hardy makes available through the work of analogical complementarity a sense of that which is otherwise 'immeasurable to human comprehension' (*TT* I.IV.30), as he does when Louis Glanville, Viviette's brother travels by train to Melchester:

> Louis entered the train at Warborne, and was speedily crossing a country of ragged woodland, which, though intruded on by the plough at places, remained largely intact from prehistoric times, and still abounded with yews of gigantic growth and oaks tufted with mistletoe. It was the route to Melchester (*TT* III.X.237).

There is more than a little irony in this passage, inasmuch as the narrative observation is both of the train's 'intrusion' into the otherwise timeless – prehistoric – landscape, and also *from* the train. We see what Louis sees presumably, even if he does not give to the landscape the reflexive attention that the narrative demands of the reader.

Here, the train acts as tropic supplement to the plough, one more technology imposing itself as both the work and sign of humanity on the natural world, shaping and breaking up the countryside. Despite this, there remain to be observed *still* the yews, oaks and mistletoe, archaic survivors of a pre-Christian Wessex, remnants of that other world. In the one image, three worlds thus vie for our attention, the mistletoe or yew arguably serving as the 'illumination' of what is already dead in a manner analogous to that of the stars seen by Lady Constantine and Swithin St Cleve – or, indeed, similar to the constant reference to Sir Blount Constantine in Africa, even though he dies there, and is never witnessed 'in person' in *Two on a Tower*. Worlds are twined around and through one another, as contesting marks of differing historicities intersect without communicating – except to the eye of the reader, who must bear witness to all such communications. For between impossible distances and equally impossible proximities, the 'landscape' of Hardy's fictional worlds operate according to an 'economy of proximity-distance' (Plotnitsky 1993, 91), in a thinking of a visionary continuum made available only to the mind's eye in face of what remain, otherwise, incommensurable discontinuities. Hardyean complementarity – the simultaneous registration of different times and different worlds through the remains, ruins and traces that are observable – serves to bring to phantom visibility the spirit of the modern world in the anachronistic site of Wessex, that partly-real, partly-dream world, in which continuity and rupture, the past and present coexist. As Swithin seeks '[b]y figures of speech and apt comparisons' to take Viviette's imagination 'into leading-strings' (*TT* I.IV.30) by which to imagine the unimaginable, so Hardy translates the material remnants of other times and sites in order that similar 'leading-strings' might take up the reader's vision also.

III.   GAZING INTO THE ABYSS

We see how, in complex fashion, the historicized, historicizing modes of representation that inform Hardy's writing mark and remark the time of their having taken place, but the signs of history are those that, whilst offering access, serve to defeat translation or explanation, producing as a result an affirmative resistance to consciousness in their alterity. They remind the viewer or reader that he or she is always at a remove from such traces, and always alone, isolated in his or her world, and shut out from another's, even if that other's is given representation. Viviette and Swithin gain this

insight, standing, ironically, in close proximity to one another on the tower, looking through Swithin's telescope:

> the knowledge that scarce any other human vision was travelling within a hundred million miles of their own gave them such as sense of the isolation of that faculty as almost to be a sense of isolation in respect their whole personality, causing a shudder at its absoluteness. At night ... the infinitely great ... strikes down upon the infinitely little, the mind of the beholder. ... (*TT* I.VIII.57)

Additionally, such modes record both image and mental image, the world and mental reflection on or image of that world. As with Henry Knight's trilobite, so a comet, in its singular appearance, affords apprehension of and access to the idea of 'thousands of years' (*TT* II.I.93). In such imaginary moments, Hardy's historicizing records are themselves memento mori, archived collections of heterogeneous traces, the ruins of the past signalling, sending themselves into an unprogrammable future, and risking everything on reading or unreadability. Hardy shares with photography the ability to bear the burden of memory through the inscription of the haunting trace, as Tim Armstrong makes plain. Of photography he remarks: 'alongside its status as an index of the real, the photograph itself becomes ghostly; it comes to represent mourning, abstracting and estranging its subject-matter' (Armstong 2000, 59). In the singular image, epistemological engulfment is threatened, leading to abstraction and estrangement.

Abstraction and estrangement are fully operative in the opening sentence of *Two on a Tower* as it plays on temporality, phenomenal perception, and mortality, and does so, not only from within a recognizable language of rural representation but from within literary, cultural, and psychological registers also. The clarity of the early winter afternoon is recorded as belonging to a 'vegetable world' (in an inaugural sentence to which we will give more attention), in which trees and other plants are observable stripped of their foliage. The oddity of this image resides perhaps in that absence of simile, and, counter to that, the insistence of the metaphor, whereby the world does not *seem* but *is* a weird multitude of skeletons, through which the sun shines. If it is not too fanciful to suggest this, it is almost as if the image of the vegetable world were a translation of some medieval text in its encoding of the 'natural' through the visual echo of a *memento mori*. Fanciful or not, the presentation of the world in this manner reminds us, if we read carefully enough, that we are in a textual rather than a merely 'natural' world, and that there is a degree of signification beyond the purely mimetic.

The finality, not to say mortality, acknowledged here serves along with seasonal temporal register and concomitant narrative pause, to make the reader conscious of time, while placing him or her outside the temporal.

The first three paragraphs of *Two on a Tower* (1882) are thus particularly instructive with regard to seeing and envisioning the historicity of one's being in relation to the 'natural' world, if we attend to their principal figurative relations. At the same time, they also begin a process of opening consciousness to itself, which is mapped across the novel. Here, as in most if not all Hardy's novels, the presentation of the visible world is striking for the ways in which such scenes demand that the reader is expected to come to a halt, to pause, to observe, and to reflect on detail to such a degree that reception of the passage, its interpretation, would be in excess of the general narrative information conveyed. Consider, for example, the very first sentence of *Tower*:

> On an early winter afternoon, clear but not cold, when the vegetable world was a weird multitude of skeletons through whose ribs the sun shone freely, a gleaming landau came to a pause on the crest of a hill in Wessex. (*TT* I.I.3)

The opening temporal indicator, 'an early winter afternoon', is deceptively simple. It is deceptive because, arguably, that adjectival modifier, 'early', could be taken to indicate either the time of the season (winter), that of the day (afternoon), or both at once. The phrase 'an early winter afternoon' imposes itself on me as available to this double reading. In this, two times are therefore present, two different temporal registers and speeds, the seasonal and the diurnal. The formal 'problem' in the sentence is both a singular disruption and also a material differentiation, neither of which will be resolved, rendering the reading of time undecidable, and leaving the sentence open. *Mise en scène* gives way to *mise en abyme*.

The sentence thus anticipates as well as finds precise expression of its operation in a narrative remark later in *Two on a Tower*, as St Cleve and Lady Constantine perceive the universe as 'the presence of a vastness they could not cope with even as an idea and which hung about them like a nightmare' (*TT* I.IX.58). The immensity of the abyss becomes ever greater, ever more intimately apprehended, if this is possible, when Swithin inspects the skies from the Southern Hemisphere:

> The inspection of these chasms brought him a *second* pulsation of that old horror which he had used to describe to Viviette as produced in him

by bottomlessness in the north heaven. The ghostly finger of limitless vacancy touched him now on the other side. Infinite deeps in the north stellar region had a homely familiarity about them, when compared with infinite deeps in the region of the south pole. This was an even more *unknown* tract of the *unknown*. Space here, being less the historic haunt of human thought than overhead at home, seemed to be pervaded with a more lonely loneliness. (*TT* III.XII.250; emphasis added)

The repetition of the phrase *infinite deeps* contrasts the perspective on the two skies, and in doing so strikes the comparison between the homely familiarity and the unfamiliar and unhomely condition that produces the iterable pulsation as a physiological trace of haunting memory. The uncanny sensation is doubled and intensified. Everything we see has been tending towards this absolutely unhomely experience, as the abyss, once opened from the very first, gapes ever larger to lone consciousness as the singular experience of analogical, anxious apprehension, which is not to be dispelled. Worlds overlap worlds within the iterability of vision, as the ineluctable reception of the sky brings together time and space in the ineffable awfulness of Swithin's dawning consciousness of what it means to dwell as a modern being on the earth. And this consciousness is doubled, moreover, and as if in miniature, in the haunted disquiet that Viviette, Lady Constantine feels on a number of occasions throughout the novel, through a sequence of uncanny apprehensions (*TT* II.II.102, III.VIII.227, III.IX.234) leading to a remark of Mr Torkingham's, sometime after her marriage to the Bishop of Melchester: ' "Lady Helmsdale is not Lady Constantine. No; put it as you will, she is not the same. There seems to be *a nameless something* in her mind.... Beyond that, *her life is strangely like it is* ...' (*TT* III.XII.254; emphases added). The same, yet not the same, Viviette suffers her own abyssal consciousness, which makes strange the familiar from within.

But coming back to that initial sentence, we perceive how the world is produced through perception but the language given to that consciousness causes representation to tremble from within. The taking-place of the abyssal opens like a black hole within the *mise en scène*. Within the scene of mimetic representation, framing and so forth, the scene opens itself in singular fashion to differing temporalities, which are different not only in speed or rhythm but also in the 'form' of their movement. On the one hand there is the cyclical nature of seasonal or cosmic time. On the other, there is the linear progression (haunted though by iterability) of a singular moment in the day, a day which can never be repeated as such. Within the same, the singular emerges, promising in its coming to

pass to be iterable, to return as the same and yet not the same. That might appear a somewhat wire-drawn reading of a three-word phrase, but the broader context, which the sentence opens onto, is that of the consideration of time and the cosmos, archaic time and modernity, the place of the subject in an infinite universe, and the function of the world's 'shrinkage' through technologies of communication, all of which involve temporal displacements and the marking of the world of different times, different ages. Of course, it may be argued that logic, grammar, syntax, all might be said to dictate one reading over another. Nevertheless, the shade of the other reading, the subordinate counter-logic of the image, remains at work as a somewhat disruptive, albeit minor, supplement. A double temporal oscillation is thus at work, which the remainder of the sentence does nothing to calm. In addition, the senses are called into play, as the reader is invited to imagine that kind or quality of clarity of winter, which is not suggestive of cold. A perceptual distinction, subtle in its gradation, and comprehensible only if one has intimate experience of such gradual seasonal differences informs the representation, and is of a kind more *felt* than recorded.

In this, Hardy's distinction – if one were to desire a comparison by which the nuance might be apprehended more nearly – anticipates another seasonal and temporal perception, by T. S. Eliot, in 'Little Gidding', when he writes 'Midwinter spring is its own season / Sempiternal though sodden toward sundown' (Eliot 1963, 214). As Eliot continues, the moment, in our becoming aware of it, is 'suspended in time', and it is precisely this phenomenological effect that Hardy achieves in his opening sentence. Yet at the same time, poised in this suspension the reader becomes aware, to paraphrase *Four Quartets* (this time, 'Burnt Norton'), that words (and indeed for Hardy *worlds*) move towards the silence of the suspended seasonal image. They move through the detail of the pattern, as Eliot has it (1963, 194, 195), which is at work within, and as the invisible base for, the inaugural image of the first chapter of *Two on a Tower*; and thus, of course, of the novel itself, in which it is not only the natural but also the human image suspended in time, moving towards a still point against which one gains consciousness of the temporality of one's being.

This is envisioned in the image of 'Palaeolithic dead men feeding' the roots of the forest (*TT* II.II.102). It is also in play in the scene of Viviette's visit to the church:

> She knelt till she seemed scarcely to belong to the time she lived in, which lost the magnitude that the nearness of its perspective lent it on ordinary

occasions, and took its actual rank in the long line of other centuries. Having once got out of herself, seen herself from afar off, she was calmer, and went on to register a magnanimous vow. (*TT* I.XI.70)

Seen in perspective, the enormity of one's own historical and material being is diminished, when placed at a distance. 'Seeing' thus anachronistically gives to the abyssal immediacy of the modern an alternative, if ambivalent perspective, which temporal and ontological opening is made possible from what appears at first glance to be merely the image of a decaying natural landscape, from which *Two on a Tower* departs. The clarity of the early winter afternoon, recorded as being of, belonging to a 'vegetable world', in which trees and other plants are observable stripped of their foliage, is thus both literal and metaphorical, pertaining to what may be envisioned if one distances oneself. Abstraction and estrangement are not necessarily appalling, whether they arrive in the phantasmic apparition of a skeletal and vegetable world, or in the arrival of the seventeenth-century orthography and penmanship of Swithin's grandmother's letters, in which is substituted *J* for *I* in referring to herself (*TT* III.XI.246–7). The trace of an older, other world arrives *as a moment of interruption in the present*, as it does in the same manner of substitution, when Joan Durbeyfield writes in her 'wandering last-century hand' (*TD'U* IV.XXXI.191).

The oddity of Hardy's opening image resides perhaps in that absence of simile, and, counter to that, the insistence of the metaphor, whereby the world does not *seem* but *is* a weird multitude of skeletons, through which the sun shines. It is almost as if the image of the vegetable world were a translation of some medieval text in its encoding of the 'natural' through the visual 'echo' of a *memento mori*. The finality, not to say mortality acknowledged here serves along with seasonal temporal register and concomitant narrative pause, to make the reader conscious of time, while placing him or her outside the temporal. We enter a world comprising many worlds, the reception and perception of which is always mediated by the signs of other times and worlds. Once more, the disturbing echo gives the reader pause, as there simultaneously comes to consciousness and into focus, an awareness of a cultural history of the hauntedness of being, and the always untimely condition of one's dwelling. Recognizing such registers and their contrapuntal interanimation is made possible through Hardy's juxtapositions of 'a real and a dream-country … the presentation of Wessex illuminates Hardy's understanding of how *imagination and observation are combined in*

perception' (Pite 2002, 3; emphasis added). Phantasy and the real, the past and the present determine both how we see and how we come to be, who we are and where we find ourselves placed in the world.

Not everyone comprehends the vision they are given, however. For Viviette, Lady Constantine, gazing into the abyss produces an 'apocalyptic effect', the persistent, indirect unveiling of a 'nameless fear' (*TT* II.II.102), an 'indescribable dread' in the face of a vision of an apparently phantom child (*TT* III.VIII.227), and a 'horrid apprehension' (*TT* III.IX.234). Vision of the universe takes away perspective and engenders the uncanny in what Martin Heidegger comes to describe, just over a generation later, as the unconcealment of being to itself. She seeks to flee the very aspect of being which, though 'indefinite' is nonetheless 'so close that it is oppressive' (Heidegger 1992, 289). Seeing into the strange detail of the world and the universe estranges Viviette from herself. The abyss into which she gazes is not merely that of space and time, it is the uncanny condition of being itself, the dread of which, because it is 'nothing in the sense of "nothing definite and worldly"' (1992, 290) or, let us say, the worldly is precisely that which discloses the unworldly. Were she to look at the world as it is, as Hardy in fact makes it possible for the reader, through those weird details of trees, fungi, decay and fog which 'adhered to the ground like a fungoid growth from it, and made the turfed undulations look slimy and raw' (*TT* I.VII.46), she would have the possibility of comprehending how being persists, as Heidegger argues, only through dwelling, that is to say in perceiving an essential relation of being in its reflexiveness to its groundedness in the material and natural world (Heidegger 1993, 359). This, in effect, is what Swithin perceives in 'seeing' a temporal vision that extends beyond the immediate and empirical world of the present, in imagining the agricultural labourers as being brought to the nave a final time. And if this glimpse into a futurity or commonality of being in the infinitude of death might be too disturbing a vision, we might also recall how, at the end of the novel, in looking up for help over the already dead body of Lady Constantine, Swithin sees 'Tabitha Lark, who was skirting the field with a bounding tread – the single spot of colour and animation within the wide horizon' (*TT* III.XII.261–2). As her surname suggests, Tabitha belongs in and to the landscape: hers is an authentic expression of being and dwelling. Whether or not Swithin comprehends it at that moment, his line of sight directs that of the reader to a focal point, to a singular articulation of surviving.

IV. DISPROPORTIONING REALITY

The interwoven patterning of lives, locations, narrative strands, discursive traces, and other material details of Hardy's writing – whether topographical, architectural or archaeological, spatial or temporal – can be said to produce a matrix of reiterative and recursive structures, which, as we have argued, has troubled critical comprehension, and disrupted its ideological efficacy and institutional purpose. Moreover, Hardy's interlacing of countless aspects and facets that go to comprise his narratives finds its echoes in both the formal levels of the text and their archival and encrypted preservation of disparate, heterogeneous literary, cultural and historical traces. Every Hardy text, it might be said, offers a singular archaeological or archival formation, albeit one from the reading of which an origin or source cannot be traced. Seen from another perspective, Hardy's text displays repeatedly a rhizomic ingenuity, through a complex of endless interdependencies that are unavailable to any architectonic prioritization or ontological ordering. The patterns of tension and resistance to easy comprehension suggest that the more we seek a single narrative thread, the more we come to realize how each thread is interwoven into, shot through by, and generative of countless others. There is thus given us to read in Hardy's fictions a haunting surplus irreducible to the very site from which such flows are glimpsed is read.

The staging of excess and rupture as the arrival of historical disordering of the narrative present takes place within vision given formal coherence through mimetic representation of reality through Hardy's acts of 'disproportioning'. That matter of that other vision within vision, of the apparition of other worlds in other times within the present moment already discussed, is figured by the eruption of the past within the present moment of recording, as the representation of the sheep-shearing barn in *Far from the Madding Crowd* makes apparent. It announces with visionary force the necessity for comprehending the historicality of one's being as this is enfolded in the disclosure of how one's being dwells in time, a time greater than a single life.

The passage with which we are concerned is long and complex, but worth quoting *in extenso*:

> They sheared in the great barn, called for the nonce the Shearing Barn, which on ground plan resembled a church with transepts. It not only emulated the form of the neighbouring church of the parish, but vied with it in antiquity. Whether the barn had ever formed one of a group of conventual buildings nobody seemed aware: no trace of such surroundings

remained. The vast porches at the sides, lofty enough to admit a wag-gon laden to its highest with corn in the sheaf, were spanned by heavy pointed arches of stone, broadly and boldly cut, whose very simplicity was the origin of a grandeur not apparent in erections where more orna-ment has been attempted. The dusky, filmed, chestnut roof, braced and tied in by huge collars, curves, and diagonals, was far nobler in design because more wealthy in material than nine-tenths of those in our mod-ern churches. Along each side wall was a ranging of striding buttresses, throwing deep shadows on the spaces between them, which were per-forated by lancet openings combining in their proportions the precise requirements of beauty and ventilation.

One could say about this barn, what could hardly be said of either the church or the castle, its kindred in age and style, that the purpose which had dictated its original erection was the same with that to which it was still applied. Unlike and superior to either of those two typical remnants of mediaevalism, the old barn embodied practices which had suffered no mutilation at the hands of time. *Here at least the spirit of the builders then was at one with the spirit of the beholder now. Standing before this abraded pile the eye regarded its present usage, the mind dwelt upon its past history*, with a satisfied sense of functional continuity throughout, a feeling almost of gratitude, and quite of pride, at the permanence of the idea which had heaped it up. The fact that four centuries had neither proved it to be founded on a mistake, inspired any hatred of its purpose, nor given rise to any reaction that had battered it down, invested this simple grey effort of old minds with a repose if not a grandeur which a too curious reflection was apt to disturb in its ecclesiastical and military compeers. For once mediaevalism and modernism had a common stand-point. The lanceolate windows, the time-eaten arch stones and chamfers, the orientation of the axis, the misty chestnut-work of the rafters, referred to no exploded fortifying art or worn out religious creed. The defence and salvation of the body by daily bread is still a study, a religion, and a desire. (*FMC* XXI.125–6; emphasis added)

Initially, of this description of the barn divided into two paragraphs by Hardy, the first paragraph is the more straightforwardly 'doc-umentary' or representational. There is a mimetic fidelity to the paragraph. It records in detail the barn, drawing attention to particular aspects of its medieval structure, which are situated in contrasting context through reference to the similarities in design and appearance to a church. Utility and beauty are registered in equal measure, and the overall aesthetic impression given is deter-mined by the announcement of a preference for the aging barn over the design of the majority of 'our modern churches'. So Hardy 'draws a picture', the order of description following, responding to, the architectonics of pictorial order, observation of the spatial relations admitting of historical knowledge, and serving to contrast the medieval with the modern.

Were the passage to stop there, one might be mistaken in reading this as a continuance of that the utopian, idealist and romanticized medievalist aesthetic captured in the work of Tennyson, William Morris, or the Pre-Raphaelites. However, Hardy's second paragraph gives form precisely to those more ostensibly abstract issues previously sketched. Not only does there occur a shift from a minimally inflected but largely objective observation, resulting in a largely realist representation, to one in which the mind's eye of the 'seer' (as Hardy has it) takes over. There is also an overfolding as well as an unfolding of discrete temporal moments and the indirect perception of those absent times in the experience of the subject's translative gaze as it is touched by the traces, fragments and signs of the barn's 'memory work'. The spirit of the past arrives in the present moment of observation, to exceed the empirical and realist, and to disorder the time of the modern through its resonance and revenance. This is most immediately captured in those sentences highlighted. Two spirits conjoin and communicate as an inner vision is unveiled from within the reportage of everyday function. This is, of course, already anticipated, if not captured, in the intimation of cyclical function, the barn being put to use in the same fashion generation after generation, and century after century regardless of the histories and ideologies for which churches and castles serve as symbolic reminders – and of which they, unlike the barn, are also ideological and temporal anachronistic remainders in the modern moment. Thus it is that the ghosts of labour, of building and shearing, return, given a material archived and archival presentation in the barn, and furthermore cited and recited, even as they haunt the actions of the present farm hands who occupy the scene.

Hardy's interpretive description is significant also, in that perspective is doubled. First, it is a question of *what* one sees. Perhaps more germane, the point is that there is someone at least hypothetically or in the imagination *to see* in the present moment what is otherwise overlooked. An invisible gaze hovering liminally at the edges of the present presentation (and implicitly the ghost of the reader to come) opens that present through the gaze to the traces of cultural memory that inform the present scene. Perspective doubles and divides itself. It stages itself as a structure or formation rather than being some essential, fixed position because narration envisions someone who could be on hand to see in this particular phantasmic manner. Narration, itself a phantom articulation, posits an imagined perspective on, and opened from the constructed performative of an imagined viewer. There appears after a fashion some shadowy figure neither of the scene nor in it exactly, but capable of

gazing at the barn (or landscape, or church, or cliff face). Hardy thus enacts the Fichtean condition of *Darstellung* (staging, presentation, presencing) as the 'activity of consciousness that consists in representing the empirical subject as *Vorstellung* [an *a posteriori* general representation, conception or mental image]' (Helfer 1996, 67). The staging or presencing is not part of the empirical consciousness. That which comes to be represented serves to mark the limit of the representational force in its ability to produce a mimetically controlled and controlling image. However, this is complicated because between *Darstellung* and *Vorstellung* there arrives a mental image that is between and other than either gazing consciousness and image. From this, what emerges is that it is a question of *how* one sees and, therefore, *what* one comes to see and what comes to be seen in a visionary communion with that which is of the past but irreducible to the material reality of the structure. In this act of envisioning, an act which disproportions reality, the aesthetic perception figures not only 'a transformed *encounter* with' the empirical world, but instead and more forcefully 'an epistemic *overcoming*' of that world (Seel 2005, 7). Hardy deploys a mode of 'aesthetic attentiveness' as an articulation of the 'here and now' of being in relation to the phantasmic world and its temporality, 'as it becomes accessible only in openness to the play of appearance of a given situation' (Seel 2005, 16–17).

The 'openness' is precisely that which gives the possibility of such revenance as we witness above, in which the historicity of spirit comes to be articulated, the echoes of the past apprehended in such a singular fashion, like the shimmering of a heat haze or the glimpse of a memory at the edge of consciousness, by which one becomes suspended temporally. Hardy exploits this through the echo of details from the first of the two paragraphs in the second. In their structural return, they present the reader with an apprehension that, because of the somewhat ghostly presence of Hardy's modern 'beholder', perspective on mere architectural detail has been transformed. The *now* of the scene is translated by the persistence of the past. While it is true then that the 'synchronic and diachronic ... intersect in Hardy's metaphor of landscape' (Bivona 1990, 96), the landscape is not the only place in which this occurs. In Hardy's writing it can take place in buildings, through the play of documents, in marks left on roads or on walls, or in the practice of rituals such as midsummer dances, mummers' plays, or the repetitious seasonal lighting of bonfires as a 'custom of the country' in *The Return of the Native*, a novel set in the 1840s, as Hardy remarks in his Preface to the 1895 edition (*RN* 429).

Having described the activity around the bonfires, through the vision of another of those hypothetical lookers-on (who move like so many phantoms throughout Hardy's narratives; *RN* I.III.18), the narration provides another markedly trans-temporal vision of countless previous moments similar to, and therefore haunting the present one being recorded. The idea of the present is haunted by the cyclical revenance of the event, and the phantoms of all those who reiterate the moment and experience its taking place. Again the 'present' moment (already displaced, in the past, sometime between 1840 and 1850 and so at a generation's remove at least from the time of Hardy's readers) is disproportioned and with it literary realism:

> It was *as if* these men and boys had suddenly dived into past ages, and fetched there from an hour and deed which had before been familiar with this spot. The ashes of the original British pyre which blazed from that summit lay fresh and undisturbed in the barrow beneath their tread. The flames from funeral piles long ago kindled there had shone down upon the lowlands as these were shining now. Festival fires to Thor and Woden had followed on the same ground and duly had their day. Indeed, it is pretty well known that such blazes as this the heathmen were now enjoying are rather the lineal descendants from jumbled Druidical rites and Saxon ceremonies than the invention of popular feeling about Gunpowder Plot. (*RN* I.III.20; emphasis added)

That *as if* (which is an echo of the exact same phrase in the previous paragraph, and thus a material enactment of temporal iterability) introduces us into the realm of the fictional, the phantasmic. Multiple historical singularities are implied in such traces as are witnessed here. Hardy's disruption of the real is felt forcefully not because any single past is recorded as leaving its traces in the present, but instead because the passage signals several times – of Druids and Saxons, Vikings and other pagan cultures. The pasts do not simply erupt from within, overflowing the present. The ritualistic nature of the activity suggests the fiction of time travel on the part of the heath's inhabitants, the disquieting, uncanny suggestiveness of the moment found in the suggestion that it was *as if* those involved in the ritual had travelled back in time to return to the present expressly for the purpose of bringing those 'past ages' into their own time. Is Hardy borrowing on the resources of a modern conceptual epistemology, such as phenomenology, or is this Hardy's narration of some more archaic discourse articulating the practices of folkloric magic? Modernity *and* atavism co-exist and correspond across time, across cultures, within the same culture. One cannot decide on how to read the scene. One cannot gain access unequivocally to the right

code. As with the scene of the barn, the 'spirit' of pagan revellers is *seen* in that visionary manner to be in communication with, as Hardy puts it, *the spirit of the beholder now*. (Which beholder we might ask? That ghostly figure, who may have seen the bonfires, had he or she been there? The narrator, so-called? Or the reader?) The scene is disturbing for other reasons also. For not only are there multiple times, thereby informing the moment with the perception of anachrony, but through this, knowledge is overthrown and one reads a subversion of received historical wisdom, and with that the location of the 'origin' of bonfires being linked to the Gunpowder plot of 1605. As a result of such disruptive temporal flows emerging out of any one given location, Hardy's art can be said, with all justification, to be 'a haunted art' (Reilly 1993, 65).

Whether historical 'reality' and its representation concerns a barn, then, or a castle (as in *A Laodicean*), a family genealogy (as in *A Laodicean*, again, or in *A Pair of Blue Eyes*) or else is revealed through cyclical ritual events, here we are given to read the signs of Hardy's difference as a novelist concerned with the problem of history and representation in the nineteenth century, both from many of his English contemporaries but also, significantly, from his immediate historical and generational predecessors. Disregard for, and disproportioning within, the conventions of formal coherence has also been observed in Hardy's presentation of that hybrid and heterogeneous discursive effect we call the 'narrator' (medium might be a better word in Hardy's case). If shortly before his death Dickens can still locate in the 1860s an originary place from which the fiction of the narrator 'does the police in different voices' (in his own well-known phrase concerning the description of Sloppy's reading and mimicry skills in *Our Mutual Friend*), Hardy's acts of narrative have no such easily attributable origins or essential location. The myth or fiction of the editor or narrator given particular historical form in *The Pickwick Papers* and finding its most majestic, Olympian 'voice' in *Middlemarch* has reached a certain impasse by the 1870s. There is no Boz for Hardy. His narratives are, instead, glossolalic and spectral. As Simon Gatrell remarks, 'the narrator in any Hardy novel is a complex organism ... [it] speaks with (at least) three different accents' (Gatrell 2000, 56). Furthermore, most, if not all, of Hardy's novels function – and thereby disable or disarm easy comprehension – through 'generically mixed plots', as Suzanne Keen has it (1988, 129). Such complexity enfolds and unfolds within the heteroglossic, hetero-affective field of signs that compose Hardy's texts for the reader's perception – and occasional discomposure – of the numerous layers of narrative form, the interrelation and interactions

of its characters, and, in active interanimation, the intercalation of signs, times, phenomena, events, and that network of places constituting Wessex. Such disproportioning is unending in Hardy. It is an endless work that demands an endless reading of the signs of history, the past, occluded cultural memory, and the necessity to go beyond the present in an archiving process of staging witness to the past. Indeed, the disproportioning of reality *is* Hardy's primary concern, his commitment to the other of history.

V. POSTING, TRANSLATING, IL/LEGIBILITY

In order that different worlds may communicate at all, or become legible from one time to another systems of transmission and translation, factors and agencies have to be in place and take place, by which signs, images and messages are couriered. The 'postal' or 'mediumistic' condition of narrative can hardly be overstressed. Yet, it is, as I remark elsewhere, of the nature of such messages to go awry, to be mislaid, to fall into the wrong hands, or to be misinterpreted. Viviette, Lady Constantine marries Swithin St Cleve, on the mistaken belief that her husband, Sir Blount, has died of 'dysentery and malarious fever', this information brought to her by Mr Torkingham, having received it in a telegram (*TT* I.XI.72). The mistake is in the identity of the victim, Sir Blount not dying until sometime after the wedding, his 'second' death conveyed, via Lady Constantine's solicitor's clerk, in a newspaper report (*TT* III.III.194–5). Even hand-delivery is no guarantee, as Tess finds out when she slips her written confession of her seduction and rape under Angel Clare's door, at Talbothay's farm (*TD'U* IV.XXXIII.210–11). Furthermore, as with the signs on Lady Constantine's tower, what is perfectly legible in one age becomes, through time and wear, either partly or wholly illegible. In addition, legibility is dependent not only on literacy but also on epistemological frameworks by which the conceptual, cultural and historical as well as the semantic operation of a sign, inscription or trace maintains its valence. There are countless hazards that the sign and its transmission undergo. If you recall, it is Michael Mail in *Under the Greenwood Tree* who delivers the address to his contemporaries that *times have changed from the times that used to be*. This simultaneously clear *and* enigmatic statement demands a recognition of the times of reading. What is read in one generation may not be accessible to another; what is legible for a particular world is obscure in another. What is not read, and therefore not received in its initial posting or transmission, may be read at a later date, or arrive unexpectedly demanding reading, like

a telegram or email delivered by some ghostly postman – Michael *Mail?* – from the dead letter office.

Post arrives, via French and Italian, from the Latin *ponere* meaning 'to place'. Historically the *post* was not simply what arrived; it was also the courier, the person or vehicle, in short the agency, by which the post was carried. *Translation* shares, if not etymologically, then semantically, in this question of delivery or motion, coming, again from the Latin *translatus*, the past participle of *transferre*, meaning to carry across. What happens to Hardy in his critical reception comes down precisely to problems of carriage and delivery, and from there to a question of reading, as Hardy strives to produce a matrix within his novels constituted by 'alternative texts of collective memory' (Lorentzen 2006, 6), which misses being read. Reading for Hardy and in Hardy often concerns the problematics of perspective, vision, and the deciphering of the invisible within the visible, the pasts within any present. In the matter of textual misreading or misapprehension concerning what the author may be up to, there is a chance irony here. For many of Hardy's novels involve, or structure themselves around, the uncertain reception of texts, the fact that texts can go awry, can be misunderstood, or received in fact without ever being read. Texts can have effects when quite unintended by the author, beneficial or detrimental. Hardy understands and demonstrates the strange powers of communication throughout his texts in its material forms such as letters, notes, or telegrams and their transmission. They are everywhere in Hardy. One might even say that Hardy's novels constitute, or come to be constituted in no small measure by, a network of postal effects, and mark their epoch as one determined by the *postal* system or relay. If we consider enumeration of the postal economy in *Two on a Tower* alone, we see that there are more than twenty forms of written or printed despatches, whether letters, telegrams, newspapers, or scribbled notes (*TT* I.V.35, I.VI.42, II.II.104–5, II.III.108, II.IV.112–14, III.II.188–9, III.III.194–6, III.IV.197, III.IV.198–9, III.VI.210–11, III.VII.221, III.VIII.225–6, III.IX.233–4, III.XI.245, III.XI.246–7, III.XI.249). Much of what happens in any Hardy novel, therefore, occurs as a result of some mode of communication, some vehicle of transport or transmission, which through its various forms and iterability constitutes a network. Stephen Smith's education in *A Pair of Blue Eyes* is one valuable example of the reliance on tele-technological media, whilst the telegraph installed in Paula Power's castle offers another.

Moreover, in nearly every example where transmission bears the burden of significance, characters either come up against the limits

of reading, being unable to decipher or otherwise being led into misreadings, or they become, in a particular manner, the addressees of such messages. Yet again, there is a repeated emphasis on the untimeliness of delivery. Communications go astray, they are delivered at inappropriate moments causing discomfort or precipitate action, or they arrive too late. As Patricia Ingham has illustrated in her introduction to Hardy's *The Woodlanders*, texts interior to the narrative are crucial to that narrative's development and form, and to the fortunes of its characters. Ingham comments of Hardy's 1887 novel that, by the time he came to write it, 'he had given much attention to the subject of decoding words and other phenomena' (W xviii). Of *The Woodlanders* itself, '[t]he importance of the written word is enacted by the reliance of the narrative dynamic on written forms: in letters, legal documents, the marriage service and, in one instance, graffiti'. Ingham continues: '[e]pisodes involving documents are the characteristic events of the narrative and the triggers for many changes and crises' (W xix). The lives of Hardy's characters are therefore 'acted out and partly determined by reading or misreading, by using or misusing what is written' (W xx).

To come back to the novels of the years 1871–1882, what goes for *The Woodlanders* holds particularly true of *Desperate Remedies*, *A Pair of Blue Eyes*, *Two on a Tower*, and *A Laodicean*. In each of these, other forms of 'text', such as paintings, telegrams, photographs, and even a tattoo structure the many acts of misreading, revelation, catastrophe, and the determination of the reading subject's subsequent identity. The texts of modernity and tele-technology flow through and interrupt realist narrative form and representation, deforming it as they re-form it. At the same time, however, the texts of modernity encounter alternative flows, those 'alternative texts of collective memory', including discourses of superstition, folklore, rural tradition, the interpretation of natural signs as part of an 'organic literacy' (Lorentzen 2006, 6), and so on. Structured to greater or lesser degrees by writings and the fortunes of reading (both for the reader and for the characters), Hardy's narratives, taken singly or together, are nothing less than sustained meditations on the wager of reading, and how the past demands to be read but without any surety for the reader of getting it right. One must read but one cannot govern that act. How one reads or fails to read signs depends on one's epistemological or location, even while no one mode of reading can master all signs or, indeed, have access to the signs except to stand in mute witness before what seems unreadable. At the same time, the modern reading subject runs the risk of being transformed by the reception

of some interpreted or translated text. This principle informs both form and content. We read and see how Hardy's characters must risk reading, wagering their futures, if not their lives on the deciphering and translation of signs. In *Far from the Madding Crowd* Farmer Boldwood's future is destined by the receipt of a Valentine sent as a joke by Bathsheba Everdene, which bears in it the 'pert injunction' to 'marry me' (*FMC* XIII.87). Boldwood, the recipient, becomes the subject of the card, subject to its address, through acts of reception and misreading. Hardy goes so far to signal the significance of writing and reading, coding and decoding, by titling the chapter in which Boldwood receives and reads that Valentine 'Effect of the letter: Sunrise' (*FMC* XIV.87).

However, the risk of reading with which the sign is invested is not confined in Hardy's worlds to the more modern technologies of the post, the newspaper or the telegram. Everything is there to be read, if we know how and have access to the epistemological matrix from which signs are generated. Such potential signification is presented from the very start of the novel, with its description of Gabriel Oak, whose face owes much to traditional representations of the Green Man (*FMC* I.3). There is a kind of correspondence – a relationship as well as a communication – in and between Oak's face (his surname invites the comparison also) and that of the foliate persona of mythical and folkloric convention. Oak's archaic 'roots' are, however, residual, immanent, inchoate. His is anachronistic in form and appearance, with a 'coat like Dr. Johnson's ... [a] watch ... several years older than Oak's Grandfather' (*FMC* I.4), and a face in which 'the hues and curves of youth had tarried on to manhood; there even remained in his remoter crannies some relics of the boy', to the extent that his features of his face had 'not yet arrived at the stage wherein they become united again ...' (*FMC* I.4–5). Much is to be read in Oak, if we have access to the various keys by which to unlock the signs.

Many of those signifiers belong to human consciousness of the natural world. Oak, for instance, understood holly as 'a cipher signifying a proposal of marriage' (*FMC* IV.27). Such significance and its communication may be obvious to some, inaccessible to others. Hardy generalizes this principle when he observes how '[t]o a shepherd,'

> the note of the sheep-bell, like the ticking of the clock to other people, is a chronic sound that only makes itself noticed by ceasing or altering in some unusual manner from the well-known idle twinkle which signifies to the accustomed ear, however distant, that all is well in the fold. (*FMC* V.31)

Similarly, not everyone can judge the time by examining the position of the stars; from seeing that 'Charles's Wain was getting towards a right angle with the Pole star, ... Gabriel concluded that it must be about nine o'clock.... This small astronomical calculation was made without any positive effort' (*FMC* VI.38). Oak and others belonging to the rural world can read more than just the position of the stars; toads, slugs, weather are all legible signs, translatable by some, illegible to others (Lorentzen 2006, 7). Thus we perceive how Gabriel belongs to a particular world, composed of different worlds and, more importantly, he apprehends to a degree the epistemologies that make those worlds intelligible. Gabriel's knowledge and his powers of interpretation or translation are not absolute, though. It is also the case that there must be a mediator or translator, in the form of the narrator or another character, who make intelligible or legible particular signs. In another scene Gabriel Oak and Jan Coggan take pursuit after figures they believe to be robbers. Losing the sound of their quarry, they have to resort to tracking, at Coggan's suggestion. At this juncture, Coggan stops before some tracks, of which the narrator records that 'the footprints forming this recent impression were full of information as to pace: being difficult to describe in words, they are given in the following diagram' (*FMC* XXXI.184). On the page before the reader appear two parallel, hand-drawn lines within which are shapes resembling horse's hooves. Hardy reproduces such prints several more times (*FMC* XXXI.185–6). In these pages Coggan deciphers the tracks, for both Oak, whose knowledge is scanty and of the most general kind at best, but also, importantly, for the reader. Not only is the pace translated, so too is the fact that the horse being tracked is recently shod, and that it is lamed eventually. Such is what we are given to read in the 'mystic charactery' of the hoof-prints (*FMC* XXXI.186).

Hardy's depiction of a world in which reading must take place and yet can cause the reader to falter or to be 'translated' is not only a portrayal of the world of Wessex, or the world internal to his novels. It is also a representation of the 'modern' world of the 'Victorian' reader. The past is a series of signs. It amounts to so many networks of transmissions. But, importantly, the 'past' is that rural world, which, though intelligible to Oak or Coggan, remains illegible to many urban readers, both those of the late-nineteenth and the early-twenty-first centuries. Who today would know that a 'God-forgive-me' is a 'two-handled tall mug' called this in Weatherbury and its vicinity 'for uncertain reasons; probably because its size makes any given toper feel ashamed of himself when he sees its bottom in drinking it empty'? (*FMC* VIII.48) And given the

specificity of place as context for the euphemistic name, who beyond Weatherbury would have known such a name in the 1880s, without the suppositious translator, whose speculation has to be presented, given that the origin of the nomenclature is unavailable? Without the narrator-translator, who is aware of the extent to which 'a (hay) rick burns differently from a house? (*FMC* VI.39) These webs of signals and traces, marks and flows, fluctuations of pulses, come and go either remaining to be read, or, in their arrival and reception, transforming the Victorian subject – and the present day reader – as he or she is opened to the other of history, and is made to confront composite and heterogeneous world-fragments that are both ours and not ours.

A telling representation of such coterminous cultural correspondence is presented in Chapters Four and Five of *The Return of the Native*, in which the preparations and presentation of the Christmas Mummers' play of Saint George occurs (*RN* II.IV.122ff.) Ancient British urns 'dug from a barrow' are mute reminders of an older, pre-Christian world, while the play itself is described as a 'fossilized survival' performed 'with a stolidity and absence of stir . . . in this refurbishing age' (*RN* II.IV.121, 122). A sinister relic of older worlds and archaic beliefs is given form when Susan produces the fetish doll, adding red ribbon, black thread for the hair, and inking the feet to signify shoes (*RN* V.VII.347). This 'practice quite well known on Egdon at that date *and one that is not quite extinct at the present day* (*RN* V.VII.347; emphasis added), culminates in Susan saying the Lord's Prayer backwards (*RN* V.VII.348) in order to 'counteract the malign spell which she imagined poor Eustacia to be working' (*RN* V.VII.347). Though hardly 'merry', this 'instinct', as Hardy calls it, is particular to England, lingering on 'with exceptional vitality' (*RN* VI.I.376). This last remark refers to the Maypole erection and dance, which is one of a number of 'symbolic customs which tradition has attached to each season of the year [and] were yet a reality on Egdon. Indeed', the narrative affirms, so as to make sensible in part at least such remnants to the outsider and the modern reader

> the impulses of all such outlandish hamlets are pagan still: in these spots homage to nature, self-adoration, frantic gaieties, fragments of Teutonic rites to divinities whose names are forgotten, have in some way or other survived mediaeval doctrine. (*RN* VI.I.376)

Whether the bonfires, the fetish dolls, mummers' plays, or May dances, remnants survive in one way or another. Marking practice

and language, they affirm the persistence of other realities, even though the origins, reasons and purpose of such events and discourses, can be given no greater significance than the expression of an intimate involvement with nature, in short of the correspondence between being and dwelling.

Correspondence determines the calculation of age according to seasonal agrarian practices, as in the maltster's narrative, in *Far from the Madding Crowd* (FMC VIII.57–8). ' "Fourteen times eleven months" ' and a nod of the head 'north-west-by north' succinctly, though in somewhat encrypted fashion, measures temporal duration in relation to locale, whilst turnip-hoeing and malting, being different practices determined by season are counted according to their difference, instead of being gathered together in the account of one year (FMC VIII.58). Natural 'voices', too, affirm in singular fashion, even though, as regards, natural manifestations, 'distinct translations attached to ... dumb expressions' (FMC XXXV.213), as Hardy has it regarding the signs portending a thunder storm. Thus it is that, as with the material transposition of horses' steps onto the page, so the buzzing and swarming of bees, a process 'somewhat analogous to that of alleged formations of the universe, time and times ago' (FMC XXVI.157), bear in them communications reliant on translation. Finches, robbins and squirrels, all have their expressions, as does the ploughboy, whose voice is a matter of degree rather than kind in Hardy's Wessex, and whose voice becomes meaningful in relation to those of the animals (FMC XLIII.264–5). Or, as Hardy remarks apropos Gabriel's interpretation of Boldwood's observation of Bathsheba and her motions, the 'meaning lay in the difference between actions, none of which had any meaning of themselves' (FMC XXII.138).

Returning to the Maltster's calculations, translatability and meaning is registered as the change between generations. The Maltster's son, Jacob, tries unsuccessfully to correct his father. In this, his knowledge is marked by generational difference in much the same manner as the difference between Gabriel Oak's reading of hoof prints, and that of Jan Coggan. Such epistemological and temporal measures are seen therefore to admit us partially, but these and other 'media of manifestation' (FMC XI.74) are carried over with a filter that excludes our direct comprehension. We will never inhabit the world of Gabriel Oak, any more than Hardy's urban readers. This is brought home to us when the prospect of Bathsheba running her farm without a bailiff, arises between her workers, and the conversation turns to the prospect of ruin. ' "All will be ruined, and ourselves too, or there's no meat in gentlemen's houses!" said

Mark Clark ...' (*FMC* XV.93) In the first edition of the novel, there follows a conversation on signs and portents, subsequently cut by Hardy for the 1895 edition. In this, Matthew Moon admits to having had very bad dreams in short succession, whilst ' "Sally put the bellows upon the table twice following last week." ' To this, Joseph Poorgrass replies: 'A sure sign that sommat wrong is coming ... I had a white cat come in to me yesterday breakfast-time. And there was a coffin-handle upon my sister's candle last night'. This draws forth the following admission: 'And I've seed the new moon two months following through glass. I was told, too, that Gammer Bell dreamed of bees stinging her' (*FMC* XV.93). In this, there is the implication of a collective oral epistemology, which in being shared and understood by all involved in the conversation, serves in the re-enforcement of a community of interpretation, which excludes those who do not belong.

It is perhaps pointless to speculate why Hardy cut this conversation, save to imagine that the local knowledge, which gives grounding and place, a specificity of dwelling, to human identity, was felt to be at too much a remove from the contemporary world of the late Victorian reader, more so even than when the novel was first published. What can be said is that, with its omission, the reader loses insight into rural folklore and superstition, and related modes of local interpretation and the epistemological worlds pertaining thereto. Read as we may, however, we will never have that immediacy of access that the lived experience of different epistemologies and worlds finds singular expression in at moments such as these. It is no mere idiosyncrasy or quaintness, for example, that Henry Fray, with whom Gabriel drinks at Warren's Malthouse 'always signed his name "Henery" '

> – strenuously insisting upon that spelling, and if any passing school-master ventured to remark that the second "e" was superfluous and old-fashioned, he received the reply that H,e,n,e,r,y, was the name he was christened and the name he would stick to – in the tone of one to whom orthographical differences were matters which had a great deal to do with personal character. (*FMC* VIII.49–50)

Misinterpreted as semi-literacy, such a moment conveys directly how writing and personality or 'character' conjoin; or rather say, how *character* in one sense of that word bespeaks *character* in its other meaning. Moving beyond Hardy's insistence on singular significance, a study of pronominal spellings through wills, letters, baptismal registers or legal documents up to Hardy's time would

serve to illustrate the pertinence of such orthographic singularity, and the difference that is enacted in this manner of making legible the otherwise anonymous figure behind the name. In a world where brothers, uncles, sons, fathers would 'share' names such as William or Henry repeatedly, or indeed where surnames are spelt with one or two 'o's, or with or without an 's' on the end (as with names such as 'Woolfrey, the draper', mentioned in passing in *The Mayor of Casterbridge* [MC XXXVII.261]) in order to proclaim different branches of the family, Hardy's observation is far from being merely incidental. Other worlds, different times are implied. Their messages arrive, but how they are received is left open to the chance from which all such deliveries suffer, and by which they have their chance of communicating – or not. Hardy's worlds are thus seen as being woven out of such fragile details, barely percipient signals attesting to the precarious conditions by which cultures maintain themselves or otherwise remain only as ruins.

VI. 'THIS STRANGE REALITY'

The first chapter of *The Return of the Native* is one of the most powerful, and also amongst the strangest, openings of any novel in the English language. Its representation of Egdon Heath on a 'Saturday afternoon in November ... approaching the time of twilight' (*RN* I.I.9) recalls some of Hardy's earliest landscape passages, where detail is emphasized, principal narrative trajectory suspended, and detail foregrounded so as to estrange the normative aspects of mimetic representation from within. This is 'Hardy's most elaborate description of nature before man or without man', the language of the chapter being 'curious in a number of ways' (Miller 1970, 87, 88). More than this, the first chapter eloquently attests that the 'fundamental reality of consciousness is temporality – a temporal flow or succession of perceptions (impressions and ideas) that perpetually and spontaneously glide away' (Gallagher 1998, 75). But what kind of consciousness is this, precisely? And in what ways does this consciousness manifest itself, its temporal nature, in the form of those characters who make up the world of Edgon Heath and its environs? One of the oddest things about the chapter is the way that, bereft of any human forms in the landscape, the 'narrator', a phantom figure, is oddly there though not there; it is from this spectral vision that arises the depiction of a semi-fluid topography 'unchanged from prehistoric times' (Miller 1970, 89) but appearing temporally perceived, as a series or successions of perceived moments.

Thus, the disquiet effected through the chapter is double – on the one hand, strangeness resides in the aspect of the land itself; on the other, it is the very 'presence' of disembodied voice projecting a vision both marked at a specific time and yet out of time, which remains odd, disturbing. Such persistent visionary singularity and the uncanny reality it mediates, even as it receives this, haunts the text throughout, principally through Eustacia Vye's visionary and hallucinatory moments, but also in other ways throughout, affecting and informing all the Heath's inhabitants. Indeed, Eustacia may be said to be merely one privileged agent for vision, which a greater consciousness controls. The consciousness that mediates and projects the world is thus understood, in David Hume's terms, as 'a system of different perceptions or different existences, which ... mutually produce, destroy, influence, and modify each other' (Hume 1975, 261). Differences in the consciousness of characters are simply the particular places in a matrix, which are given expression and come to appear in different forms, at differing times; and these, in turn gain access to, even as they are informed – albeit unreflexively – by the practices and beliefs that shape ritual and habitual behaviour, such as the lighting of bonfires or the mummers' play. In such a system, difference takes precedence over static form and its representation. Time creeps almost imperceptibly through a series of flows and dissolves in the details of the representation, as is expected in liminal locations and at transitory times. 'Cinematic succession' thus 'takes priority over theatrical structure' (Gallagher 1998, 75). In this manner, *The Return of the Native* projects a world that is both spatial and temporal, a world with its own strange consciousness, about which there is nothing human, and with its own temporal dimensions.

Of the heath itself, Egdon possesses an 'untragic austerity' and, in the 'almost sexual union between heath and night', the reader is forced to gaze on the material expression of 'an indifferent cosmos' (Johnson 1983, 48, 49). Out of time and older than recorded history, appearing illimitable, this brute materiality has one meagre consolation, however: it inaugurates as an 'antidote to the ache of modernism ... [an]understanding [of] the past in a new way' (Johnson 1983, 50). Whether such an understanding might be beneficial is doubtful. Whatever that comprehension might result in though, Egdon Heath certainly presents itself as an enigma, chiefly as a result of that differential motion, to which I have already alluded. It is described as a 'Face' by the chapter title and on its opening page, with additional reference to its 'complexion' (*RN* I.I.9). It is, moreover, a 'face on which Time makes little impression' (*RN* I.I.9).

Outside – older, perhaps, than – Time, the materiality of inhuman place and face is measured as greater than a metaphysical concept, or the human measurement of that. And we should not leave unremarked that strange quasi-personification here, which hints at Egdon being more than mere backdrop or setting for the action of the novel. That face is accompanied by a 'Titanic form' (*RN* I.I.10), and its 'personality', if this is the right word, is 'best … felt when it could not clearly be seen' (*RN* I.I.9). The entire form takes in the world, making it all its own, as '[t]he distant rims of the world and of the firmament', mark divisions in both time and matter (*RN* I.I.9). When night finally does arrive, the heath, having a 'watchful intentness' about it, awakes and listens (*RN* I.I.10), solitude looking out of its 'countenance' (*RN* I.I.11). Being such a 'face', the heath, which is looked on and which implicitly looks out onto its world, thus evokes the uncertain origins of the word, *face*, which etymological roots refer variously to *facere* – to make – and the prefix *fa-*, meaning to appear or to shine. The heath thus makes a world, it 'enworlds' itself in its appearance, in the power of its materiality 'shining-forth', and so illuminating its own condition as it leaves its imprint on consciousness. Other, it is comprehensible only as a being of sorts, inhuman but nonetheless appearing as if alive – and all the more discomforting for that, – which is 'withal singularly colossal and mysterious in its swarthy monotony' (*RN* I.I.11). Its uncanny 'life' has nothing of the homely or the familiar about it, and the characters of *The Return of the Native* are notable for their apparently restless, perhaps febrile, wandering across Egdon Heath in a state of uprootedness, of 'homeless drifting' (Miller 1995, 11).

Hardy draws out the image of the landscape of Egdon Heath across the first chapter as a seemingly suspended moment captured, though not quite frozen, at various small points of transition: 'the vast tract of unenclosed wild known as Egdon Heath embrowned itself *moment by moment*' (*RN* I.I.9; emphasis added). Hardy's sentence is fascinating for the ways it insinuates the relation between pictorial representation and writing, form and content, space and time. Were this the only sentence in the chapter to do so, its remarkable and singular force would alone warrant our attention, for it exemplifies in singular manner a spatial and temporal becoming, projecting a reality that is capable of apprehension, and which yet remains disquieting. What is all the more interesting in the sentence just cited, though, is its condensation of motifs and tropes that are to be observed throughout the chapter. As the chapter illustrates and traces repeatedly, there is no subject, no consciousness, no living being. There is the hypothetical furze-cutter, of course

(*RN* I.I.9), and, equally, that hypothetical 'tourist', the modern thinker as Hardy describes him, whose spirit is attuned to the 'mournful sublimity of a moor, a sea, or a mountain' (*RN* I.I.10–11). There is also the, equally suppositious, 'ascetic' (*RN* I.I.11). But, despite such projected phantoms, there is no human life in this chapter, no human figure to be discerned on Egdon Heath. There is only the inhuman and the phantom, the observer and observed, from out of which is manifested the 'strange reality' (*RN* IV.VI.271) of Egdon Heath, the perception of the world shared by certain of its inhabitants, and, indeed the world that Hardy presents his readers in *The Return of the Native*. Egdon, we would contend, is the exteriorized coming into being, the appearing and articulation of inhuman consciousness in its facticity and material externality. To see this from a slightly different perspective, the 'strange reality' we encounter in the first chapter, and which comes back to interrupt both the characters in *Native* and the reader, works through the 'personification of the heath' as 'the covert manifestation of the ubiquitous presence of the narrator's consciousness', while the 'narrator, in his turn, has got his sense of his own personality, it may be, from the heath' (Miller 1995, 27). It is as if the novel and the world it represents alternate 'between being seen as inside out and as outside in' (Miller 1995, 25)

Strange reality does not refer to the Heath, inevitably. It is the narrator's interpretation of Mrs Yeobright's shock at realizing that the stranger cutting furze before her, whose walk she had anticipated uncannily as ' "exactly as my husband's used to be" ', is her son, Clym (*RN* IV.VI.271). Clym, in losing his sight partially, loses also something of his 'modern' individuality. In becoming the strange, short-sighted begoggled furze-cutter, his physical proximity to the heath becomes the mute affirmation of his own 'return' (as the title has it), his factitious-becoming. This is given facund expression in the following passage:

> It was a sunny afternoon at the beginning of summer, . . . The ferny vegetation round him, though so abundant, was quite uniform: it was a grove of machine-made foliage, a world of green triangles with saw-edges, and not a single flower. The air was warm with a vaporous warmth, and the stillness was unbroken. Lizards, grasshoppers, and ants were the only living things to be beheld. The scene seemed to belong to the ancient world of the carboniferous period, when the forms of plants were few, and of the fern kind. . . . (*RN* III.V.202)

Typically, detail interrupts more general representation, form and colour impressing themselves on the mind's eye. In that odd

mediated-unmediated way that Hardy's phantasmic narrator has, we see the world *as if* we were witnessing the world as it was in another time; or *as if* the other time of the world were still there in the narrative present, resonating within the still of the image. Such is the ubiquity of the material vision for Clym that

> ... the scenery overpowered him.... There was something in its oppressive horizontality which too much reminded him of the arena of life; it gave him a sense of bare equality with, and no superiority to, a single living thing under the sun. (*RN* III.V.206)

The near-sublime encounter undermines Clym's humanity. He is given the vision of a consciousness no longer human and therefore no longer hierarchically or evolutionarily superior to the world in all its strange levelling force. Eventually, though, becoming conditioned to the overpowering subjection of the heath, Clym enters more closely, more intimately, into that world, where the prehistoric reality is further revealed:

> His daily life was of a curious microscopic sort, his whole world being limited to a circuit of a few feet from his person. His familiars were creeping and winged things, and they seemed to enrol him in their band. Bees hummed around his ears with an intimate air, and tugged at the heath and furze-flowers at his side in such numbers as weighed them down to the sod. The strange amber-coloured butterflies which Egdon produced, and which were never seen elsewhere, quivered in the breath of his lips.... Tribes of emerald-green grasshoppers leaped over his feet.... Huge flies ... buzzed about him.... In and out of the fern-brakes snakes glided in their most brilliant blue and yellow guise.... Litters of young rabbits came out from their forms ... hot beams blazing through the delicate tissue of each thin-fleshed ear, and firing it to a blood-red transparency in which the veins could be seen. (*RN* IV.II.247)

Yeobright is given access to a world, and thus is able to dwell in this world, to find an authentic expression of being in this reality. Clym becomes so much a part of the heath that, eventually, the vision of what it truly is in all its sublimity reveals itself to him in a symbolic moment of disclosedness: 'Instead of there being before him, the pale face of Eustacia, and a masculine shape unknown,'

> There was only the imperturbable countenance of the heath, which having defied the cataclysmal onsets of centuries, reduced to insignificance by its seamed and antique features the wildest turmoil of man.... A consciousness of the vast impassivity in all which lay around him *took possession* even of Yeobright.... (*RN* V.II.316-17; emphasis added)

The countenance returns, Clym being placed 'face-to-face' with the other. Consciousness of temporality and the temporal consciousness return also here, as the world and time of the heath gather Clym into their consciousness. That daemonic implication signifies the extent to which Egdon claims its creatures, and the one distinction remaining between Clym, the lizards, rabbits or insects, is consciousness, as the exterior and interior sites are enfolded the one in the other, each as the palimpsest, and bearing the imprimatur, of the other in a reciprocity and flux separable only by distinguishing between the 'who' from the 'what'.

From the narrative trajectory I have just traced, it can be argued that the 'return of the native' is not Clym's return to Egdon, the place of his birth, or at least it is not this solely. For what returns 'in' Clym, so to speak, is the 'native' element, that which marks and informs the world of the heath, stretching back to times before Roman occupation and the making of the barrows, with which the novel concerns itself. The 'return of the native' is thus the return of what most powerfully, unconsciously, calls *in* and *to* Clym. Loss of sight only serves to hinder Clym looking further afield beyond the strange reality of Egdon, whilst opening to him another vision, and returning to him that, which was properly his, for 'Clym had been ... inwoven with the heath in his boyhood' (*RN* III.I.168). He was, the narrator informs us, 'permeated with its scenes, with its substance, and with its odours. He might be said to be its product' (*RN* III.II.173). What Clym comes to consciousness, what vision and insight reveals to him is what is always already written on him therefore. Clym's is a vision that touches most nearly on his being, so that one realizes the intimate relationship between being and dwelling. With that comes the realization that 'there is no presentation of character without terms borrowed from the landscape ... [and] no presentation of landscape without personification' (Miller 1995, 27).

That local moment of estranged perception in which Mrs Yeobright's vision is 'cheated', and the more general experience of a revelation of Clym's selfhood in correlation to the Egdon's identity, is somewhat typical of the many singular moments of experience, encounter, insight and dawning consciousness that inform the novel. Clym's mother receives a vision of the heath not dissimilar from Clym's: 'All visible animation disappeared from the landscape, though the husky notes of the male grasshoppers from every tuft of furze were enough to show that ... an unseen insect world was busy in all the fullness of life' (*RN* IV.VI.282). Despite this connection between mother and son, a difference is marked conversely between

her vision and that of Clym in a subsequent observation, which expresses her mistaken belief that she has been ' "cast off by her son" ', as she puts it (*RN* IV.VI.281). What follows the image of the desolate world brings Mrs Yeobright's consciousness more closely in alignment to that of Aeneas Manston, in *Desperate Remedies*: 'In front of her a colony of ants had established a thoroughfare across the way ...'

> To look down upon them was like observing a city street from the top of a tower ... this bustle of ants had been in progress for years ... doubtless those of the old times were the ancestors of these.... (*RN* IV.VI.282)

Such distance and estrangement, rather than possession, appears inevitably as the precursor of tragic destruction. The intrusion of the temporal dimension adds to the image a visionary spontaneity, so that the imagined height from which the ants are envisioned as urban inhabitants implies a kind of vertiginous opening, itself the presage of Mrs Yeobright's imminent death. In effect, the strange reality is not only a vision of alterity but of death also.

To come to Eustacia: as has been mentioned already, Eustacia is but one privileged agent to whom, and through whom, visionary insights of strange realities manifest themselves. Often, such moments of vision are associated with Clym, as on the occasion when she overhears of his return from Paris, not yet knowing who he is. As a result of this information, she has 'visions enough to fill the whole blank afternoon', while her 'colourless inner world' became 'as animated as water under a microscope ... Myriads of imprisoned shapes arose where had previously appeared the stillness of a void' (*RN* II.I.110). While this psychic transmogrification is expressive of Eustacia's desire, and so that sexuality that will lead to her destruction (Boumelha 1982, 50), we should not overlook the language of her visionary transport. Generated as a response to the image of a 'young and clever man', a stranger to Eustacia made all the more desirable because of his association with Paris, and thus with a cosmopolitan, modern and exotic world in marked contrast to the world of Egdon Heath, Eustacia's 'inner world' is driven by a busy and restless motility. Again, the microscopic animation recalls other images and visualizations in Hardy, thereby suggesting a web of vision by which the world is given to consciousness, and by the representation of which Hardy seeks to impose a vision of the world's alterity on the reader. Whilst this 'microscopic' world is one of the imagination, it is iterated in exteriorized form, later in the novel, in the representation of the 'timid animal world' in 'great

animation, in the pool 'outside the bank of Eustacia's dwelling' (*RN* III.IV.189).

Elsewhere, the narrator observes that, following a first encounter with Clym, 'Eustacia's features went through a rhythmical succession of' emotional, 'minute' changes, the outward physiognomic inscription of ideas, a 'cycle of aspects, produced by a cycle of visions' (*RN* II.III.117). Once more, we encounter the mute revelation of Eustacia's desire, an inner world in this example given through motion as the indirect register of otherwise invisible apparitions. At the same time, what is peculiar to Eustacia's face here is, in its outward 'translation' of those inner and invisible visions, analogous with the miniscule changes that take place over the face of the heath in the opening chapter. Such transformation of the invisible vision to the visible sign belongs to a broader phenomenological world of perception. It is generalized by Hardy, in moving from the specific examples of Eustacia and Mrs Yeobright, to the more wide-ranging, if still gendered reflection on female powers of 'insight' (*RN* III.III.188). Of this somewhat inadequate term, Hardy admits that this is what 'we call' what is the ability to 'watch the world they [women] never saw, and estimate forces they have only heard' (*RN* III.III.188). In this, women might be perceived to be in some fashion as having a different access to alternative realities within the one world in which all Hardy's characters exist, to which access Clym can only attain through the partial loss of sight. However, this is complicated through the figure of Eustacia, for her sight is always turned either inward or to some distant point beyond Egdon. So desirous is Eustacia for alternative vision that Clym becomes the singular image, a vision more than a real man for Eustacia (*RN* II.III.119) and, in a transport of passion, 'it seemed as if her ears were performing the functions of seeing as well as hearing ... the body ... having become ... so sensitive to vibrations' (*RN* II.III.116). Though Clym Yeobright provides the focal point for her, Eustacia is already displaced within her world. Eustacia is alienated from the world that is most properly hers, and thus homeless, without proper dwelling, as a result of the force of her consciousness, signalled not in modes of thought but in a more immediate surfacing of the flux of desire, and signified also in that sense of not belonging or wanting to belong, to be rooted, in one particular place. As she puts it to Clym, ' "I wish we didn't live here, Clym. The world seems all wrong in this place" ' (*RN* IV.VII.284).

The difference between the visions of the world given to Clym, to his mother, and to Eustacia, is a difference of degree, but also in Eustacia's case one of kind. For what Mrs Yeobright glimpses,

and what Clym becomes possessed by, is precisely the inextricable nature of one's being and the place from which one comes. Eustacia signally fails to perceive that there is always relation, an intimate and mutual dependency between the 'who' and the 'what' in *Native*. It is not that this relation does not exist elsewhere in Hardy. Rather it is that Hardy repeatedly foregrounds the question and the mystery of the 'who' and the 'what' through consciousness and vision in this novel. Clym's 'who' becomes subsumed by Egdon's 'what'. Eustacia fights against this from her very first appearance, striving as she does to retain an illusory individuality in a world in which vale, upland, barrow 'amounted to a unity', and were apprehensible as 'strangely homogeneous' (*RN* I.II.17). What is missing from this homogeneity is the figure standing atop the barrow, a human figure with a lantern, who, too, is part of the unity described in the narrative. This 'figure' gives to the scene a 'perfect, delicate and necessary finish' (*RN* I.II.17). It is, furthermore, described an 'organic part of the entire motionless structure' (*RN* I.II.17), as if the barrow had given birth to the figure, or as if the figure had emerged from out of the pagan burial mound. In moving away from the initially static position or, as Hardy expresses it the 'discontinuance of immobility' (*RN* 18), the figure produces 'confusion' (*RN* I.II.18). Emerging as a female figure, her 'sudden displacement' (*RN* I.II.18) shows to the world and the reader that she 'had no relation' to those who replace her on the barrow (*RN* I.II.18).

Eustacia is thus figured as *of* the world of Egdon, but struggling to be free of it. She strives to hold out against becoming consumed by the community of the heath and the various cyclical returns of 'Paganism', which the barrow initially announces (*RN* IV.III.255). Yet, the strangest reality may be that of Eustacia herself. Struggling all the time against that which gives her identity, she appears as a transitory and disruptive force in the dark world of Egdon, a 'figure in a phantasmagoria' as Hardy has it, 'a creature of light surrounded by an area of darkness ...' before being 'absorbed in night again' (*RN* V.VII.342). Eustacia is thus a sacrifice to the strange reality of Hardy's world, a world which exists as the 'condition under which being ... is given' (Lacoste 2004, 10). Because Eustacia ignores her 'givenness', this gift of the other, and because she turns away in visions and dreams to alternative realities channelled through desires, she ignores the 'immemorial presence' of that world which is at 'the bottom of every conscious life, as the condition of our carnal being' (Lacoste 2004, 11–12). Eustacia's mistake is to believe that the exotic, the strange, the luxurious, the unexpected take place and are conditions of other worlds elsewhere; she fails

to perceive how such events are 'always within the horizon of the world' (Lacoste 2004, 12) that gives us the particular manifestation of our being. Against this malady of misperception and forgetfulness of one's being Hardy's strange realities struggle to mediate, the face or countenance of his world seeking to express to the reader's mind's eye an authentic vision of being.

4

Uncommon Events: *The Trumpet-Major* (1880), *A Laodicean* (1881), *The Mayor of Casterbridge* (1886)

I. UNCOMMON FANTASIES

Consider two remarks of Hardy's, concerning the writing and purpose of fiction. They are striking for their recognition of that in fiction which should by-pass, flow out of, or exceed merely realistic representation. In 1881, Hardy notes:

> the real, if unavowed, purpose of fiction is to give pleasure by gratifying the love of the uncommon in human experience ... uncommonness must be in events ... and the writer's art lies in shaping that uncommonness while disguising its unlikelihood. (*LTH* 150)

The following year, Hardy observes how:

> Coleridge says, aim at *illusion* in audience or readers – *i.e.*, the mental state when dreaming, intermediate between complete *delusion* ... and a clear perception of falsity. (*LTH* 152; emphases in original)

While much criticism of Hardy has been given over to explorations of character psychology, historical context, or a combination of both, what should be obvious from Hardy's comments is that his literary focus is, in addition to these interests, directed toward event

and reader. Concomitantly, also of significance is the uncommon or singular, as that which marks and serves to remark the event *qua* event, something out of the ordinary and unrepeatable as such. This is only recognized, if at all, inasmuch as fictional narrative must *disguise* its singularity and 'eventness'. The second observation taken from Hardy's *Life* is significant in its emphasis on the phantasmic and phenomenological projection, as that which produces a particular condition, a sympathetic resonance perhaps, in the reader through the character's experience of the fictional event. It is *as if* reader and character were somehow aligned, *as if* one came to be possessed by the other's encounter with the impossible event – impossible because, as a reader, that to which I bear witness is not there, strictly speaking, whether the account is of a 'real' event, historically verifiable, or 'purely' fictional. What distinguishes Hardy from other novelists in this process is his use of the uncommon, the visionary, or the strange, which moments invent the apprehension of the impossible, through interruption of the everyday.

Neither purely fictional nor occupying and reporting on the real in some disinterested manner, Hardy's novels produce from the unstable space between 'fiction' and 'reality' events and encounters which transform irreparably characters' lives. That space is where the question of what we call 'history' reveals itself in all its complexities as, also, the problem of reading. In the process of transformation, in undergoing and being subjected to the uncommon in event and experience, Hardy's characters invite the reader to reconsider the correlation between 'fiction', 'reality', and 'history' as matters of interpretation and cultural translation. Hardy writes of 'the events that may or may not become history, and he illustrates . . . the unknowingness . . . of ordinary people involved in daily events' (Shires *TM* xxxix). Such production engenders the uncommon within the everyday, resisting accommodation to historical or generic expectations, even as it plays off these, thereby introducing a further level of teasing the reader. Hardy thus 'shapes' the reader's

> consciousness neither by utter fidelity to an 'accurate' past nor by having present knowledge of fulfilments to come. Rather he reveals ironies of circumstance and ideological contradictions, which lead to our disjunction from the past and our closeness to realities we may not expect. (Shires *TM* xxxix)

In this, the event of the past is rendered *as if* it were taking place anew, as if the text were able to invent, to find that which marks the event in its singularity. And in this, the narrative of the event,

produced in its singularity, invents for the reader the historical, the temporal and cultural memory.

Thus it is, Hardy 'offers us a series of interpretive challenges' (Shires *TM* xix), through the readerly experience of heterogeneity, irregularity, anti-realism, explored through matters of history, the past, memory, spectrality, the inmixing of discourses without appropriate regard for hierarchies, and an 'anti-real' intensity of scrutiny regarding natural detail. In this, alternative voices and perspectives emerge from within broadly realist and historicist modes of representation, to project alternative histories and cultural memories, which remain to resonate for the present reader. Hardy thus 'interweaves competing claims of large historical processes with those of individuals engaged in the routines and roles of daily life' (Shires *TM* xix). Whilst, in *The Trumpet-Major*, the Napoleonic wars inform individual lives, elsewhere geology, astronomy, and folkloric tradition inform Hardy's text. To this there is the formal interanimation between various 'generic strands', these being, in *The Trumpet-Major*, 'history, romance, and comedy', all of which making-complicated in the work of the fictive serves to 'shape other incongruities to reframe utterly how we think about our positioning in time and place', thereby enacting 'discontinuity and alienation in a peculiarly modern and radical way' (Shires *TM* xix). As the inauguration of a narrative concerned with historical forces two generations before the moment of being written, we read therefore that we will find ourselves '[i]n the days of high-waisted and muslin-gowned women, when the vast amount of soldiering going on in the country was a cause of much trembling to the sex, there lived in a village near the Wessex coast two ladies of good report, though of limited means' (*TM* I.I.11). There is a fascinating, though small instance of temporal layering at work in this opening sentence. More than merely a statement concerning the past, the first sentence of *The Trumpet-Major* performs that past as if it were being written without direct knowledge of the enormity of historical events about to be enacted in Europe. If not a sentence lifted from Jane Austen exactly, the past, constrained through observations of fashion, and the personalities of the shabby-genteel, is presented initially in tone and style as if this were, perhaps, an early novel by Charles Dickens. (Compare, for example, Hardy's sentence with those which open *Nicholas Nickleby*.)

The purpose here is to go against the grain of realist historicism, and to recognize that 'history' as it is represented in novels of previous generations in the nineteenth century is out of date; both mode of representation and the conception of what constitutes

'history', 'historical narrative', and so on are seen to be anachronistic, and from this revelation Hardy intervenes in the historical process at the level of narrative form. When Elfride observes of the fifteenth-century romance she is attempting to write in *A Pair of Blue Eyes* that '"such writing is out of date now"' (*PBE* I.I.39), there is a conscious irony at the expense of Walter Scott. Whilst Scott's historical novels had 'initiated the modern celebration of a romanticized medieval England', which mystification of the mediaeval was to be continued throughout the Victorian epoch and conjoined with a sentimental and 'tearful regret for the passing of a rural way of life identified with the distant English past of legend' on the part of the 'Pre-Raphaelites, Ruskin, Morris and Tennyson', Hardy's purpose was very different, offering a countersignature to such writers and the ideology their writing embodied. In Hardy, 'the past does not simply irrupt into the present ... [its revenance] foregrounds a cultural "repetition compulsion"' (Bivona 1990, 92–3). Hardy depicts a culture of modernity striving to 'convert the past into the present so that it may be safely stowed away', given a heritage makeover so it can no longer 'threaten the present' (Bivona 1990, 93). Against this, Hardy illustrates how the past can never be contained, once structured phantasmically so as to be felt *as if* this were *my* experience. To this end, part of Hardy makes uncommon the commonplace in the otherwise realist representation of history, and in so doing, places us *in* the event, albeit as spectral witnesses.

It is, more precisely, to place the reader within the currents and contradictions of a moment rendered as an illusion in order that the phantasm, conjured through the work of fiction, might have more powerfully an emotional pull, making the reader *see* and *feel*. It is the vitality of sympathetic imagination that allows a 'labouring man', on visiting the British Museum, to stand before the base of a pillar, and imagine 'that stone once echoed / The voice of Paul' (*CP* 381–2). The difficulty for Hardy, though, is how to make the reader apprehend in innumerable ways, when, as he observes in his preface to the 1895–96 edition, what is left of the past are merely the

> casual relics of the circumstances amid which the action moves ... [such as] an outhouse door riddled with bullet-holes, ... a heap of bricks and clods on a beacon-hill, ... worm-eaten shafts and iron heads of pikes for the use of those who had no better weapons, ... and other such lingering remains. (*TM* 3)

All such 'remains' bring to the imagination the events of the past 'more vividly than volumes of history could have done' (*TM* 3).

Fictional witness, neither wholly factual nor fictional, risks everything on the fragment or ruin. It risks everything further in translating the auratic effect (such as the imagined echo of St Paul's voice perceived indirectly), as that is engendered through the encounter with that material remainder, translated into the materiality of the letter. Such translation is effected in order that the phantasms of the past might touch the reader with an immediacy more forceful than any mere historical account. And this is what remains when 'oral relation' of the everyday is all that is left (*TM* 4), and when '[t]hose who have attempted to construct a coherent narrative of past times from the fragmentary information furnished by survivors' acknowledge 'the difficulty of ascertaining the true sequence of events' (*TM* 3). The difficulty remains and is only available to comprehension if one admits that, in passing from 'history' to 'literature', the discontinuity is maintained through the invention of narrative that stages events *as if* they were uncommon, *as if* they were happening for a first time, *every time we read*. Hardy thus strives to fill the role simultaneously of 'someone who stands in the presence of being in the past (when he is waiting for the disclosure), in the present (when it takes place in the . . . acts of history), and the future (when . . . his work will maintain, for others, a mediate form of contact with being)' (de Man 1993, 65).

II. DISRUPTED RECEPTION

Hardy marks and re-marks the otherwise unbridgeable gap between generations that is presented powerfully in *The Trumpet-Major*, as that novel struggles with its fragmentary information. Though a domestic and largely parochial romance with some comedic interludes, Hardy's lyrical seventh novel stages its narrative against and in confluence with the undercurrents and effects of the Napoleonic Wars. *The Trumpet-Major* addresses itself, therefore, to the lives of Hardy's grandparents' generation. Of all Hardy's novels, it is the most cruelly ironic in its perception of the importance of the past, and the ways in which the traces of the past can inform, or become occluded in and by the present. For, while the novel foregrounds the romantic experiences and intertwined lives of Anne Garland and her suitors Robert and John Loveday (the former a sailor, the latter the titular trumpet-major), and the squire's nephew Festus, it calls all generic expectations into question through the intrusion of the historical as both literary mode and material reality. The writing of 'history' violently erupts and interrupts narrative, making its demands, and demanding a mode of witness otherwise unavailable,

inasmuch as it is impossible for those who experienced, and suffered, the war to speak. To write (of) romance after the trauma of conflict is both impossible and necessary for Hardy. The novel disrupts its own reception by upsetting generic convention, causing the traumatic eruption in the past to return to an act of reading, as a reminder of what will not go away, but which remains to be read as a belated apprehension of a specific determinate of Victorian modernity and identity.

As we will see in *The Mayor of Casterbridge*, the past is always with us, as are our previous generations. They haunt us forcefully, shaping who we are. Nowhere moreso is this announced in *The Trumpet-Major* than in the narrative's ending, in which Hardy is at pains to disrupt fictional closure through the narrative of historical consequences, and, in so doing, opening to the reader the transmission of the experience of historical rupture and violence, through the experience of history's others, Anne, Robert, and John, civilians, soldiers and sailors who have no historical voice in conventional, broad historical accounts of war. In the final chapter, John is recalled to his regiment to join 'Sir Arthur Wellesley, in the Peninsula' (*TM* III.XLI.299). Hardy's passing reference to Wellington, and the Peninsular Wars (1808–1814), marks the fiction rudely with the intrusion of its historical context. It demonstrates, moreover, through the reception of a message, how lives are subject to the decisions of others, through a network of transmissions by which political history operates, and the currents that are made to flow as a result, with consequences, which are, if not unforeseen, at the very least unpredictable as to their eventual arrival and after-effect.

The final chapter is brief, as if the weight of what is always already in place creates a density leading into the night of its setting and the abyss onto which it opens. Beyond showing the 'traces ... due to the natural wear and tear of time', John 'showed no signs of gloom' (*TM* III.XLI.299). This was, after all, an 'exciting time', and a 'period when romance had not so greatly faded out of military life as it has done in these days' (*TM* III.XLI.300). Yet, Hardy continues, recounting how, of 'the seven' who take their leave of Anne on the night mentioned in the final chapter, 'five, *including the trumpet-major*, were dead men within the few following years, and their bones left to moulder in the land of their campaigns' (*TM* III.XLI.300; emphasis added). The titular protagonist leaves the book for his death. From the time of *The Trumpet-Major*'s deadly conclusion, death overseas was a growing concern in the nineteenth century. From the Afghan wars of the 1830s, through to the Indian Mutiny, and on to the colonial campaigns in Africa and Burma in the

1880s and '90s; and then to the revenant *Dynasts* and 'Drummer Hodge', who is thrown into a grave 'uncoffined' (*CP* 90–1), the prospect of dying intensifies in Victorian culture over Hardy's career, and beyond. In this, we perceive how 'history' cannot be contained, consigned to the past – for whilst the Trumpet-Major's death is that moment in the Peninsular War, in the early years of the nineteenth century, overseas posting and death in general was a contemporary reality and anxiety for Hardy's readers.

Hardy re-emphasizes the destruction to come in the last paragraph, as, seemingly needlessly, in an excess of repetition, death returns once more for John. His face is seen briefly by candlelight, as he backs across the doorstep into the

> black night; and in another moment he had plunged into the darkness, the ring of his smart step dying away … as he … went off to blow his trumpet till silenced for ever upon one of the bloody battle-fields of Spain. (*TM* III.XLI.301)

Hardy gives his reader no preparation for what is called the 'coming time' (*TM* III.XLI.300), even though we know, historically, it is to come, and has come to pass. It remains uncanny in this simultaneous futurity *and* having happened in this manner, Hardy maintains the disjunction between the 'then' of John and Anne, of whom it is remarked that she smiled in reply to John, 'not knowing that the adieu was for evermore' (*TM* III.XLI.301), the 'now' of publication, and that of every subsequent reading. Hardy seeks to make that 'then' a 'now', for even though we read prior to this that five of the seven would be dead, like Anne we are not privy to the identities of those five, or whether John is amongst them. Indeed, when John Loveday, the Trumpet-Major, turns at the threshold of the door, poised with a smile between past and future, public and private roles, the warmth and comfort of the dwelling and the dark and death of a military campaign, the reader comes to know of his death before Anne. Time is suspended momentarily in this visionary moment before John's steps anticipate his material death, in the trope of their 'dying away', (*TM* III.XLI.301).

Interestingly, disturbingly, Hardy creates a tension between private and domestic identity – John Loveday, the miller's son – and public, historical function – the Trumpet-Major. It is as if John arrives finally at the title of this novel; as if this were the identity for which he is destined. His living self is elided under the memorial weight of title and military function. The title reinforces this sense of historical intrusion and determination, as the fictional figure

becomes memorialized, even as that same title erases or promises to efface, John's personal identity. In the impersonality of the title, the reader is called on to recognize the historical anonymity of so many lost in wars. Additionally, the reader witnesses the departure of the dead, before they are dead, walking towards that death unmindful of its certainty. And while the reader is haunted by this recognition, within the dated time frame, it might be said that the dead arrive unexpectedly as the ghosts of their living selves, as ghosts from the future. The trace of history thus arrives as a memento mori, a message dispatched and destined to be read by each and every reader of Hardy's. History is intercepted by the subject, who is translated, transformed by this arrival, a revenant inscribing the self through the opening of cultural memory.

One might suggest also that Hardy is commenting on a specific transformation of literature in this historically inflected gesture, as well as being a gathering of the generations of the Victorian era, as a community in death. His narrative stages an irreversible, epochal translation of the responsibilities of narrative witnessing. Hardy records the sign of modernity for fiction through the inscription of its ethical responsibility to allow the dead to speak. Fiction thus bears witness to hetero-affective forces and signs of history, the past, and cultural memory, as these are intimately entangled in the previous generations who are, hypothetically, one's direct forebears. Who we are, Hardy affirms in the staging of national identity as a community-in-death, *is* figured through our belated apperception of those others, of whom we speak as generations. To see this from another perspective, Victorian identity is generated by the traumatic experience of obliteration and transformation that the nation undergoes in various ways over the decades from the 1780s to the 1830s. Death conjoins without making continuous by understanding the tropic difference of past and present, then and now, as historical difference, where otherwise there would only be a formal relativism.

III. UNDECIDABILITY AND OCCLUDED HISTORIES

But *The Trumpet-Major* is not solely concerned with the Napoleonic Wars. Its interests in historicity, temporality and identity are more broadcast, albeit that the final chapter's density draws all that goes before it into its darkness, so as to register all the more forcefully the singularity of the event. If Hardy's violent ending appears unnecessarily cruel, it might be posited that brevity and density are in inverse proportion to the enormity of historical event. There is a question here concerning an ethics of representation. How does one

figure such a moment? Is the condensed force the only appropriate means of giving the reader reflective pause, intended to engender an 'epistemological awakening'? (Ricciardi 2003, 143) Such an awakening might have to do with reflection on the connection between individuals and the economy of conventional historical representation. When we read the following:

> Anne now felt herself close to and looking into *the stream of recorded history*, within whose banks the littlest things are great, and outside which she and the general bulk of the human race were content to live on as an unreckoned, unheeded superfluity (*TM* I.XIII.93; emphasis added)

We apprehend our own relation to history, being more likely to belong to the 'outside', being just one more 'unreckoned, unheeded superfluity' who 'live[s] on'. Importantly, Anne's awakening – a single irreversible event – is *felt*. She apprehends a distance, despite her proximity to the military display she is watching, between herself and those who become abstracted as the stream of recorded history. Anne perceives herself in this, and in relation to the scene, as one who remains beyond, other than inscription; except that Anne cannot know that Hardy has written her down, and that such inscription is part of Hardy's greater project.

Anne's momentary vision of herself opens to the reader alternative historical flows and modes of representation, which in turn uncover otherwise occluded narratives and images flowing from, but not limited to the individual. Regarding the occlusion of English family histories, and the fortunes of historical inscription, we read that:

> Miller Loveday was the representative of an ancient family of corn-grinders whose history is lost in the mists of antiquity. His ancestral line was contemporaneous with that of De Ros, Howard, and De La Zouche; but, owing to some trifling deficiency in the possessions of the house of Loveday, the individual names and intermarriages of its members were not recorded during the Middle Ages, and thus their private lives in any given century were uncertain. ... It was also ascertained that Mr. Loveday's great-grandparents had been eight in number, and his great-great-grandparents sixteen, ... at every stage backwards his sires and gammers thus doubled and doubled till they became a vast body of Gothic ladies and gentlemen of the rank known as ceorls or villeins, full of importance to the country at large, and ramifying throughout the unwritten history of England. (*TM* I.II.18)

A fascinating passage in its complexity, it registers the undecidability of those who, outside all recording, remain unknowable. Indeed,

in something approaching historical parody, of those who remain otherwise unrecorded all one can say is that each earlier generation doubles its later descendents. Rather than tracing a lineage to an origin, Hardy implicitly posits the origin in the 'present' of Miller Loveday, as the family line is disseminated exponentially into an unrecorded past, an historical abyss. All one is led to are unfamiliar nouns, 'ceorls or villeins', which serve as tropes for the partial unreadability of the past, even as they surface to erupt in that present without presence of reading. In this small, performative manner, Hardy thus inscribes illegibility at the level of the historical materiality of the letter. The past exists ultimately as such material traces, which return to remind us that historicity is always a matter of the remainder and the impossibility of a full translation. More than this, the word situates itself in Hardy's representation as a representation that remains alien and other, much as the people it figures without representing them.

Anne's perspective and those of the anonymous ceorls and villains come to find echoes on the day of 'a review [of the troops] on the downs by the King'. At various points in the day, unidentified by-standers cry out, '"There's King Jarge!" "That's Queen Sharlett!"' (*TM* I.XII.89). The voices of the spectators arise as 'Confused acclamations'. The anonymous voices imprint themselves from their perspectives as not wholly distinguishable historical traces. The phonetic spelling of Dorset or 'Wessex' accent maintains materially regional identity, thereby giving to the scene juxtaposition between inside and outside, known and unknown, the named and the unnameable. Thus, Hardy generates a narrative in which history is positioned against historicism, as trope and voice oppose fact and date, thereby producing a 'rhetorical' reading of the texture of historical event.

Regarding Hardy's handling of history in Chapter XII, other small details of cultural history announce themselves:

> The miller wore his best coat on this occasion, which meant a good deal. An Overcombe man *in those days* would have a best coat, and keep it as a best coat half his life. The miller's had seen five and twenty summers chiefly through the chinks of a clothes-box, and was not at all shabby as yet, though getting singular. But that could not be helped; common coats and best coats were distinct species, and never interchangeable. (*TM* I.XII.88; emphasis added)

Here, again, we bear witness to a small history, against which Hardy balances the greater historical narratives. Using Miller Loveday as the exemplar, Hardy takes the uncommon occasion of wearing the

best coat to offer a cultural history of dress etiquette. It is likely that what pertains here to the men of Overcombe in general would have applied also to other communities. It is, however, this local detail of cultural registration with which Hardy is concerned, and is perhaps typical of the kinds of information transmitted orally on which Hardy comments in his Preface to *The Trumpet-Major*, as that locution 'in those days' attests. Its imprecision, historically speaking, adds weight to its rhetorical resonance, as a spectral voice offering a different perspective. A similar phrase is found elsewhere, when Hardy observes that 'afternoon sermons at ... church [were] of a dry and metaphysical nature *at that date*' (*TM* II.XVI.120; emphasis added); the date in question is that of the novel's setting – and, indeed, much helped by the subsequent publication of such sermons, allowing later readers to get a taste of what their forebears had to endure on Sunday mornings. (Conversely though, the historical trace slips out of sight and out of mind; today's casual Hardy reader would not necessarily know such sermons.) Risking a counterintuitive reading, phrases such as 'in those days' and 'at that date' are, in fact, neither Hardy's nor the narrator's. Instead, they are transcriptions of anonymous, marginal voices, which, passing from speaker to speaker enter momentarily into the *stream of recorded history*. Even though Hardy uses them as convenient marks of historical distance and narrative continuity, such idioms, in being just that, enter into the medium of the novelist's discourse. In doing so, they trouble the apparent boundary between fiction and reality, soliciting the certainties of both, even as in their locution they interrogate the ontologies of both. But, returning to the cultural memory of coats, if the source of particular locutions remains undecidable, it can be seen that Hardy does intervene in the translation of the tale through that Darwinian trope, concerning their 'distinct species'.

Despite the different facets of historical record in the chapter (and elsewhere), few appear to acknowledge awareness of what is to come. Only once in Chapter XII is there an exception, which anticipates *The Trumpet-Major*'s final chapter. Hardy's conscious reference to history in this passage provides a fulcrum on which the doubleness of the scene rests:

> They still spread their grassy surface to the sun as on that beautiful morning not, historically speaking, so very long ago; but the King and his fifteen thousand armed men, the horses, the bands of music, the princesses, the cream-coloured teams – the gorgeous centre-piece, in short, to which the downs were but the mere mount or margin – how entirely have they all passed and gone! – lying scattered about the

world as military and other dust, some at Talavera, Albuera, Salamanca, Vittoria, Toulouse, and Waterloo; some in home churchyards; and a few small handfuls in royal vaults. (*TM* I.XII.92)

Representation doubles because it opposes both the 'before' and 'after' of events. Equally, though, it situates the brightness and heat of the day, the colour, movement and intimation of music, ordering these as a somewhat impressionistic aesthetic, if 'confused' whole, in contrast to which the ruined aftermath of war arrives, as the sparest of representations telegraphed violently through the proper names of battlefields. The whole is scattered, representation left in ruins.

It is not only the people of Wessex to whom Hardy bears witness, however. Locations, the landscape, architectural forms – all have histories to be invented. Of Oxwell Hall and its immediate environs, it is observed:

> As for the outside, Nature, in the ample time that had been given her, had so mingled her filings and effacements with the marks of human wear and tear upon the house, that *it was often hard to say* in which of the two or if in both, any particular obliteration had its origin. The keenness was gone from the mouldings of the doorways, but *whether worn out by the rubbing past of innumerable people's shoulders*, and the moving of their heavy furniture, *or by Time in a grander and more abstract form, did not appear*. The iron stanchions inside the window-panes were eaten away to the size of wires at the bottom where they entered the stone, the condensed breathings of generations having settled there in pools and rusted them. (*TM* I.VI.43; emphases added)

What is given us to read is erasure, effacement, obliteration, the assignable origins of obliteration undecidable. We thus read the limits of reading, perceiving multiple inscriptions of the undecidable. All the narrator can do, inviting the reader to bear witness in the process, is admit that time has left its mark, whether through human or inhuman agency. Not all signs of the past are elided anonymously, however. Those to whom history 'happens', whilst remaining 'outside' and oblivious of its currents, often aid in the removal of the material signs of cultural history. In anticipation of a visit, Anne's mother helps clean Miller Loveday's home: 'the tawny smudges of bygone shoulders in the passage were removed without regard to a certain genial and *historical value* which they had acquired' (*TM* II.XVI.115; emphasis added). The inquiry has to be made – *historical value* to whom? Certainly neither Mrs Garland, nor the reader. The only people to whom such signs can have historical value are the Miller and his two sons.

Here is a private history, therefore. Hardy is making a case for an excessive historical significance to be found in marks, signs, remainders, ruins and fragments everywhere. At the same time, Hardy seems to be confessing that one cannot be mindful of one's own historicity all the time. This being so, by what criteria do we judge historical value? What is to be saved? Not every history or memory is recorded. The preservation of one narrative often occurs at the price of another, and certain historical traces have accumulated historical 'worth' in being reiterated, the weight of which only buries the seemingly insignificant deeper. Against this, it might be, the work of literature is to offer a countersignature to such occlusion, even if it can only remark what it cannot interpret. Hardy addresses this problem in the poem 'The Roman Gravemounds', as he remembers an encounter with another walking around a Roman burial site. This encounter causes the poem's speaker to reflect that, while Rome's 'long rule' has been frequently 'A theme for the sages of history', the stranger's cat, whom the stranger has brought to bury on the same site as the remembered Romans, was a 'small furred life was worth no one's pen' (*CP* 396–97). However, this is not quite true, or no longer true after the writing of the poem. Hardy's penultimate line perjures itself in a performative manner. In the event of its being written, especially as a reflection on the witnessed burial of an animal, 'Whose life never won from the world a thought', the line, and therefore the poem, archives the otherwise unremembered. Importantly, it gives to the nameless stranger a, perhaps sentimental, memorial accord analogous with that shown to the cat by its owner, both of whom have now entered into textual record.

Again, we are confronted with a question of the ethics of representation. Hardy posits such minor details as of irrecoverable historical significance at an historical moment when, for many Victorians of Hardy's parents' and grandparents' generation, English cultural life is *felt* to be undergoing various ineluctable epistemological and cultural shifts. In the face of this, and although the conclusion of *The Trumpet-Major* cannot cease to haunt us, Hardy inverts narrative precedence apropos the materiality of history, subverting the significance of historical narrative in the process. In a novel nearly 300 pages long, the greater and recorded events of history are maintained at the threshold of anonymous, provincial life. Direct effects, though devastating, are few and far between. Overturning the 'inside' and the 'outside' of 'recorded history', and 'disproportioning' emphasis and significance, he brings back to the mind's eye various details of everyday life, from muslin gowns to metaphysical sermons, from best coats to the smudges of bygone

shoulders, all of which otherwise unremembered details speak quietly and eloquently of the irreparable loss of and to provincial English life. The common is thus made uncommon through being remembered, brought to the reader's attention. Hardy delineates traces of cultural and impersonal memory, offering an alternative stream, recording and simultaneously filtering, or editing, what in the 1880s was not necessarily recorded, and it remains for the reader to choose which history is the more significant. In this choice resides the meagre possibility for Hardy that history might awaken 'in us a true sense of our temporality' (de Man 1993, 88). For, in *The Trumpet-Major*, as in *A Laodicean*, and to lesser extent elsewhere in Hardy, 'History ... is what allows recognition to originate in a truly temporal perspective' (de Man 1993, 88), in which perspective, keeping to the custom of when to wear one's best coat, is of more immediate cultural significance than a battle taking place elsewhere. Such perspective directed to various, heterogeneous details illumines for us that history does not persist 'as a memory of a unity that never existed, but as the awareness, the precarious condition [of loss, occlusion, and erasure] that has never ceased to prevail' (de Man 1993, 88).

IV. THE 'UNRECOVERABLE'

Hardy's anti-realist endeavours in superficially realist narrative thus serve to remind one not only of the impossibility of producing coherence and unity regarding the representation of the past, but also the problem of one's own time and place. There is a diachronic tension that remains irresolvable, if one becomes conscious of the extent to which one's modernity is informed and determined by anachronistic traces that haunt any ontological formation oblivious to the complexities of historicity and cultural memory. In this, Hardy reminds us through the strategic, putative aesthetic awkwardness of his texts that a thick description of history is possible, which rhetorically radicalizes and transvalues a more normative historicism belonging to realist narrative. Emphasizing detail, making clear occlusion, recovering the forgotten – adding to narrative history those incidentals that make up the material and phenomenal experience of a given moment translates dispassionate representation into a more intimate sensate apprehension. That we perceive this at all serves as a reminder that Hardy's is readable not as aesthetic failure but as a constantly differentiated discourse on the historicity of being. Modernity in Hardy is not an assured, albeit embattled, ontology; it is a site for competing ontological affirmations. As Jim Reilly puts it,

the tension of the age is enacted in Hardy's *A Laodicean* ... where Paula Power ... owns and puzzles over the style – Gothic or classical, faithfully restorative or boldly redesigning? – in which to revamp a castle so old that its origins – Saxon or Norman? – seem unrecoverable. (1993, 13)

As *The Trumpet-Major* shows, the recoverability of a more recent past is equally problematized. How does one hear, thereby invent, recover, that which speaks through a bullet hole, the fragment of a staff, or a pile of bricks? Hardy insists on the paradoxical historical problematic, and with that the contest within, and as the sign of, being's historicity throughout *A Laodicean*, which is remarkable for its power to disturb the idea of the present from within. It enacts in numerous ways the condition of placing 'the modern flower in a mediaeval flowerpot' (*L* I.IV.32). Indeed, it goes further, staging the present and modern identity as constantly contested anachronic, and ultimately undecidable sites, as the very title registers economically.

A Laodicean's full title is *A Laodicean; or, the Castle of the De Stancy. A Story of To-day*. The word *Laodicean*, described by the *OED* as archaic, can be employed as either an adjective or a noun. It signifies the quality of being indecisive regarding religious or political beliefs. Someone who is a Laodicean evinces such vacillating habits of thought ideologically or theologically. If we extend the use of the term to the title itself, it might be said that Hardy's title is appropriately 'Laodicean' in that use of *or*, which signals the oscillation between the former and the latter parts of the title. It is as if Hardy could not make up his mind, or was only half-heartedly committed to either choice for his title. The archaism seems fitting, however, albeit unintentionally. The second part of the title acknowledges as its subject a castle, specifically that belonging to the De Stancys. This name with its qualifying Francophone 'de' indicates another sign of the past, specifically the Norman conquest and usurpation of lands belonging to older, occluded societies and cultures belonging to Wessex and the other kingdoms of the Heptarchy. (Saxon churches with Norman towers in Hardy figure the contest of cultural identities acutely through their representation.) The title appears to be haunted by that which is not of the present. Though arriving in the 1880s, the very material from which the title is 'built' is glaringly anachronistic. And it is as if Hardy perceives this in his further addition to the title, when he adds a second subtitle: 'a story of to-day'. Archaic and obscure terminology, references to medieval architectural structures and possibly Norman families – all figure the title and in doing so whisper suggestively of that condition of haunted modernity. If *A Laodicean* is a story

of today, it is a story inescapably haunted by the traces of the past. 'To-day', as the title has it, is always already woven by all the 'inherited traits' that make themselves appear, and so impress the mind of the modern subject, taking 'possession' of her (*L* III.II.166). The 'modern' as non-synonymous supplement for 'to-day' is received as an ontological determinant shot through with those 'hauntological' ruins, the very marks of which arrive as if to affirm that modernity only takes place by virtue of anachrony and uncanny possession.

To be modern, then, is to be *Laodicean*; not in one's personality or consciousness necessarily, though both Paul Power and George Somerset are depicted as being, in some degree, 'balanced between believing and not believing' (*L* I.I.5). Rather, being or belonging to the modern is to be nothing other than indecisively enfolded in heterogeneous temporal and historical, and, therefore, cultural flows. *A Laodicean* works by staging unbridgeable aporia within any discourse concerning generations, historical locatability, provenance or authority. This is immediately recognizable in that this is as much a novel of telegraphy, trains, photography and other technologies of the late nineteenth century, as it is one concerned with Gothic and earlier manifestations of architecture. Both inhabit the same temporal and narrative space, and yet neither the ancient nor the modern has precedence; nor, for that matter, is one privileged over the other. If origins are unrecoverable, so too is a source for modernity, compromised as it is by the anachronistic signs and frames out of which it comes into focus.

The signs of such logical or representational disjunctions in logic and representation, along with other instances of undecidability, manifest themselves even in the way a person looks. Of George Somerset's appearance, we are informed that '[t]hough he would have been broadly characterised as a young man, his face bore contradictory testimonies to his precise age' (*L* I.I.4). Somerset recalls a number of architects and professional men in Hardy's novels, suspended as it were between modes of existence and figuring a liminal location between country and city, practical and theoretical 'experience', past and present. Not least amongst these is Stephen Smith, an architect's apprentice, from *A Pair of Blue Eyes* and the three architects of *Desperate Remedies*. However, in Somerset the problematic of modernity is more intensely focused. Part of the problem for Somerset is the modern age itself, a restlessness in fashion and epistemology symptomatic of the 'unlimited appreciativeness' and kaleidoscopic change' from which 'modern malady' George 'had suffered . . . as much as any living man of his age', resulting in 'his not having been able to make up his mind which . . . was the true point

of departure for himself' (*L* I.I.5). As a result, such impermanence of focus and reflection creating a 'Laodicean' culture, externalizes itself in Hardy's narrative in Somerset's appearance. A further consequence is that the 'youthfulness about the mobile features', in contrast to 'mature forehead', results in a face unfamiliar 'in past ages' and an aesthetic typicality more 'of the future human type than of the past' (*L* I.I.4). In such confusion and its larger ramifications we may not unreasonably read the reason for Hardy's having subtitled *A Laodicean*, 'a novel of to-day'; for, to stress an abiding and germane matter for Hardy, 'today' announces modernity without fixing the present to a specific date. It unhinges the present moment in favour of a mutable 'now' caught up in, and transformed, if not haunted by the traces of past and future.

V. DISCOMPOSING MODERNITY

Whether folkloric or architectural, oral or written, Christian or pagan, Hardy foregrounds the remnants of embedded pasts without narrative, or those in danger of being erased from modern narratives of cultural identity, treacherous traces always open to a misreading that perceives them as quaint, nostalgic, while at the same time, tracing the eruption of pasts into a present that is never stable. That the present is never stable is attested to not simply in Somerset's particular knowledge and its limits, even though Somerset is the initial conduit through which such matters are focussed or transmitted. Beyond the narrative, such limits come to be announced in those acts of criticism unable to account for what they do not know, and for which they cannot therefore read. It might be said that Somerset sees but does not always comprehend. His vision gives him access to other times, even if Somerset is only a medium for the narrative's meditations on the time-torn condition and the temporal layering that composes – and discomposes – the modern.

Paula Power, daughter of a wealthy railway magnate, who buys the castle belonging originally to the De Stancy family, also embodies and acts as a conduit for the conflict of knowledges and discourses. Like Somerset, she perceives without full understanding, and so is caught in the 'Laodicean' tensions of an anachronistic modernity. It should be noted that Paula, like George, has a 'modern' look: 'She was, in fact, emphatically a modern type of maidenhood, and she looked ultra-modern by reason of her environment; a presumably sophisticated being among the simple ones' (*L* I.II.11). Here, again, Hardy plays off modernity and archaism,

complexity and simplicity, through an intermingling of a psychology and phenomenology of appearance given a specific material context.

George Somerset's first 'exposure' to Paula Power (although he does not yet know it to be her) is in a 'recently erected chapel of red-brick' (*L* I.II.8), to which he is drawn on hearing 'New Sabbath', a tune which calls to mind his childhood. Here, again, the past erupts into the present, and, in doing so, opens for the reader a history greater than Somerset's own, but for which he is the conduit or medium. Once recalled, Somerset remembers that the tune 'appertained' in his childhood 'to the old west-gallery period of church-music, anterior to the great choral reformation' (*L* I.II.8), which is partly the subject matter of *Under the Greenwood Tree*. On seeing the new chapel from which issues the sound of 'New Sabbath', Somerset apostrophises the encounter with the remark, '"Shade of Pugin, what a monstrosity!"' (*L* I.II.8) However, ironically, the narrator intrudes with his own parenthetical intrusion that countersigns Somerset's commentary: 'this exclamation (being one rather out of date . . .)', thereby offering a punctuation that anachronizes Somerset's perspective. Pugin's own architectural influence in the second half of the nineteenth century, with its invention of the neo-Gothic, was itself a deliberately anachronistic-modern style, but already a generation or two old by the time Hardy became an architect. The chapter then continues, offering the reader a description of the architecture:

> The building was . . . a recently-erected chapel of red brick, with pseudo-classical ornamentation, and the white regular joints of mortar could be seen streaking its surface in geometrical oppressiveness from top to bottom. The roof was of blue slate, clean as a table, and unbroken from gable to gable; the windows were glazed with sheets of plate glass, a temporary iron stove-pipe . . . an oblong white stone [was] let into the wall just above the plinth, on which was inscribed in block letter: ERECTED 187-, at the sole expense of JOHN POWER, ESQ., M.P. (*L* I.II.8–9)

Typical of many of Hardy's descriptive passages, whether of architecture or landscape, strong lines mark the representation, forming interruptions in the mode of representation as much as they serve it. At the same time, a bold yet restricted palette of colours in stark juxtaposition – in this case, white, blue, red – inform the sketch. Hardy's writing disrupts the flow of narrative through a self-conscious foregrounding of representation's own material constructedness in writing. The force of description is contrasted with the earlier description of the first chapter: 'the dissimilitude between the new utilitarianism of the [chapel] and the scenes of

venerable Gothic art ... could not be well exceeded' (*L* 9). And all the time the reader is recalled to the fact that what we read is not merely the narrative representation but also, always a representation as filtered through the mind, the perceptions of George Somerset: 'His mind was arrested by the intense and busy energy which must needs belong to an assembly that required such a glare of light [as emanated from the chapel]' (*L* I.II.9). The arrest of which Hardy speaks is that which the narrative is apprehended as undergoing in its own motions and construction, and is thus typical once again of Hardyean suspension intended to focus the eye of the reader on detail. Hardy doubles the effect, all the while taking care to maintain, however narrowly or invisibly, a distance between the effect as translated through Somerset's psyche, the translation of the imagined reality and the materiality of the text. Thus we see more than Somerset, seeing also that he does not see fully, as Hardy marks the limits of vision and perspective symptomatic of the modern condition.

How Somerset comes to find out Paula's identity is by a chance of modern technology. The question of technology is a significant matter in the novel. William Dare, who seeks to discredit Somerset with Paula, has a '"patent photographic process"' (*L* III.II.171), by which he causes a photograph of George to look as if the latter were drunk (*L* I.III.23). Dare's alignment with modern technology pairs him with Paula's father, through the latter's professional involvement with railroads. Both men serve as figures for modernity, while it is architectural history and the genealogical longevity of the De Stancy family that serve as the indices of antiquity and other histories. The most significant technology in *Laodicean* is, though, a telegraph wire, by which Somerset discovers Paula's identity. Not merely a narrative device, the telegraph, along with telegrams and telegraphy thread their way through the novel (*L* I.V.35, I.VI.43, III.IV.182, III.X.214–15, IV.II.240–41, IV.IV.254). On leaving the chapel where he first glances Paula, Somerset sets off across the fields towards the inn at which he is lodging. His 'attention was attracted ... [by a] single wire of telegraph running parallel with his track' (*L* I.II.16). The humming of the wire Somerset takes initially to be the hum of a night bee. In this brief moment, Hardy rudely introduces the modern in the technological form of communication and transmission. More than that, he marks what might be described as a sylvan scene with a line that, picking up figurally the shadows of trees streaking 'like a zebra' the lane with their shadows (*L* I.II.16), provides the reader with an analogical graphic interruption on the field of vision signifying not nature but human intervention in the natural. For while the shadows are an inevitable

'natural' temporal mark on the scene, the telegraph wire most obviously is not. It is strung across the scene as a means to disorientate through its modernity.

Following the 'lead of the wire' across the countryside (*L* I.II.16), Somerset comes eventually to a spectacle standing in anachronistic contrast to the telegraph wire on the one hand, and the natural world on the other: 'there appeared against the sky the walls and towers of a castle, half ruin, half residence' (*L* I.II.17). On closer inspection, the decaying erection is seen to have a 'comparatively modern wing' (*L* I.II.17). Of no one time itself, and therefore having no stable or proper identity, the castle, described in the metaphors of nineteenth-century science as 'this fossil of feudalism', is found by Somerset to be 'the journey's-end of the wire' (*L* I.II.18). There is noticeable also a modern wing, but the rest of the castle is notable for its 'neglect and decay' (*L* I.II.17). George then 'walked up to a modern arch . . . the wire . . . vanished through an arrow-slit' (*L* I.II.17–18). Hardy emphasizes the anachrony of the vision for Somerset, a vision that presented through temporal but also technological and epistemological juxtaposition of cultural identities situated in the 'stolid antagonism of the interchange of ideas' as these are represented by the castle and the telegraph wire. On the one hand, the former signifies synecdochally 'hard distinctions of blood and race, of deadly distrust of one's neighbour in spite of the Church's teaching, and of a sublime unconsciousness of any other force than a brute one' (*L* I.II.18). On the other hand, the wire, as metonymic trace, affirms beyond it a 'machine which beyond everything may be aid to symbolize cosmopolitan views and the intellectual and moral kinship of all mankind' (*L* I.II.18). Feudalism and modernity, past and present, isolation and communion, brute materiality and, via that tele-technology, the spectral affiliation of a disembodied modern culture: as that wire crosses into the castle, witnessed and heard in its function by Somerset, so too do the signals of profoundly different cultural identities historically riven intersect with one another to produce a perceptual contest, which discomposes the modern understood as distinct temporal location from within.

The first two chapters play out the ancient and modern, therefore, in this 'story of to-day' as if to define 'to-day' as always already irreparably sundered, this rent being the condition of its identity. In this manner the 1870s and 1880s are defined through such interplay and tension. Into this play and the gap between temporally absolute or discrete moments or historical instances is inserted the modern subject who seeks to interpret the conflicting signals. As the telegraph and the castle highlight, composition involves the interaction

between line and mass, motion or trajectory (and in the case of the wire its 'singing' or electric oscillation as the resonance of the tele-technological or spectral condition of modernity) and material structure. As Hardy expresses the – to George – unexpected juxtaposition of the feudal and the modern there is an encounter between, on the one hand, 'a stolid antagonism to the interchange of ideas' and, on the other hand, the machinic production of kinship (*L* I.II.18). This is not necessarily only Hardy's view, if it is his at all. For, in the next sentence, he observes that '[i]n that light the little buzzing wire had a far finer significance to the student Somerset than the vast walls which neighboured it' (*L* I.II.18).

The metaphors concerning 'neighbouring' and light have ironic significance here. We are not reading of a literal or empirical act of illumination, but an interiorized illumination, Somerset's perceptual and reflective processes. The modern subject's mind is illuminated for the reader, even as it illuminates that selfsame subject. Structures of translation and apprehension are delineated. However, Hardy takes a more distanced view than Somerset's, so reopening the space that Somerset's mind comes to close in its reflections. In doing so, he thereby reintroduces for the reader that problematization of reading the past in the present, bearing witness to the past and reflecting on one's relationship to it, which is temporarily – and it may be suggested, temporally – elided. Hardy issues a cautionary interruption in the following manner: 'But, on the other hand, the modern mental fever and fret ... was also signified by the wire; and this aspect of to-day did not contrast well (at least in his moonlight meditations) with the fairer side of feudalism ... and such a living power in architectural art as the world may never again see' (*L* I.II.18). The first two chapters, therefore, offer the reader an exemplary model of the perception of the anachrony intrinsic to modernity. Hardy effectively illuminates the necessity for determination of the latter as being rooted in the conscious interpolation of the former. That the mind is itself intrinsic to the perception of the modern as modern, and that the perception involves the mind as being the place between ancient and modern, is itself telling of the 'modern' condition.

Indeed, to backtrack a little, it has to be said that the novel demonstrates this from its opening pages. In the opening paragraph of the novel, the reader's attention is drawn to a 'chevroned doorway' (*L* I.I.3) formally noted as one element in the overall composition before George Somerset's vision, his interior subjective perspective and that of the sketch he carries out; his drawing of the building, along with its 'tall mass of antique masonry', the 'battlemented parapet', and the 'moulded stonework' (*L* I.I.3). All such traces bring

back the past, as it were, into present, a moment which is effectively suspended by this foregrounding of the trace of the old in the new. As soon as the material of the past is sketched it is as if it were there, as if it were in the present moment of reading and perception, but also as if one were removed temporally to the moment of its having been constructed. The reader is privy also to a double time in the opening chapter: the double time of Somerset sketching and of his own being sketched – for the reader. All that has 'passed into the unseen' six hundred years prior to this inaugural narrative moment returns to be illuminated, and in the fact that the material scene is itself haunted by the 'performers', as Hardy puts it, who had constructed the church originally, as well as those who, before the church had been given material manifestation, had traced the envisioned contours, sketching a design not yet come into being. A curious effect is produced here, in the final paragraph of the novel's first page. Somerset is observed in the process of 'copying the exact contour[s] of each moulding to his drawing ... mark[ing] down the line thus fixed' (*L* I.I.3).

Hardy shows us the observer observed, the sketcher sketched, as I have already indicated. What he also illustrates is another sketcher, another observer, himself. He presents a figure in the shadows, engaged in the auto-occlusive work of penumbral adumbration to be sure – but one more figure tracing the lines of that prior figure, who only comes to appear, to be observed in inverse and anachronic order. Hardy thus reveals the extent to which what we call history is always a process of reiteration, of transference, of the singular moment of following the lines in order that the unseen traces come to be seen once more. What is also made visible in this is the relay and multiplication of gazes and the concomitant dislocation of any central or originating position or perspective, either within the scene or across time, Yet of course what is also revealed in this moment of suspension and oblique reflection – which is intended undeniably to give pause to the act of reading-as-witness in order that reading might become a moment of being 'brought to reflection' concerning 'human decline and death that [the scene] illustrates' (*L* I.I.3) – is the belated disorder of all temporal reflection on being and the events of history and the traces of the past. As with the title of the novel, any story of to-day must necessarily have folded within it the traces of the past, the ruined architecture of other historical and material moments. *This* is the story of to-day. This is, in effect, Hardy's apprehension of modernity: to be modern, one traces, copies, illustrates and reflects, and so becomes aware of oneself historically, reading oneself in relation to those echoes. The unseen is invoked

through the illustration of the seen, if reflective perception (seeing oneself obliquely through what one is directed to see elsewhere) is caused to take place. Hardy makes possible such reflection by the deliberate and stark juxtaposition between present and past, the living and the dead, the figure of the sketcher and the intimation of the dead hand behind the material remnants of the past.

VI. MAKING VISIBLE

A Laodicean's is a disquietingly hybrid novel, all the more so because it admits of no origins or sources, no 'genuine', authoritative identity out of which hybridity is formed. Neither feudalism nor modernity is given as the locus of meaning. The groundlessness of the novel is opened through moments such as those described, and repeatedly throughout the text in its concern with transmission, motion, flow and flight, with intersection, intercommunication and miscommunication in the constitution of the subject in history. The self's constitution by, and location within, 'history' in this novel is central to its interests, even as the very idea of self is traced in its mutability and protean flux. This makes it all but impossible to read identity, whether one's own or another's. This is all the more pointedly addressed in that the impossibility of choice leads to the self becoming a Laodicean: someone historically determined as vacillating, rendered inactive by an aporetic experience of the traces of history. The 'modern' subject is a passive sufferer of his or her time, subsequently given over simultaneously to a kind of cultural restlessness or febrile activity (that is captured formally in aspects of the prose) or else, ennui. Of course, Hardy is not alone in producing a subject whose modernity is defined by such sufferance. What is different in Hardy's victims of ennui from those of other writers in the fin de siècle is often precisely the burden of the past that reminds one of one's present location, allied to a self-conscious experience in the face of undecidability and various aporetic instances. To counter the symptoms of modernity whilst offering a critique of the same, Hardy works to make visible the various, differing temporal strata and flows. In this, he makes visible also those perspectival angles by which the reader gains insight into the framing and positioning of the subject.

As Somerset enters De Stancy Castle via 'a flight of stone stairs', the stairs are made to bear witness to 'Tudor soldiers and other renowned dead men [who] had many times walked' on them (L I.III.19–20). Whether or not this is the young man's thought

is not apparent. As this and the following lines in this particular paragraph demonstrate, the narrative traverses Somerset's reflections but remains neither wholly outside them nor inside them. At one juncture Somerset is observed observing the walls, while at another the reader is admitted to his suppositions (*L* I.III.20). Thus narration partakes of the telegraph effect, entering into consciousness and transmitting its signals, as these are, themselves, reverberations generated sympathetically in response to the materiality of the environment. If what we read is inescapably temporal in its being remarked, then the anachrony of a clock, not 'coeval with the fortress itself, but new and shining, and bearing the name of a recent maker' (*L* I.III.20) is not an insignificant memento of history's passage. Yet one more technology, it appears to intrude into its setting, interrupting its harmony and surface, thereby remaining at odds with that environment, rather like Paula amongst the congregation or the 'electric wire' and the arrow-slit.

Hardy provides a figural conceit for the transition, the temporal effect, around the remainder of the trace that informs and infests the modern and its representation, when Somerset, 'left to himself' (*L* I.III.20), is seen by the reader observing the gallery in which are housed the portraits of the De Stancys. Family transmission enacts a kind of genealogical and representational telegraphy, as if one could read particular ghostly effects within the same modern moment. Most noticeable in the representation of the paintings is the condition of material decay of the canvasses rather than anything peculiar to aesthetic effect. Time intrudes and forces interpretation in another direction than the aesthetic. This is further amplified when the narrative announces that 'many of the frames were dropping apart at their angles' (*L* I.III.20). Framing is incomplete, the frame fails, and as a result of time, upon which we are enjoined to reflect from our own inescapably temporal and historical locations, whenever we might come to read the novel. The frame being open, there is implied that which no attempt at representational closure or enclosure can maintain.

Into this broken image come Somerset's reflections: 'He wondered how many of the lofty foreheads and smiling lips ... could be credited as true reflections of their prototypes ... Somerset felt that it required a profounder mind than his to *disinter* from the *lumber* of conventionality the *lineaments* that really sat in the *painter's presence*, and to *discover* their *history* behind the *curtain* of mere tradition' (*L* I.III.21; emphases added). Hardy's language is fascinating here. Between notions of disinterring and discovering there is the sense of archaeological uncovering, of digging up the dead and

making visible what was invisible. At the same time, the passage relies on the historicity of representational convention, apprehended as convention and therefore of another historical moment because capable of being reflected upon at a distinct and different historical instance. The implication of distinct moments is further marked in the acknowledgement of a painter's presence. This acknowledges the presence of an actively intervening, interpretative observer, as had the opening of the novel in its image of Somerset as sketcher. Again, in the rhetorical motions of the opening passages another, shadowy observer is also implied.

There is an implicit parallelism in this scene (*L* I.III.21), which in its representation, in what and how it represents, is both temporal *and* structural: between painter to the novelist an analogy is made. This carries also from subject to subject, from the observer observed to one – the phantom 'narrator' or the artist generally – who observes unseen, and from there to the reader; from one observer to another, and, therefore, also, from one group of observed beings, the De Stancys, to another observed figure, that of Somerset, who in turn is observed observing, his function once more doubled, and in that doubling, figured confessionally as someone materially and historically caught at a moment that no frame can maintain or contain. As 'behind' the portraits is a painter, and as behind Somerset there is the narrator, behind whom is Hardy, and then each and every reader of the novel; so, there is also the strong implication of a true identity behind the historically, culturally and ideologically determined parameters of aesthetic representation. And historicity is captured in this: while convention dictates that subjectivity is either not to be revealed or cannot be transmitted across decades, much less centuries, so at another moment, in another medium – writing rather than painting or drawing – there is no representation without the phenomenological interpretation of another, and another observer.

VII.   POSSESSION OR, THE EXPERIENCE OF HISTORY

Paula Power's perception of modernity is different from Somerset's. She describes herself in the following way: 'I am not a medievalist myself … I am Greek' (*L* I.X.70). How accurate this is, is beside the point. More telling is Paula's argument over repairs to De Stancy Castle. Instead of creating 'deceitful' imitations of the original fabric, anachronistic patches should be made, so that past and present are thrown into stark relief (*L* I.VIII.60–1). This attitude is all the more comprehensible, and indicative of a certain

late-Victorian sense of modern identity, when we gain access to Paula's rooms, into which George wanders by accident. Here he sees: 'popular papers and periodicals ... [s]atirical prints ... books from a London circulating library, paper-covered light literature in French and choice Italian, ... the latest monthly reviews ... [and] the telegraphic apparatus ... ' (*L* 31) In an adjacent room, there are: 'a Bible, the *Baptist Magazine*, Wardlaw on Infant Baptism, Walford's County Families, and the *Court Journal*. ... knickknacks of various descriptions, and photographic portraits of the artistic, scientific, and literary celebrities of the day' (*L* I.IV.31). The range of reading material is heterogeneous, suggestive of interests in lineage, law, institutional constructions of identity, and so on. Furthermore, it also figures an intermixing of differing cultural, and therefore, historical moments within the one representation, as if the image itself were only constructible through the anachronic interplay. Of all that Somerset observes and its context in his 'study of ancient architecture', Hardy goes on to comment that 'These things, ensconced amid so much of the old and hoary, were as if a stray hour from the nineteenth century had wandered like a butterfly into the thirteenth, and lost itself there' (*L* I.IV.31). Interestingly, time itself becomes the figure of transport, that 'stray hour' being the metaphor and displaced trope for Paula Power. Paula's gadfly interests, gathered into a desultory scene and temporal moment, suggest her distracted and diffuse, *Laodicean* personality, the Modernity of being captured here through the details of the domestic locus, dwelling cut adrift from any stable ground or identity.

Furthermore, it is as if Paula's life is nothing other than a series of partially read texts, all of which aim to communicate in varying languages, but none of which can communicate or connect directly with one another. Indeed, it seems as if Paula feels a longing for a greater sense of dwelling and home, when she remarks to Somerset '[b]ut I wish I had a well-known line of ancestors' (*L* I.XIV.96). Somerset's response that 'Archimedes, Newcomen, Wall, Telford, Stephenson, those are your father's direct ancestors' is hardly comforting (*L* I.XIV.96), but it does suggest a pseudo-genealogy of discontinuous technological and epistemological transformations. Despite or perhaps because of her phantom-line, though, Paula finds herself pulled by the medievalism she initially disavows. In this, she re-enacts the contest of Mid-Victorian cultural identity, as modern 'progressives' who owned steel mills bought Pre-Raphaelite paintings, named steamships after characters from Tennyson, and worshipped in Pugin chapels. Even as her rooms are indicative of

displacement from the nineteenth to the thirteenth century, so Paula, on a visit to Lisieux, finds herself, in the midst of a somewhat hallucinatory scene,

> *transported* to the Middle Ages. [The street] contained the shops of tinkers, braziers, bellows-menders, hollow-turners, and other quaintest trades, their fronts open to the street beneath stories of timber overhanging so far on each side that a slit of sky was left at the top of for the light to descend, and no more. A blue misty obscenity persuaded the atmosphere, into which the sun thrust oblique staves of light. It was a street for a medievalist to revel in.... She had never supposed such a street to exist outside the imaginations of antiquarians. Smells direct from the sixteenth century hung in the air in all their original integrity and without a modern taint. The faces of the people in the doorways seemed those of individuals who habitually gazed on the great Francis, and spoke of Henry the Eighth as the King across the sea ... (*L* VI.I.350–1)

The passage offers strange and estranging, uncanny attestation to that which haunts, that which emerges from and is other than the otherwise unremarkable. An event arises from the human experience of the encounter with the uncommon that resonates within the everyday, and, subsequently, the recording of that experience, an event the singularity of which is only knowable through the transformation from one materiality – that of the brute world – into another – that of writing. Uncommonness, as Hardy calls it, is shaped, given form in its occurrence. It emerges from, in excess of, mere observation. We are caught, observing along with Paula, a world existing in two times simultaneously. Uncommonness is shaped through the projection and production of what Hardy describes above as *illusion*. The singularity of experience is apprehended through the phantasmal tenor of the event.

Illusion of a particularly haunting kind takes hold of Paula much before the encounter in Lisieux, however. When Miss De Stancy brings her brother to meet Paula, Captain De Stancy inspects the paintings of his ancestors in the castle gallery. The figures in the paintings have already been described, on George Somerset's first encounter with them, as 'phantoms that looked down from the frames' (*L* I.III.22), but this mere conceit is superseded by what can only be described as an uncanny experience for Paula during the Captain's visit. Somerset had already noted the haunting resemblance between the portraits of the De Stancys and Miss De Stancy, observing in particular a genetic 'degeneration' or 'defective reprint' (*L* I.III.23) in the present Miss De Stancy, absent from her

ancestors. However, Paula's apprehension of family likeness is far more troubling:

> As he moved hither and thither, the various expressions of De Stancy's face made themselves picturesquely visible in the unsteady shine of the blaze. In a short time he had drawn near to the painting of an ancestor whom he so greatly resembled. When her [Paula's] quick eye noted the speck on the face, indicative of inherited traits strongly pronounced, a new and romantic feeling that the De Stancys had stretched out a tentacle from their genealogical tree to seize her hand and draw her into their mass *took possession of* Paula. (L III.II.166; emphasis added)

Initially romantic, the apprehension of possession soon changes. We read subsequently that a 'strange spell cast over her by something or other ... which was as if the historic past had touched her with a yet living hand' (L III.IV.182). Clearly, history is as much to blame for Paula's feeling of being haunted as any living figure. Such moments, though few, lead, along with Captain De Stancy's interest in Paula, and her disillusion over Somerset as a result of Dare's photograph, to departure for France, Paula remarking to her aunt: 'I will never return to that castle as Miss Power. A nameless dread comes over me when I think of it – a fear of some uncanny influence of the dead De Stancys ...' (L VI.III.368)

So possessed is Paula by a certain spirit of medievalism that, in the last part of the novel, Hardy's narrative takes on an increasingly Gothic tone. This culminates in the narrative's detail of a shadowy figure 'flitting in and about those drafty apartments, and making no more noise in doing so than a puff of wind ... the figure went from door to door ... and then ... it was seen no more' (L VI.V.373–4). This results in the conflagration that destroys the castle. Ironically, only when the castle is destroyed by fire, are Paula and Somerset 'released' from possession, left 'unencumbered with the ghosts of an unfortunate line' (L VI.V.378). In a remark that hints at a belief in ghostly possession, Somerset tells Paula that she will be herself again and '"recover from the warp given to your mind ... by the medievalism of that place"' (L VI.V.379). Paula's response, thought, is striking for its rejection of such an idea: '"And be a perfect representative of "the modern spirit"?' she inquired; "representing neither the senses nor understanding, nor the heart and the imagination; but what a finished writer calls "the imaginative reason"?' (L VI.V.379). However contested a modernity inflected by other historical traces may be, it is better to be possessed, inhabited or haunted by other times, than to have no time other than one's own, cordoned off from every trace of the past that makes one's identity.

Possession, experienced in the reading of Hardy's texts and also as that imposed on his protagonists, is nothing other than the experience of history. Positing the problem of historicity, and with that of modernity as the dawning of a self-reflexive perception concerning identity and materiality towards the end of the nineteenth century, historical transmission in Hardy's novels is given singular form through the juxtaposition of subjective perception and the 'historical' as this inevitably involves 'complementary movements of the discovery (loss) and the recovery of the past (love) that constitute the realm of historical experience' (Ankersmit 2005, 9).

It might be observed, apropos his star-crossed lovers, that Hardy's tales are more concerned with focussing on loss, or discovery, than on love, or recovery. If there is love, then all too often, love is lost. Hardy, it might be argued, transforms the writing of the novel and marks the historical moment of his productions by abandoning the 'past' conventions of much Victorian realist fiction. Marriage as the gesture of utopian closure in the novel of the nineteenth century attempts to deny, displace, hold of history, to suspend the movement of time in effect. The figure of marriage seeks to establish an 'endless present' in its idealized unity. Rarely do Hardy's novels offer such closure or consolation, in a gesture that places the end of narrative at a remove from historical flow for all time.

Generally, though, Hardy repeatedly forestalls this evacuation of the material and historical conditions of experience, structuring instead the experience as a haunting eruption of the traces of the past on the subject's awareness. In this he discovers history and with that the loss that is memory and historical experience. Thus, a hotel in *A Laodicean* is materially the encrypted record of 'stage-coach memories' (*L* I.XII.87), while the present silence of the chapel of Stancy Castle, evocative of temporal passage through the memory of the lost voice of 'priest or deacon ... for generations utter[ing] the daily service' (*L* I.XI.76), brings to Somerset's mind a sense of his own mortality: '"so, too, will tie triumph overall this further within me"' (*L* I.XI.77). And finally, it is this which, at the close of *A Laodicean*, authorizes Paula Power to remark to George Somerset, while standing before the smouldering ruins of her castle, that she wishes she still had her relic of the past intact, and that Somerset were not of the future, but belonged to the anachronistic De Stancy family: '"I wish my castle wasn't burnt; and I wish you were a De Stancy!"' (*L* VI.V.379)

Knowledge, like desire, can only search after that which is impossible to attain. Even when knowledge is achieved, it is only partial, illuminating with its enlightenment all that remains in shadow. *A Laodicean* concludes therefore with impossibility, with

the discovery of the irrecuperable past as the subjective, historical experience of the world. What cannot be recovered is precisely the past, and the memory's ability to bring back, to dis-cover what is hidden about the nature of the past – that it is only available as ruins, traces, fragments – , serves merely to intensify the experience of loss as the condition of hindsight. Our knowledge tells us this much, at least, and there is scant comfort in it. Coming face to face with loss, absence, impossibility, the present is structured as always already haunted by the very condition of reflection and encounter that makes any present possible. The conclusion of *A Laodicean* thus allows not only Paula Power belated insight but the reader also. The reader is given insight into Paula's subjectivity, and perhaps subjectivity in general, not only through reflection on loss, but through the constitution of identity by loss. In this bitter-sweet frustration, the mnemotechnic relay of consciousness, inscribed by a history that can never belong to it properly because the past is irrecuperable as such, projects from within itself the remembrance, if not of things past in themselves, then of that which affirms what one is. What, in short, being reveals to itself about itself, is that to grasp fully the condition of being historical is to expel oneself from the illusion of homely familiarity with one's world; it is to be left with an ineluctable sense of *Sehnsucht* – a feeling of yearning, without determinate object.

VIII.   HAUNTING'S PERSISTENCE

Throughout this chapter, I have spoken about the haunting nature of the past, and the ways in which it persists in any narrative 'present', returning to disrupt, disturb, and disquiet. The sense of yearning or longing captured in the German notion of *Sehnsucht* to which I just turned in concluding discussion of Paula Power might also be considered as a manifestation in the modern subject of one's being haunted. In the final part of this chapter, I wish to turn to what is perhaps Hardy's most 'haunted' text, *The Mayor of Casterbridge*.

Nowhere in Hardy's work is the insistent revenance of the past's trace acknowledged more persistently or blatantly than in *The Mayor*. In this short chapter we shall see how spectres, phantoms, phantasms and the work of haunting leave indelible marks on the novel, and the town and inhabitants of Casterbridge. The dead and their spectral manifestations appear even in the faces or actions of the living. Casterbridge is a haunted place, its topographical, architectural and archaeological structures resonating with the traces of the spectral. The ghosts of other textual forms, of which the tragic

is only the most persistent or obvious, also haunt the very structure of the novel. Though he is not alone in being ghost-ridden,
Michael Henchard especially is troubled by the past, by certain spectral returns that determine the direction of his life and the choices
or decisions he believes he makes for himself.

From one perspective, haunting is simply, if provisionally, determined as the ability of forces that remain unseen to make themselves
felt in everyday life. Thus 'haunting' is both modern and archaic: its
work defines both a psychoanalytic dimension at personal and cultural levels, whereby the return of the repressed resurfaces, and also
the effects by which past, often archaic practices and beliefs leave
residual traces come to be felt in the modern moment. Spectrality
is that force whereby ancient and modern come into confrontation,
interrupting the quotidian. Such interruption in the everyday causes
one to anticipate, to fear, to act or to respond in ways that we
do not fully comprehend. Thus, 'all the major characters reveal
a capacity ... of responding to experience as the working-out of
inevitable courses' (*MC* xxxi). This assessment catches the sense
of a spectral movement of the invisible within the visible. Such
haunting can also cause us to feel unsafe, uneasy, in places where
we had always felt at home. Haunting creates, then, the sense
of the unfamiliar within the familiar. Its operation is thus a structural, as well as a temporal disturbance. Haunting inhabits and, in
creating an uncanny response, manifests itself as not arriving from
elsewhere, but instead makes itself felt 'surfacing ... in a return of the
repressed as a foreign element that strangely seems to belong to
the very domain that renders it foreign' (Wigley 1993, 108). As we
shall see, haunting, ghosting, spectrality: all articulations inhere in
The Mayor and the topography and history of and around Casterbridge, haunting with an aggressive immanence the very places,
narratives and forms they serve to articulate.

The persistence of the past in the narrative and historical present
of *The Mayor of Casterbridge* is represented as the unsettling or
uncanny recurrence of the past trace. A 'strange peculiarity in the
presence of the present' (Lukacher 1998, 156–7), the past produces
also in the disturbed subject the structural sense of uncanny displacement and doubling, that 'uneasy sense of the unfamiliar within the
familiar, the unhomely within the home' (Wigley 1993, 108). There
are numerous signs of 'the return of the repressed' in relation to
'centuries-old tradition', in addition to which 'residual' customs and
forms, along with 'archaic practices', make their impact felt (Keen
1998, 127, 132, 140). Such spectral force also informs genealogical
patterns and familial structures: 'as a 'spectre', the genetic product

is at once the reincarnation of a figure from the past and an image that has been raised by a guilty party's imagination' (O'Toole 1997, 18–19). Moreover, the spectral inhabits structure or identity in such a way as to displace or disrupt the propriety of the form from within. 'Hardy's is a haunted art' in which 'material reality is displaced as the goal of representation by shadowy and spectral unrealities' (Reilly 1993, 65). Hardy is thus read as working within a fictional paradigm that, though indebted to mimetic realism, nevertheless disrupts that realism repeatedly and violently from within its own conventions, as has become apparent in discussion of other novels.

When we speak of the 'past' in relation to *The Mayor*, this might signal equally a number of differing forms of manifestation. Of personal returns and manifestations of the past there are those who come back from Henchard's personal past: Susan, Lucetta, Elizabeth-Jane, even Newson. There is also the furmity woman, through whom the wife-sale returns to haunt Henchard's public identity, even as it has perpetually haunted his private sense of self. The impersonal past of Casterbridge is acknowledged in a number of ways, not least in the history of mayoral office, and in the various ancient artefacts and structures found in the land surrounding land, such as the Ring, Mai Dun, and Diana Multimammia. A rural past is also acknowledged through and traced in the return of events such as the fair at Weydon Priors or the skimmington ride. In each historical past an alternative world intrudes into the present, disordering the perception of temporal unity. Then there are the 'past' texts that inform the structure of the novel – Greek and Shakespearean tragedy, the Old Testament, references to French novels, to Miltonic monsters, or the novels of Walter Scott, and Gothic fiction. Such 'remains' are not 'the remains of something that was once present'. They are, instead, that which, in being spectral, prevent 'any present, and any experience of the presence, from being completely itself' (Royle 1995, 61). This ghostly trace has the ability to disrupt not only the present moment but also any sense of identity. It may even write itself as 'dead men's traits' in the sleeping face of Elizabeth-Jane (*MC* 126).

This is not a simple or single instance in itself. It reiterates in part an earlier moment in the novel, when Susan and her daughter return to Weydon Priors, the mother's features being figured imperfectly in the daughter's as the manifestation of 'Nature's powers of continuity' (*MC* 21). Thus, ghosting returns, while the return is always ghostly. Furthermore, the earlier scene that anticipates the haunting of Elizabeth-Jane is itself a return. The question of the return is not limited to the reiteration noted between the faces of the two women,

as the text suggests. For as Hardy tells the reader, '[t]he scene in its broad aspect had so much of its previous character ... that it might ... have been the afternoon following the previously recorded episode' (MC 21). This is but one instance of the persistence of return as evidenced through 'particularities within a continuum', which in turn establish 'the anthropology of a location ... explicitly relating the behaviour of present individuals to that of countless predecessors' (Hardy, ed. Kramer 1987, xxiii, xxii).

In that we can read a doubling movement of revenance, where movement haunts moment, we can suggest that the entire order of the novel is predicated on the troping of return as the spectral persistence disordering order and identity from within, as an otherness within the text. Even as Elizabeth-Jane's face is haunted by Susan's, and even as this recalls the earlier moment of return on the part of the two women, so that moment of return, in recalling the supposedly 'initial' scene of arrival at the Fair and the subsequent wife-sale, implies the continuous structural movement of displacement and disjointing. To this can be added a reading of the wife-sale, not as some simple or single originary event generating the unfolding of the narrative but as itself a moment of a form of 'archaic survival' that, in turn, belongs to forms of economic 'traffic' that 'structure the novel' (Keen 1998, 140). This 'structuring' is also at the same time a disturbance that inhabits the structure, disordering as the necessity of an ordered form, as an internal 'other' that haunts and makes possible the very form itself. It disturbs the unity or identity of all structures, whether we are speaking of the human subject, an architectural form, the mapping of the town, or the form of the novel.

The spectral can be seen on occasions in acts of uncanny doubling, a form of return. For example, Elizabeth-Jane, on visiting her mother's grave, encounters a figure 'in mourning like herself ... [who] might have been her wraith or double' (MC 134). Lucetta – described as the 'wraith' – is also an uncanny double of Susan Newson / Henchard on one occasion, the 'double of the first' (MC 250). Elizabeth-Jane is herself a double of sorts. Not Henchard's but Newson's Elizabeth-Jane, she doubles even as she is haunted by the dead child whose place she has taken, whose identity is signed and simultaneously displaced in the reiteration of the name. That 'Elizabeth-Jane' is a proper name given to two characters sharing the same mother (whose features 'ghost' the second daughter's face) is important. For it alerts us to the importance of textual haunting, of haunting as textual, where even the act of writing can return, though never quite signifying that which it had done. This is a sign of repetition *and* displacement, return *and* disturbance. In addition,

Henchard sees in Farfrae's face the double of his dead brother (*MC* 49), and this has an 'uncanny appeal for Henchard' (*MC* xxv). Finally, Henchard is presented as uncannily doubled by the skimmington ride effigy, as is Lucetta. That dummy comes back to haunt both of them (Keen 1998, 140).

Apropos effects and figures of doubling: (*MC* xxviii): such patterns and the 'phantasms' of which they are composed (for all involve the images and memories of the dead) do nothing so much as signify the operations of each other, rather than intimating either a 'reality' beyond the text or an origin or source of which the text is a copy. Indeed, the uncanny mo(ve)ment of revenance and disturbing reiteration comes from within a figure or face to disturb identity and disconcert the subject. In this operation, the ghostly trace, which in reiterating constantly operates in a manner similar to the simulacrum, 'calls into question the authority and legitimacy of its model' (Durham 1998, 3). Such doubling and the rhythm of return of which it is a part destabilize more than the identity of particular characters. It is disruptive of 'distinct domains and temporalities ... [to] the extent to which they increasingly appear as the echoes or doubles of one another' (Durham 1998, 16).

Haunting's disruption is not restricted to characters in *The Mayor of Casterbridge*. The various spatial and temporal boundaries of the novel that are found increasingly to be permeable and capable of being transgressed signify one another's functions and potential interpretative roles in the novel. This is the case wherever one is speaking of the 'haunting' of the present by the past, signalled in the numerous returns discussed above, all of which permeate arbitrarily defined temporal boundaries. This can be read at the level of particular words themselves. Through archaic, untimely words such as 'burgh and champaign' (*MC* 30), the present of the narrative is disrupted. Words such as 'furmity' and 'skimmington' also signify an anachronic haunting. We recall in this Hardy's reflections on the nature of language itself, composed as it is of traces of other times and other modes of expression. Such linguistic revenants remain ruinous and fragmentary, giving no access to an originary discourse or context, or otherwise reminding us that whatever access or understanding we may have is mediated, the word's 'lived' use and sense out of our reach. I can never speak of a skimmington as if such an event were part of my lived, communal experience, no matter how much knowledge I might gain of it. Additionally, there is also spatial movement across boundaries, which involves a temporal emergence of residual archaic practices, as in the eruption of Mixen Lane into the 'proper' or familiar space of Casterbridge (Keen 1998, 132).

The margin overflows the centre, as the fluxes of the past disorder the present, and this is to be understood keenly in Hardy's implicit image of Casterbridge as a centre into which come various forces, memories, and people, as well as being an urban site around which in the landscape are those ruined structures of other worlds and times.

Structurally internal to the town, part of it and yet other, the liminal site of Mixen Lane haunts the town, returning through the manifestation of 'archaic practices of an ancient environ' (Keen 1998, 132). Its return is untimely and uncanny, displacing the familiarity, the modernity, and domesticity of Casterbridge that Hardy has worked so hard to project. Yet Mixen Lane is but one figure in the novel simultaneously 'at once removed from and infinitely proximate to' (Durham 1998, 17) what we consider to be the novel's present moment and its present action. Thus the world of Michael Henchard and the world of Casterbridge are disturbed in their identities from within by the articulation of alternative structures – others of, within and as a condition of textual form – that signify, and thereby double, the operations of each other. Hardy's 'use of place resonates with personal and social significance' (Greenslade 1994, 55), but such resonance is internally unstable, even as it destabilizes the form in which it emerges. While a form of return, such haunting is not simply a straightforward temporal arrival from some identifiable prior past. We witness instead 'underground doublings which arise from differential interrelations among elements which are all on the same plane. This lack of ground ... means that there is something ghostly about the effects of this ... type of repetition' (Miller 1982, 6). In its untimely, not to say anachronistic, fashion, this spectral trace articulates a dissymmetry comprising a non-identity within identity.

IX. WESSEX-GOTHIC

In the last chapters of *A Laodicean* things take a decidedly Gothic turn at De Stancy Castle, with mysterious shadows seen to walk the halls, shortly before the outbreak of the conflagration. Equally, short stories such as 'The Withered Arm' rely on the familiar effects of the Gothic. Whereas earlier I had recalled Hardy's analogy between poetry and architecture, with his insistence that poetry should work with the unexpected, the unforeseen and the irregular as learnt from Gothic architecture, so another analogy suggests itself, in order that we read the ways in which haunted structures are significant to Hardy's texts in general and *The Mayor of*

Casterbridge in particular: the analogy between Gothic as architecture and Gothic as narrative mode, genre, or concatenation of tropes, images, and motifs. Hardy does not simply put aspects of Gothic to work in his fiction, however. In drawing on what was, by his generation, an already anachronistic genre, he conjoins elements of Gothic in narrative proximity with pagan superstitions and other elements of folkloric belief and practice. The signs of the phantom-text are to be found everywhere, then. Not particularly Gothic in itself, though nonetheless appearing as the trace of a reference to such genre fiction, there is the doxical acknowledgement of Susan as '"The Ghost"' (*MC* 83), and a '"mere skellinton"' (*MC* 85). Almost immediately upon her death, Susan is reported as having something of a headstone–appearance by Mrs Cuxsom: '"And she was as white as marble-stone"' (*MC* 120). Susan is immediately replaced in this comment, her face equated with – and ghosted by – the second- or third-hand signification of a material which will form the architectural symbol of her being dead. Of Henchard, Nance Mockridge comments, in that knowing, prescient manner peculiar to working women in Gothic novels, '"There's a bluebeardy look about en; and 'twill out in time"' (*MC* 86). Not that the Mayor has a dungeon, in which to chain Susan, yet his figure is haunted with a powerful Gothic resonance. Moreover, Nance's prediction points to the 'persistence of the unforeseen' (*MC* 334), as Hardy will put it on almost the final page. Her phrase is both economical and excessive: it is an utterance belonging to the cheapest of Gothic thrills, while also resonating in a somewhat uncanny, if not haunted, fashion. Structurally, therefore, her phrase, having to do with time, is disturbed from within, being both timely and untimely, having to do with the persistence of unreadable traces as a condition of temporal disturbance, with which the novel is so concerned.

Other characters are also marked in ways that suggest Gothic convention. Newson is given a ghostly quality in relation to the question of the return (see Keen, above). Specifically, he disturbs Henchard: '[t]he apparition of Newson haunted him. He would surely return' (*MC* 300). Conjuror Fall lives outside the town, and therefore outside the boundaries of society, as is typical of figures associated with alchemy and the black arts. His habitation and narrative preparation for the encounter between Henchard and Fall confuse discursive boundaries, intermixing the Gothic, the folkloric and fairy-tale. The way to Fall's house is 'crooked and miry' (*MC* 185), and Henchard's approach to Fall's home is suggestively eerie: 'One evening when it was raining ... heavily ... a shrouded figure on foot might have been perceived travelling in the direction of

the hazel copse which dripped over the prophet's cot' (*MC* 185–6). That *might*, in any other Hardy novel a typical conditional phrase, here echoes with a sense of the ghostly. Even the furmity woman gets in on the Gothic act, for, upon her return, it is remarked that she 'had mysteriously hinted . . . that she knew a queer thing or two' (*MC* 202). Of course, what she knows is all too material, of this earth, being merely the information concerning Henchard's past, but her return is part of the general movement of return in the text, while Hardy carefully frames her ominous comment in a manner designed to amplify its portentous aspect.

What will return in this instance is the narrative that already haunts Henchard, as the furmity dealer's citation. While the old woman returns, what returns through her is the trace of the past and, with that, the suppressed truth as that which haunts. Indeed, Hardy engages in a narrative economy of recurrence, by which truth is apprehended as always revenant and revelatory. To put this differently, truth is always spectral and is only known in its iterable appearances, as such, regardless of the logic or rationality of a given narrative moment. The Gothic is one mode of production that allows for an economy of explanation, a logic of representation, to order and rationalize, even as it relies on the non-rational. Yet within that mechanism, there is always the spectral element. Gothic convention is precisely this: convention, structure and law. Within such convention, however, is that which is irreducible by explanation. What cannot be explained is that the return happens, and that it happens moreover not as the return of some presence to the present, but as the haunted trace. The truth of Henchard's past is coincidental to the general movement of spectral revenance, which the Mayor of Casterbridge is incapable of reading, and which *The Mayor of Casterbridge* barely glimpses.

The technique of repetition at work throughout the novel provides this barely seen spectral condition, even while, within the structures of the text, such reiteration is locally domesticated through the recourse to particularly familiar textual forms, such as the Gothic. Not only are characters read and written as if in a Gothic context, therefore. They behave as though they were characters from a Gothic novel, even as the narrative voice mimics or is haunted by the trace of the Gothic. Elizabeth-Jane is 'startled by the apparition of Farfrae' (*MC* 136). Lucetta's face is altered by an encounter with Farfrae also: her face 'became – as a woman's face becomes when the man she loves rises upon her gaze like an apparition' (178). There is something decidedly strange, *uncanny*, about Farfrae, something of the trickster about him (as his 'magic' with the spelt grain implies)

that his appearance to two women should be described as an apparition, on both occasions. It even disturbs Hardy in the act of writing, for notice that pause signalled silently in the dash as the writer seeks the most appropriate simile. However, we will have to leave the Scot for a moment.

There are other Gothic traces, too, improper references and ghostly citations without specific origins. The keystone-mask above Lucetta's door (*MC* 142) and the decaying sign of the Three Mariners (*MC* 42–3) have a certain Gothic appeal. Furthermore, their ruined decaying qualities hint at the uncanny, the unfamiliar within the familiar. Suggesting forms of temporal persistence, of the past's ability to return and to disturb, they both signify a certain sinister ineffability that gives the lie to the familiarity and homeliness of the structures – the public house and Lucetta's home – of which they are synecdochic figures. Both serve economically in tracing that 'structural slippage from *heimliche* [homely] to *unheimliche* [unhomely] [in which] that which supposedly lies outside the familiar comfort of the home turns out to be inhabiting it all along' (Wigley 1993, 108). Most immediately, however, their function is to create that *frisson* so typically desired in the Gothic. Both the sign and the keystone serve a textual, that is to say a haunting, function, in that they remind us that a 'house is not simply an object that may be represented, but is itself a mechanism of representation' (Wigley 1993, 163), whereby in the perception of an image, one encounters a structure of iteration. It might be added that what goes for a house holds true of Hardy's novel structures also.

We can read such effects at work when we are told how Jopp's cottage is 'built of old stones from the long-dismantled priory, scraps of tracery, moulded window-jambs, and arch-labels, being mixed in with the rubble of the walls (*MC* 221). Those scraps, the ruins of the priory, long since gone, operate as references in a number of ways. Priories are, of course, favourite ruined sites, often haunted, in Gothic discourse. There is in this image, with its fragments of clauses, the return of the past in the present structure once more, the structure of the cottage and the structure of the sentence. The former is structurally (dis-) composed by the material traces of a former structure; the latter is structurally (dis-) composed by the haunting traces of Gothic discourse that, in their phantomatic inscription, enact a ghostly transference in the image of the cottage, from its being simply an object to be represented, to being a mechanism of representation. In this, the text does nothing so much as displace itself, endlessly. For the operation of haunting signals not simply a prior moment, if that is even the purpose.

Instead, it serves to signal a certain spectral dislocation that belongs to the novel as a whole, signalling the ruins of other ruins, the keystone, the decaying sign, the Ring (Chapter XI), even as they in turn signify other traces, and the other of the trace. This movement, the Gothic 'oscillation', is not merely an intertextual feature; it is of a different order. The priory stones are readable, therefore, as are other structural and architectonic features, in a manner similar to more explicitly narrowly textual referents, such as those from the Old Testament or tragedy, as we have already suggested. The 'stones', in being the traces of an absent discourse, being performative fragments and ruins, are not there to suggest that the reader simply turn back to the literary past, to some prior form as the novel's inheritance or what might, too blithely, be described as 'context'. Instead, they acknowledge an inescapably haunted quality within the structure of any textual form, by which one is haunted because one can never decipher in full the trace that demands to be read.

X.   HENCHARD'S HAUNTING

We have seen already how devices of doubling and repetition, which are intrinsic to the novel's structure and identity, articulate *The Mayor of Casterbridge*, and yet disturb that very form from within. Additionally, following Suzanne Keen's argument, I have already argued how, in witnessing his double in the form of the skimmington effigy, Michael Henchard is plagued by this uncanny double. Thus, arguably, the entire novel may be considered as an exploration of the uncanny condition that Henchard in particular experiences repeatedly. There are numerous local and immediate instances of the experience of the uncanny in the novel. Henchard feels haunted by Newson, as we know already. Moreover, the reader is told repeatedly that he is a superstitious man. Henchard is first revealed as 'superstitious' through his decision to visit Conjuror Fall (*MC* 185). Though this moment is not in itself uncanny (though arguably Henchard's trip to Fall is meant to induce an uncanny sensation in the reader), the next instance of Henchard's superstitiousness is, and deliberately so. Henchard is ruminating on his misfortune over the reckless crop selling:

> The movements of his mind seemed to tend to the thought that some power was working against him.
> 'I wonder', he asked himself with eerie misgiving; 'I wonder if it can be that somebody has been roasting a waxen image of me, or stirring an

unholy brew to confound me! I don't believe in such power; and yet –
what if they should ha' been doing it!' ... These isolated hours of superstition came to Henchard in time of moody depression ... (*MC* 190–1)

While we may read the passage as remarking the residue of a
superstition imbued with the discourse of folkloric mythology, the
passage is notable nonetheless for its sense of the uncanny, of that
internal power and the sensation of 'eerie misgiving'. Later, following the skimmington ride, we are told that 'the sense of the
supernatural was strong in this unhappy man' (*MC* 297). In this
assessment of Henchard's response to the effigy, there is the sense
that Hardy may be read as explaining away the uncanny feeling
through recourse to the idea of superstition, even as Henchard experiences it. Yet uncannily, perhaps, that earlier speculation concerning the waxen image may also be read as one more example of the
'persistence of the unforeseen', while the effigy marks a form of
return of Henchard's fear, even as it physically returns via the river.

Freud acknowledges that the writer, any writer, in creating
uncanny effects in a narrative world otherwise predicated on
'common reality' through the use of events that 'never or rarely happen in fact', appeals to the 'superstitiousness' that we have allegedly
left behind (Freud 1997, 227). In a novel concerned so much with
residual forms of haunting, however, the very trope of superstition
as archaic pre-modern residue is readable as the uncanny manifestation of the haunting trace. Hardy's narrative is constructed so as
to reveal Henchard as haunted by superstition, while playing on
the possible residue of superstition in the reader, and yet maintaining a distance from such irrational sensations by doubting whether
'anything should be called curious in concatenations of phenomena'
(*MC* 204).

There are, however, clearly uncanny moments for Henchard that
have little or nothing to do with superstition. Towards the end of his
life Henchard is described thus: 'He rose to his feet, and stood like
a dark ruin, obscured by "the shade from his own soul upthrown"'
(*MC* 326). One of the most complex and overdetermined of sentences in the novel, this delineation of Henchard addresses both his
own being haunted, suffering from the disturbance of the uncanny,
and the uncanny haunting to which *The Mayor* is prone. The ghostly
citation with which the sentence concludes traces a double movement at least. It comes from Shelley's *Revolt of Islam*, as does the
phrase 'dark ruin'. While reading a citation, and one that, in its signifying operation, refers us to those other ghostly citations, we are
impressed by the figure, not merely of the soul, but of the 'shade'

also. Conventionally, the reading of that 'shade' should imply a shadow. However, there is also at work in this image the more archaic sense of 'shade', meaning 'ghost' or 'spectre'. The phrase 'dark ruin' is itself a ruin, a fragment, an improper citation that haunts the sentence and that does service as a simile for Henchard, even as it echoes beyond the image of Henchard, or, indeed, any animate creature, to hint at the Ring and other architectural sites and remnants out of which Casterbridge is composed, and by which it is haunted.

Not long prior to this moment, at which the return of Newson prompts Henchard's sense of being haunted once again, Henchard returns to the place from where the novel begins (*MC* 318–19). In this instance of reciprocal return – Henchard's return is counter-signed by the return of place – Susan's own words return to Henchard, and, uncannily, to the reader also: for her words are reported directly, from her own initial utterance, while they are also adrift from her, from the grave as it were, as a disembodied voice, the voice of the other, haunting Henchard's memory (*MC* 319). The sense of the uncanny is quite startling here, for even as we read the words on the page, so we hear and see those words imprinted in the memory, arriving from some other place, and yet from within at the same time. In this, Susan's voice is doubly haunt-ing, for in its movement of return and address that, shockingly – uncannily – places the reader in the place of Henchard as addressee, it carries in it the anticipation of Henchard's will, which is reprinted onto the page, and there for every successive generation of reader (333). The will is most appositely perceived – and read – as a 'terrifying series of negative performances, spoken from the grave' (Miller 1998, 110), a 'kind of ghostly negative that . . . has positive existence' (Miller 1998, 112). Directly before us, Henchard's will comes back as a fragmented 'recording', a ghostly transmission, of his voice that, despite its commands to forget him, haunts us all the more.

'That Elizabeth–Jane Farfrae be not told of my death, or made to grieve on account of me.
'& that I be not bury'd in consecrated ground.
'& that no sexton be asked to toll the bell.
'& that nobody is wished to see my dead body.
'& that no mourners walk behind me at my funeral.
'& that no flours be planted on my grave.
'& that no man remember me.
'To this do I put my name.

'Michael Henchard' (*MC* 333)

What this act of narration from beyond the grave suggests is nothing less than the ghostly condition of all narrative: 'all narration is a murmur from beyond the grave . . . killing it as living speech and resurrecting it at the same time as ghostly, remembered speech' (Miller 1998, 112). Henchard's address provides exemplary and undeniable proof of, on the one hand, the fact of his death and, on the other, the return of his death, the paradoxical iterability of his finitude that also and at the same time turns us back to, and returns to us, as other than itself, the text of *The Mayor of Casterbridge* awaiting the act of reading, while signalling in this movement and spacing (that spacing which is the effect of haunting) that reading is always an endless work, remaining to come, again and again, as part of the structural openness and instability of historicity. It is through this that the sense of the uncanny is produced, the spectre glimpsed. Through this redoubling, displacing and regenerative rhythm, the ghost survives, and we as readers are uncannily transformed, destined to be the addressees, the recipients of the will.

XI. *DÉJÀ VU, DÉJÀ LU*

If the will offers a formal example of the temporal troubling of writing within itself through the difference on which it relies to communicate beyond any initial context or intention, Hardy does not limit the haunting experience of iterable eruption to the act of writing. We read so many instances in *The Mayor* in which something appears to come back or anticipate a return to come. So many events and signs remind us of so many others, and our having experienced them before that we may well read the text with a growing sense of that tedious, even oppressive familiarity, or else an apprehension of *déjà lu*, if not *déjà vu*. However, perhaps this is the point, structurally at least. There is still the question of structure haunting us here, with which we began. To return to the question of return: what cannot be stressed too often is the proposition that, whether we are speaking of the proper name, the matter of architecture or archaeology, the question of textual traces or cultural events, the office of the mayor in relation to the social order, or a communal identity based on the supposed stasis of civic office, each figure repeats every other. Consider the resounding bells heard by Susan and Elizabeth-Jane on entering the town as one exemplary moment in the novel:

> They came to a grizzled church, whose massive square tower rose unbroken into the darkening sky. . . . From this tower the clock struck eight, and thereupon a bell began to toll with a peremptory clang. The curfew was still rung in Casterbridge, . . .

> Other clocks struck eight from time to time – one gloomily from the
> gaol, another from the gable of an alms-house ... a row of tall varnished
> case-clocks ... joined in one after another ... then chimes were heard
> stammering out ... so that chronologists of the advanced school were
> appreciably on their way to the next hour before the whole business of
> the old one was satisfactorily wound up. (MC 31)

Each sound reiterates every other in this, even though time is 'out
of joint', so to speak. The passage in its movement from clock to
clock, from chime to chime, performs the gradual and erratic sounding of the hour, as the narrative moves. The hour is displaced from
and within itself, even as each clock re-sounds the temporal punctuation of every other, and spaces the very idea of time. This one
scene uncannily suggests the structure of the novel itself, where every
form of return or reduplication signifies nothing so much as every
other similar form. The clocks set the tone, if you will. Moreover
in this temporal disjointing, the performance of which hints that
there is no time like the present, there is no single present moment
not always already divided, the spectral structure makes itself felt in
that residual trace of another time sounding within the present, the
medieval curfew bell. Furthermore, the chimes in this scene anticipate and return in the moment, just prior to the election of Farfrae
as Mayor, when the clocks strike half-past eight, and the streets are
'curiously silent' (MC 151).

The resounding of the time out of time with itself figures aurally
spacing and strata, as well as inevitable temporal registration. The
clocks trace the spatial and temporal movements that haunt the
town, but, also, analogically offer a figure for the composition of
the novel, in its understanding of subjectivity and historicity. The
architectonic resonance is common, and worked out in a particularly
rich way in the opening of Chapter Eleven, when Hardy describes
Casterbridge:

> Casterbridge announced old Rome in every street, alley and precinct ...
> It was impossible to dig more than a foot or two deep about the town
> fields and gardens without coming upon some tall soldier or other ...
> Imaginative inhabitants who would have felt an unpleasantness at the
> discovery of a comparatively modern skeleton in their gardens, were quite
> unmoved by these hoary shapes ... (MC 70)

In the same chapter, the Roman amphitheatre, the Ring, is discussed,
in particular, the history of recurrence associated with the ruin:

> Apart from the sanguinary nature of the games originally played therein,
> such incidents attached to its past as these; that for scores of years the
> town gallows had stood at one corner; that in 1705 a woman who had

murdered her husband was half strangled and then burnt there ... In
addition to these old tragedies pugilistic encounters almost to the death
had come off down to recent dates in that secluded arena ... though
close to the turnpike-road crimes might be perpetrated there unseen at
mid-day. (MC 71)

What is merely suggested in the first passage by the mention of architectural and archaeological detail is made clearer in the second. The
past persists as trace, setting the tone through its ghostly persistence
in and disturbance of the present. The remains of architectural detail
are 'announced' through the present structure of the town, so that
the present is represented as disturbed by such traces; the land itself
is built upon the remains and return of the past. In the case of
the Ring, it is not a question of architectural structure or archaeological remainder. Rather, the persistence is of a particularly spectral
kind. Events of a similar nature recur within the same space, so that,
as Hardy gradually dematerializes the return of the past – moving
from overt structure, to what is hidden or sedimented, and then to
forms of recurrence that are altogether more haunting – so he traces
a temporal structure of revenance and insistence, of iteration, that
is all the more disturbing and uncanny for the return of violence to
the same location, as an effective figure of spectral dislocation.

What haunts here, whether one is speaking of the sound of the
bells, the description of the town, or the history of the Ring, is the
ineluctable recurrence of a ghostly trace. In perceiving this, we might
say the novel is less a narrative than a haunted archive, in which
the structure is haunted by virtue of the fact that every trace in its
return refers to every other trace having the power to do the same,
and so overdetermine the present. This is hardly new in *Mayor*,
but Hardy intensifies the effect he had elsewhere put to work, and
which he continues to manipulate throughout his poetry until his
death. Hardy capitalizes on the force of repetition, on the returns
that he accumulates in a mode of writing describable as archiviza-
tion, whereby the numerous traces, citations, references, allusions
are gathered. That the novel may be read as having the power to
create uncanny feelings in its readers through the endless and differentiated reminders that the present is the storehouse of past echoes
and elements is one sign of its being haunted. That every subsequent
generation of readers is enjoined to forget Michael Henchard by his
will and yet receive his communication so unforgettably is another
sign. The haunting condition is that effect by which language effaces
itself even as its trace and injunction remain, whether by 'language'
we signify spoken or written signs or the material traces of other

human remains. If we do not read these remains in their disseminating signification of one another and the ways in which they both structure and discompose identity within a given moment and across history, we run the risk of misunderstanding to what extent this is a phantom-text. A haunted and haunting space, *The Mayor of Casterbridge* offers a disorientating experience by which we enter into the true revelation of the historical and one's subjective production as a properly conceived historical being. Not perceiving this, we risk missing Hardy's ghostly communication, and so doom ourselves to live out haunted lives, much as is the case with Michael Henchard, consigning himself as he does to perpetual afterlife.

5

Confessions of the Other: *The Woodlanders* (1887), *Tess of the D'Urbervilles* (1891), *Jude the Obscure* (1895)

I. INVENTION AND AUGURY

I turn finally to Hardy's last novels, *The Woodlanders*, *Tess of the D'Urbervilles*, and *Jude the Obscure*. I reflect on what speaks without speaking, attesting to unwritten history and shared memory. I consider that which would remain otherwise, without witness and without voice. And, I explore, again, what is lost in translation when phenomena pass beyond living memory, or when the modern subject fails to read, or reads incorrectly. As what is to come will make clear, Hardy's worlds are expressed through phantasmal manifestations from within the real, and voices belonging to such projections. Such voices are not simply those of humans, but belong to actions, places, and all manner of inanimate phenomena. In turning to specific manifestations and articulations, I intend to revisit particular themes that have been addressed elsewhere.

In order to do so, and to explore, and so open, the ways in which Hardy continued throughout his novel-writing career to transform his own material until he abandoned the novel in favour of poetry, I will elucidate in brief, in the following section of this chapter, two novels, *The Hand of Ethelberta* and *The Well-Beloved*, which have received far less critical attention that most of his other publications.

The purpose in the last chapter is not, though, to draw extensively tropic, thematic or conceptual readings of *Woodlanders*, *Tess*, and *Jude*. It may appear perverse not to give greater consideration to *Tess* and *Jude*, given the extent to which they are read and taught. So ubiquitous are they, that passing reference is made to them in the 1939 Broadway hit, *The Man Who Came to Dinner*. Critic, radio presenter and belle-lettrist, Sheridan Whiteside, is forced to remain in the house of the Stanleys as a result of an injury. Harriet Stanley, the sister of Whiteside's reluctant hosts, remarks that she has read much of his work, noting especially that she has read his commentaries on *Tess* and *Jude*. That this is dropped in as a passing aside indicates the novels' widespread reception, their 'cultural capital'. Both are so thoroughly explored already by critics that one might argue such familiarity and critical coverage is a reason for not commenting on them in greater detail, but instead to turn to certain scenes or features within those novels, which either have been overlooked, or otherwise placed within the context of a larger reading.

Admittedly, this will appear to some as an evasion, and to others odd. But there can be no doubt that, today, of all Hardy's novels certainly *Tess* and *Jude* arrive enmeshed within, and filtered by, such a wealth of critical commentary, that they are all but impossible to receive save for those critical interjections and translations. Additionally, I would risk an hypothesis, which remains undemonstrable here, that *Tess* and *Jude* are the least typical Hardyean productions, and it is their anomalous quality, their being least 'like' Hardy which has ensured their critical appropriation, their 'generalizable' transmissibility, which can highlight the universal and downplay the specifically Hardyesque 'idiosyncracies' or singularities. This is all outrageously indefensible, an hypothesis that remains to be proven. Having risked such a tendentious proposition though, I will instead adumbrate possible readings through attention to a few passages from each text, explicating their work in relation to philosophical themes. In so doing, I hope to gesture towards other readings that remain to come of Hardy, readings for which this present volume might serve as a preface of sorts, an *inaugural invention*.

I use *invention* here as I have throughout this book, in its less commonly understood meaning of 'finding' what is already there, rather than producing something entirely new. *Inauguration* implies beginning or introduction, but I wish to depart from this conventional sense also somewhat, to suggest that inauguration admits something, admission giving access; that which is admitted though (to play here on the semantic resonance) is also confessed – one thus

finds and so confesses, giving voice to the confession of the other, that which throughout Hardy comes to speak, continues to be admitted, to come in as the strange or odd, into the reading of Hardy. Of course, I do not wish to overstress this, because what is strange or odd about Hardy's prose is well known, much studied. But at the risk of pushing at the various semantic boundaries here, I want in this admission that is also an invention to intimate that which, in Hardy's Wessex is always – always already – the difference of *augury*.

Augury, or more specifically *augur*, has a contested etymology. As the *OED* informs us, the Latin *augur* or, earlier, *auger* may derive from words meaning 'bird' and 'talk', and before that from the Sanskrit *gar*, to shout or make known. However, an alternative Latin root is *augere*, meaning to increase or promote, from which comes *auctor*, in turn taken into Middle English as the form of *author*, but also the word from which comes *actor*. The sense of *auctor* signifies not a writer alone but any person who creates, who invents or constructs. A hypothetical conceit, therefore: Hardy as both *augur* and *author*, inaugurating Wessex, he invents that which is given him to see. Hardy's narratives are caught up in acts of invention, of finding what is already there in the world. It takes those signs, those phenomena, the traces of language, and so forth, and puts them to work, reading them, whilst reading others who do not, or cannot, read them, as augurs. Hardy, it might be said (and as fanciful as this may seem, were it not for his own insistence on the visionary in relation to the real), is the augurer of Wessex, who gathers together the auguryne manifestations from other worlds already there but passing into illegibility, and casting them in the modern world as the signs that determine the fate of those to whom such phenomena carry no memory. For, despite the overbearing weight by which the material world appears to oppress and contrive against the fortunes of Hardy's characters, without access to the phantastic in relation to what it means properly to dwell in Wessex, to be of Wessex properly, all hope is lost. And it is this motif, which I take to be most pressingly reiterated in *The Woodlanders*, *Tess* and *Jude*. Before considering those, however, let us turn to *The Hand of Ethelberta* and (*The Pursuit of*) *The Well-Beloved*, apropos phantasy, or certain manifestations of it.

II. PHANTASIES

Irreducible to a single modality, the phantastic is an acknowledged dimension of Hardy's text, and is found in most if not all his

publications. However, relatively few Hardy critics have devoted any sustained attention to Hardy's two most idiosyncratic novels, *The Hand of Ethelberta* and *The Well-Beloved*, or *The Pursuit of the Well-Beloved*, as it was published first in serial form before much revision. Both novels are driven by very different forms of phantasy at the level of form and content, and cursory discussion of them will serve to remind ourselves of the many ways Hardy's last novels are amongst the oddest works in English fiction.

A brief search of on-line journals produces more than three thousand articles on Hardy's poetry and novels. Of these, only fifty articles approximately address specifically *The Well-Beloved* and just under half that discussing *The Hand of Ethelberta*, a novel perhaps most pithily and aptly described as 'strange' (Miller 1970, 208). Were we to ask what, if anything, the two novels, written sixteen years apart (though Hardy had been toying with particular ideas that subsequently found their way into the latter novel for some time),[1] have in common, we might find the following: both are narratives that reflect on art and aesthetics in one way or another. Both develop narratives through the role of personae, and the seductive appeal the mask or presentation of another plays for the onlooker or audience. Additionally, both construct a distance between principal protagonists and the worlds they either pretend or desire to inhabit; in common with a number of Hardy's novels, *Ethelberta* and *Well-Beloved* direct our perspective towards characters who act as 'spectators of life' (Miller 1970, xiii) – Christopher Julian, a music teacher and sometime suitor of Ethelberta, and Jocelyn Pearston (or Pierston, depending on which version of *Well-Beloved* one reads), a sculptor. And both novels move between locations in Wessex and London Society drawing rooms, with emphasis given largely to the urban settings. There the ostensible similarities end.

Given the relative unfamiliarity of both novels for all but the most dedicated Hardy reader, I will take the liberty of providing a brief précis. '[F]ascinating by its very strangeness' (Gittings 1975, 15), *The Hand of Ethelberta* concerns a servant's daughter, the Ethelberta of the title, who wishes to support her family financially. Becoming the talk of London society following the anonymous publication of a volume of poetry, Ethelberta becomes a professional storyteller. So successful is she in this venture that she is able to establish a home in London for herself, with her family 'masquerading' as her servants (Page 2000, 159). The novel, a generically mixed text (and thus in its 'monstrosity' not dissimilar to *The Trumpet-Major*),[2] plays off both working-class and ruling-class identities as

well as oppositions between town and country (see Lothe 1999, 123–4). Having performed a story telling at the home of Lord Mountclere, which story is her autobiography – she fictionalizes herself in disclosing the truth of herself – Ethelberta realizes that Mountclere knows her background, and accepts his offer of marriage, which goes ahead despite efforts on the part of both her family and Mountclere's brother to prevent this. Donald Stone defines the novel as a search for home, 'the heroine ... wander[ing] from place to place in search of a protective lodging where she can be her own mistress' in a comic anticipation of Tess and Jude (Stone 1984, 296). Homelessness is thus, once more, the modern condition of one's being, albeit given a somewhat frothy representation in *Ethelberta*.

It should be noted in passing how these are not the only characters who struggle to find a home, who lose their homes or who survive for a time without one: Clym Yeobright finds no comfort on his return to home, and is left, at the conclusion of *The Return of the Native* an itinerant preacher; Paula Power's castle is ruined by fire; Michael Henchard becomes steadily more and more abject, dying eventually in another's cottage; Giles Winterbourne loses the home that had been his family's for several generations, once tenancy rights revert back to the estate controlling the leases. The material dwelling place aside, we find ourselves back at the question of the relation between being and dwelling. For Hardy true or authentic dwelling in an existential sense in the second half of the nineteenth century is inaccessible, so removed have his characters become from their worlds, as a result of their modernity.

But to come back to the novels in question, and *The Well-Beloved* specifically: Jocelyn Pierston, a sculptor, 'whose perception of and contacts with the external world are largely dominated by his imagination' (Page 2000, 457), is obsessed throughout his life by the phantasm of his ideal beloved, which spirit he finds manifested in three generations of women, who are, successively Avice Caro, Ann Avice Caro, and Avice Caro, this last being the daughter of the second and the granddaughter of the first. At twenty year intervals – the three stages of Pierston's life corresponding with Hardy's formal division of the text – the sculptor falls in love with each Avice, even though he never marries any of them. In what seems at first a somewhat odd narrative, we find a meditation on the relation between reality and aesthetic imagination, and the function of art. J. Hillis Miller sees the novel as a key statement on art in the nineteenth century, and thus deserving of attention, as well as for what he defines as its '"antirealistic" texture' (Miller 1970, 169).

If Hardy's final novel is about art in general, and the plastic arts and representation or its impossibility specifically, his fifth, *Ethelberta*, is about art also, though in this example narrative art and its power to create alternative realities, which ironically, can only be felt and never directly interpreted. In this, *Ethelberta* has genetic affiliations with Henry James' 'The Figure in the Carpet', rather than with a social comedy of manners such as Wilde's *The Importance of Being Earnest*, while *The Well-Beloved*, a novel much admired and cited by Marcel Proust, shares a genealogy with *Middlemarch* and Thomas Mann's *Death in Venice* (Page 2000, 459).

The earlier of the two 'had nothing whatever in common with anything [Hardy] had written before' (*LTH* 103). On its publication, *Ethelberta* was a moderate success, one reviewer commenting that 'it was the finest ideal comedy since the days of Shakespeare' (*LTH* 108). Another reviewer in *The Spectator*, R. H. Hutton, observed that '[a] more entertaining book ... has not been published for many a year ... a very original and a very skilled hand is wielding the pen' (Page 2000, 158). Despite this however, Hutton believed that the character of Ethelberta was 'a riddle to us, and so little of a living figure', and that she was, moreover, one of the novel's 'vivacious shadows' (Page 2000, 158). Additionally, and overall, it was generally thought to be full of impossible situations. Hardy's reaction, recorded by Florence in the *Life*, was to see the novel as anachronistic – ahead of its time by a generation. As Hardy, through the ventriloquial powers of his wife, puts it, '[i]t was, in fact, thirty years too soon for a Comedy of Society of that kind' (*LTH* 108). With hindsight and experience, it could later be observed that the work had more in common with the plays of 'Mr. Bernard Shaw' (*LTH* 108).

Regarding *Well-Beloved*, a diary entry of February 1889 indicates thoughts on one theme of the novel: 'The story of a face which goes through three generations or more, would make a fine novel or poem of the passage of Time. The differences in personality to be ignored' (*LTH* 217). The haunting persistence of the face, a motif already used by Hardy, in the representation of Elizabeth-Jane in *The Mayor of Casterbridge* several years before, hints at a ghostly sublimation, which returns to disturb its viewer. The poem in question is 'Heredity' (*CP* 434), included in *Moments of Vision and Miscellaneous Verses*, the author's fifth volume of poetry published in 1917, but Hardy also produced a poem, published in 1901 in *Poems of the Past and Present*, with the title 'The Well-Beloved' (*CP* 133). This 'fantastic tale' (*LTH* 286) gave narrative form to

the 'theory of the transmigration of the ideal beloved one, who only exists in the love, from material woman to material woman' (*LTH* 286). Again, this novel was perceived belatedly as anachronistic. For, through Florence once more, Hardy saw a similarity between what is probably his oddest publication and the writing of Marcel Proust 'many years later' (*LTH* 286).[3] Like *Ethelberta*, *The Well-Beloved* was seen as unbelievable and fantastic, though with the added opprobrium of being deemed amoral. All Hardy would respond to the criticism (Hardy described the worst of the criticism as '"mendacious malice"' [*LTH* 286]), beyond the preface appended to the novel, is summed up in a letter to a literary magazine, on the design of what became his final experiment in prose: 'underlying the fantasy followed by the visionary artist the truth that all men are pursuing a shadow, the Unattainable' (*LTH* 286).

Both novels are phantastic in one sense or another; both deal with the artistic imagination and visionary power, or what Hardy was pleased to call in a P.S. to a letter to poet Algernon Charles Swinburne a *'fanciful* exhibition of the artistic nature' (*LTH* 287; emphasis added). And in both, Hardy creates a distance from his usual phantastic modality in order to meditate on the role of phantasy and imagination. These two strikingly different novels thus bear a resemblance to one another inasmuch as they resist engaging in the visionary and phenomenal mode that is so much in evidence elsewhere throughout Hardy's work. Yet, to approach the two novels that receive the least attention – perhaps as a result of the least comprehension – it has to be remembered, following John Holloway, that Hardy's 'most instinctive mode as a writer is figurative, not analytic; his most habitual method is symbolism, not argument ... the many recurring patterns, symbols, and images' perform a tropic and visionary world always at odds with 'mimetic, formal and moral' considerations (Siebenschuh 1999, 773). In *Ethelberta* and *Well-Beloved*, we see what is lost if one represents a world where the symbolic is rationalized, given over to a realist economy of representation. When the reader witnesses the operation of or discourse on phantasy at a distance the strangeness of the tale becomes marked by a loss, and with that a desire to recover that very power of perception, which, elsewhere in Hardy's novels and poetry the idea of Wessex enables.

We must turn therefore to those strange, magically inflected phantasies of what Hardy calls the 'vegetable world' on occasions, and of which there will be more to say. The tropic and visionary, the 'partly-dream worlds' are what remains to consciousness and one's

own sense of historicized being, as necessary countersignatures to the material conditions of loss and belatedness that inform one as to the partly-real world about which Hardy writes, and which he calls, with fully ironic awareness, Wessex. Wessex is always, though, partly real, partly-dream world, for it projects from within the real 'a ghostly supplement' (Armstrong 2000, 9), which is, at once, a '*surplus*, beyond equivalence and self-presence, and that which replaces the "real". ... The supplement is both an "exterior addition" and indicative of a lack of a real presence' (Armstrong 2000, 10). And this is what is seen, when one looks closely – nothing as such and yet the pulse of all existence and being. The Hardyean supplement, that strange moment, the rendering of a phantasy or vision, the detail of nature that is more than merely natural: all tend to reveal an immanent given, an 'appearance in the duration of the phenomenologically constituted flow' (Henry 2008, 35). 'Outside' the events it narrates, narratorial consciousness nonetheless haunts the 'internal' subjective space of the reader, Hardy's representations coming to be constituted in the interplay between the fictive world and subjective consciousness, through the shuttling weave of narrative motion. Whilst *Ethelberta* and the *Well-Beloved* maintain a space and thus a fictive decorum between the reading subject and the narrative subject, they never allow one to be taken 'outside' one's being. Elsewhere, from within the most seemingly ordinary detail and the history of its existence, one becomes conscious of one's being and dwelling in all its strangeness; subjectivity is thus taken outside its own being by Hardy, becoming in the process part of 'a world, a first world, an "inner world" – all that it never truly is' (Henry 2008, 35). This, we should acknowledge, is far from an unequivocal beneficence; for it is '[t]hrough the solid barrier of cold cretaceous upland to the northward [that Jude] was always beholding a gorgeous city – the fancied place he had likened to the new Jerusalem' (*JO* I.III.22). For the 'predestinate Jude' (*JO* I.VII.44) such visionary calling leads, eventually to destruction, as if, mindful of its becoming obscure itself, Wessex demands a sacrifice. Failing to read the land that gives him identity, unmindful of what constitutes his authentic mode of being and dwelling, Jude misreads, misrecognizes another world, mistaking the phantasy of its promise in long perspective, and blind to that which remains obscurely before him, close at hand. Like Jocelyn or Ethelberta, Jude is caught up in, determined by the visions and phantasies of reading, but does not comprehend their cost. If he reads at all, Jude suffers from the tragedy that his reading is never on time.

III. CONFESSIONS, OF THE OTHER

If Hardy teaches us anything, it is that reading takes time. The time of reading, though, never moves at a single speed; there is always more than one time. The different times of reading are also those of historical transmission, manifestation, translation and reception. The good reader of Hardy perceives, therefore, that one should linger, pausing to gain perspective in a place seemingly unpropitious for narrative drama, and so in turn to reflect on the detail that comes to be revealed, from the visible to the invisible. At the same time, Hardy illustrates for the good reader the historical importance of repetition, especially where what returns is not recognized as significant. Hardy invariably presents both the 'banality of the mundane' (Henry 2008, 85) in a new light, and also marks the passage into disuse and disregard of the everyday: 'There were men at this time still living in Hintock who remembered when the gin and other [machines] like it were still in use. ... By the year 1840 the use of [man-traps] was well-nigh discontinued in this neighbourhood. But ... they by no means disappeared' (W III.XIV.351–2). The gin or man-trap appears still, the knowledge of its common use at the cusp of beginning to pass away, its presence a material and mute reminder, available only while there are those alive to recollect its use and transform that memory into narrative, to be shared amongst the inhabitants of the locality. The mundane object becomes, in Hardy's telling, a cultural phenomenon, 'something showing itself in a world' (Henry 2008, 85), having the power to make visible a way of life and, with that, another world. Dated precisely, and given a place, it returns in order to 'speak' not only of itself but another time. Its return is therefore the signature of difference in Hardy's fiction, and with that comes the singularity with which Hardy's fiction is invested.

Not all such signatures or 'voices' are so easily read or heard, however. Hardy understands this, and so gives over a lengthy exposition on the nature, use and context of the man-trap (W III.XIV.350–2), a cultural history, which in the telling, the narrativization, seeks to bridge a gap between distinct worlds and their phenomena. If we mistake such phenomena as only banal or mundane, however, we miss something about them, about the significance that makes itself manifest in their being repeated in narrative. Thus it is that a 'familiar knobbed thorn walking-stick, whose growing' Grace Melbury's father 'had seen before he enjoyed its use' (W II.XVI.229), has its own communicative power. Similarly – and this we can deduce from the significance of the stick, as it serves

metonymically or synecdochically for the work of memory, of the interrelation between being and dwelling that resonates for a given person or group of people – a particular site is not, for Melbury, merely a material sign belonging to a 'scene', as Hardy calls it, from 'the material environment of his person' (*W* II.XVI.229). Although it is very much this, it also gives place to the projection and revenance, the spectral survival, of a 'tragic vision that travelled with him like an envelope' (*W* II.XVI.229). The metaphor of the envelope expresses the communication of a message without necessarily communicating directly what the message, the address, is (though in this instance the reader is aware, albeit in a manner that has a markedly different emotional resonance, than it does for Melbury). Thus Hardy, once more, conveys transmission and knowledge, whilst simultaneously signalling the difference in perspective between one person's reading and another's.

Misrecognition, misreading, historical fatality and the cultural 'fault' of historical myopia plague Hardy's characters and narratives, as I have remarked; at the same time, Hardy also shows that there are limits to what may be conveyed, that perception comes up against subjective borders. What we may read from this as the lesson and the 'secret' of Hardy, or one facet of it at least, is that '[a]mong the phenomena of *repetition, resurgence, revival, or haunting*, it is not' Jean-Luc Nancy cautions, 'the identical but the different that invariably counts the most' (Nancy 2008, 1; emphasis added). Difference counts in Hardy, and serves as the force of all those keywords that Nancy identifies, but which, though in markedly different contexts, serve as keywords in Hardy, and in the reading of Hardy also. Difference counts, even if it is impossible to count the frequency of difference, to count on its appearance being obvious or unequivocal. For in difference, one has the only slightest possibility of hearing the other speak, and it is only the in-difference to difference that characterizes modernity and historical (and therefore epistemological) passage in Hardy, and which in turn makes such accents inaccessible, or impossibly foreign, personal and intimate, and yet also impossibly distant.

Three, somewhat extensive, but nevertheless necessary, quotations, then, from which to continue, to illuminate further the work of difference and as if to show how 'between *mimesis and mnemosyne* or creative memory ... there is this double-play of un-forgetting' (Armand 2006, 63):

> I can recollect the time when the places of burial even of the poor and
> tombless were all remembered, and the history of the parish and squire's

family for 150 years back known. Such and such ballads appertained to such and such a locality, ghost tales were attached to particular sites, and nooks wherein wild herbs grew for the cure of divers maladies were pointed out readily. (*LTH* 313)

The fresh harrow-lines seemed to stretch like the channellings in a piece of new corduroy, lending a meanly utilitarian air to the expanse, taking away its gradations, and depriving it of all history beyond that of the few recent months, though to every clod and stone there really attached associations enough and to spare – echoes of song from ancient harvest-days, of spoken words, and of sturdy deeds. Each inch of ground had been the site, first or last, of energy, gaiety, horse-play, bickerings, weariness. . . . [For Jude however,] in that ancient cornfield . . . it was [merely] a lonely place, possessing, in the one view, only the quality of a work-ground . . . (*JO* I.II.14)

Winter in a solitary house in the country, without society, is tolerable, nay even enjoyable and delightful, given certain conditions, but these are not the conditions which attach to the life of a professional man who drops down in such a place by mere accident. They were present in the lives of Winterborne, Melbury, and Grace; but not to the doctor's. They are old associations – an almost exhaustive biographical or historical acquaintance with every object, animate or inanimate, within the observer's horizon. He must know all about those invisible ones of the days gone by, whose feet have traversed the fields which look so gray from his windows; recall whose creaking plough has turned those sods from time to time; whose hands planted the trees that form a crest to the opposite hill; whose horses and hounds have torn through the underwood . . . what domestic dramas of love, jealousy, revenge or disappointment have been enacted . . . [However, if] the spot . . . lack memories it will ultimately pall upon him who settles there without opportunity of discourse with his kind. (*W* II.I.124–5)

The second and third passages are taken from *Jude the Obscure* and *The Woodlanders*, the first, from a letter, written by Hardy to H. Rider Haggard, in March 1902. Together, they make available a discontinuous narrative of Wessex life, while illustrating how repetition, resurgence, revival and haunting maintain themselves in cultural memory. They come to appear, and so to speak from some other place than late Victorian or early Edwardian England, even though this is precisely the site from which we apprehend them as issuing.

Hardy's recollection, captured in the passage from *The Life*, starts from personal memory, opening itself to an act of collective cultural anamnesis, whereby memory reveals itself as memory of place, and place, in turn, is a site of communal memory. Place can thus *take place* as a phantasmic and visionary projection. It can return as

recollected, imagined representation as a result of that which history and memory leave recorded there, maintained as a material and communal, though heterogeneously constituted archive. This is seen to be at work in the other extracts cited, and is also to be witnessed as a gesture of attestation and un-forgetting, in *Jude the Obscure*. In *Jude*, Shaston, the 'ancient British Palladour' (*JO* IV.I.199) and thus a town of two identities, is one such place, its representation structured by the traces of differing temporal, historical and cultural purposes and practices. Remarkable for its 'natural picturesqueness and singularity' (*JO* IV.I.199), it is as it has been, but now remains 'world-forgotten' (*JO* IV.I.200) – forgotten by the greater world, but also a forgotten world, with its 'twelve churches, its shrines, chantries, hospitals, its gabled freestone mansions' (*JO* IV.I.199). Additionally, Shaston was 'the burial-place of a king and a queen, of abbots and abbesses, saints and bishops, knights and squires' (*JO* IV.I.199). A place of pilgrimages, it is also, more mundanely, a place where 'horses, donkeys and men may have been seen ... laden with tubs and barrels' (*JO* IV.I.200). Lastly, the town's 'modern' singularity lay in it being a place of 'wandering vans, shows, shooting galleries, and other itinerant concerns' (*JO* IV.I.200). Such cultural memory, focused initially in the 'pensive melancholy' of a visitor, and gathered in narratives implied by 'living memory' (*JO* IV.I.200), is made up of different discourses and practices, various associations and relations, belonging not to Hardy but to the experience and memories of others. Returning to the passage from *The Life*, Parish and family are invoked, those without names – the *obscure* of the passage and parish – recalled in their nameless afterlives return, and ballads and oral tales acknowledged. Hardy's personal act of witness borne out of memory is itself a ghost tale of sorts, being the recollection of a world having passed by a generation at least, but doubly so, in being the phantasm of a world comprised of the ghost-narratives of those already dead and gone – save for the traces that remain, as iterable issue attesting to local history.

And it is local history, personal narratives, which are associated with the land in the second passage, again from *Jude the Obscure*, which Jude is either unable to read, or to which he has no access. Song and spoken word once more resonate, for a nameless subject, if not for Jude, whose reading of the disappearing world gives a landscape, a ground and dwelling place from out of which come such attestations, such confessions of the other, which admit *and* bear witness to the other even as they remain the traces of those other voices. Such voices, such spectral traces of alterity, and with these the signs of surviving, iterable difference are also present in the third

extract, from *The Woodlanders*. In its contrast between the incomer Fitzpiers, and the native inhabitants of Little Hinton, one perceives what it means to dwell authentically, to have one's being informed by that which haunts place, thereby binding one to one's others, the 'invisible ones' as Hardy calls them. Phantom tracks, hands, the motions of plough, and the daily dramas of unnamed lives live on, if one's memory is habitually informed the confessions of place, the secret affirmations that resonate in the 'old associations' whether biographical or historical, animate or inanimate. If one can read this, one is already attuned to the 'phenomena of repetition, resurgence, revival, or haunting'. All such phenomena find themselves only in the perception of the narrating subject who speaks, who utters in response to that which discloses itself, and which speaks eloquently, if, once more, mutely at the same time. Hardy's acts of representation are, therefore, acts of bearing witness to the phenomena of difference that return, and, in being translated, survive. Here are acts of confession, of being, as that word admits, in which, from the banality of the mundane one perceives and receives the possibility of utterance, hearing in this manifestation the declaration or confession, of the other.

IV. THE 'VEGETABLE WORLD'

One invents the confession of the other, then; one finds what is already being articulated. And in this invention, which is also a response, one reiterates the other's 'voice', such 'confession' being *of* the other, concerning and from the place of the other. Hardy's narratives *invent* the natural world, much as they *invent* the gin or man-trap, recovering its cultural significance albeit partially. As Melbury's stick notes, the natural world and the world of human phenomena are not distinct, separable from one another; this indeed is the interanimation between the human and vegetable worlds that Hardy maps in each of the passages so far quoted in this chapter. Every singular example, be it gin or stick, rock or furrow, speaks of and for many lives, numerous histories. In invention, Hardy's representations of the world find what is always already there, but passed by, ignored, left unread or remaining unheeded and unheard. Nevertheless, the natural or 'vegetable' world, as Hardy refers to it on several occasions, is there to be read, its voices caught. First, in *Desperate Remedies*:

> Between grey and half-overgrown stonework . . . the water gurgled down
> from the old mill-pond to a lower level, under the cloak of rank broad

leaves – the sensuous natures of the vegetable world. On the right hand the sun, resting on the horizon-line, streamed across the ground from below copper-coloured and lilac clouds. ... All dark objects on the earth that lay towards the sun were overspread by a purple haze, against which a swarm of wailing gnats shone forth luminously, rising upward and floating away like sparks of fire. (*DR* II.IV.230)

Next, in *Far from the Madding Crowd*:

It was that period in the vernal quarter when we may suppose the Dryads to be waking for the season – The vegetable world begins to move and swell and the saps to rise ... there are bustlings, strainings, united thrusts and pulls – altogether, in comparison with which the powerful tug of cranes and pulleys in a noisy city are but pigmy efforts. (*FMC* XVII.106)

And, from the same novel:

It was the first day of June, and the sheep-shearing season culminated, the landscape, even to the leanest pasture, being all health and colour. Every green was young, every pore was open, and every stalk was swollen with racing currents of juice. .... Flossy catkins of the later kinds, fern-sprouts like bishops' croziers, the square-headed moschatel, the odd cuckoo-pint, – like an apoplectic saint in a nic of malachite, – snow-white ladies'-smocks, the toothwort, approximating to human flesh, the enchanter's night-shade, and the black-petaled doleful-bells, were among the quainter objects of the vegetable world in and about Weatherbury at this teeming time ... (*FMC* XXI.125)

In passing it is worth observing that to read this last passage in conjunction with the words of Dick Dewy's song at the beginning of *Under the Greenwood Tree* – 'A Rosebud in June' – would transform and deepen an understanding of the both song and the earlier novel's introduction. This observation aside, the final reference to the vegetable world is found in *Two on a Tower*, in a passage already cited but worth recalling here:

On an early winter afternoon, clear but not cold, when the vegetable world was a weird multitude of skeletons through whose ribs the sun shone freely, a gleaming landau came to a pause on the crest of a hill in Wessex. (*TT* I.I.3)

The passages share in their representation a fetishistic fecundity; fetishistic, not because of the displaced sexuality that might be misread here in three of the four passages, but instead as a result of the degree to which Hardy's factitious rendering of the natural suggests a more than natural, a *supernatural* condition to the natural world.

In each passage, an invisible flux is made visible, binding the human to the natural world, if one knows how to read the signs. If one cannot, then such fetishism seems merely strained obsession. Reading can take place only on two conditions: if we have access to that epistemology that makes meaning available, but in addition if we are able to find the right time for such reading. Move too quickly, look from too great a distance, sum up in a general impression, to which details and contrasts give the lie, and we read nothing at all. Seen up close, given time, the vegetable world becomes stranger, not more familiar, with its multiple temporalities of growth, decay, cyclical patterns, and seasonal transitions.

For the urban Victorian reader, this is likely to be a world, which, translated onto the page, is understood as comprising and by constituted by recondite and cryptic discourses, articulated in turn by equally recherché epistemologies. Dryads and skeletal forms, fleshly blooms and racing juices; luminous, and swarming worlds, the power of which is greater than the most modern of metropolises: all such phenomena hint at the *phantasia* that is Wessex, a world in which phantasies do not merely come to appear in the real, but are, indeed, that on which the real depends for its material existence. For Hardy's fictions are *phantasies* in that they make visible the structures, networks, rhythms and fluxes of the modern world. The suspension of narrative drive to pause and reflect on the vegetable world invents an iterable phantasy, which is both imaginative vision and illuminating apparition. It is illuminating because, on the one hand, it unveils the condition of the world in miniature, independent of human consciousness, whilst, on the other hand, it is perceivable only through conscious, phenomenological translation. In this, Hardy makes unusual the habitual process, making strange the everyday, transforming it into that which is, in being unremarkable, into that which fascinates and enthralls. The modality of phenomenal representation resists naïve readings. It also admits a differential model for reading and interpretation.

Each extract where the invention and inauguration of perception and translation interrupts the realist world view introduces a 'node, a point of intersection or focus, on which converge lines leading from [and to] many other passages in the novel', throughout Hardy's fiction, and throughout Wessex. The reader, as a consequence, must 'execute a lateral dance of interpretation . . . without ever reaching a passage which is chief, original, or originating, a sovereign principle of explanation' (Miller 1982, 127). At the same time, Hardyean invention gives, if not access to how another sees, then limited but significant perspective on the process of perceiving. In this manner,

and through the vision that Hardy opens, 'the incidents of the moment … gleamed confusedly … as [if one witnessed] an outer landscape through the high-coloured scenes of a stained window' (*W* II.XVI.229). And thus it is that at a given moment, to a particular subject, 'tree-trunks, the road, the out-buildings, the garden, every object wore that aspect of mesmeric fixity which the suspensive quietude of daybreak lends such scenes. Outside [the] window helpless immobility seemed to be combined with intense consciousness; a meditative inertness possessed all things' (*W* II.VIII.166–67) Through becoming attuned to such 'suspensive quietide' expressive of an 'intense consciousness', we apprehend how reality gives way from within itself to its other, a phantasy that serves to admit us to worlds where meaning is always immanent, rather than transcendent; and this is perhaps Hardy's most percipient insight. When Hardy enfolds such moments in folkloric memories of 'mysterious sights' recounted as 'sundry narratives of [bark-rippers'] … fathers, [and] their grandfathers', the origin of which could 'only be accounted for by supernatural agency', along with other similar tales of ghostly brothers and exorcisms (*W* II.III.139), Wessex assumes a strange and estranging energy. This force, of spectral *apophansis*, is neither simply archaic nor modern exclusively, neither wholly pagan nor phenomenological. In each the work of difference is traced as that which survives and returns takes on new forms, new modalities. What both old and new ways of seeing share is the sense of letting something be seen to manifest itself in reiterating perception of the world, the essence of the world is disclosed as what becomes conscious to beings through perception and capable of being shared as such. In memory of the disappearing culture, *aletheia*, truth *as* and *in* unveiling takes place, not through the representation of what is but in the perception and reception of the aura of what is. Hardy thereby effects the disclosure of the spirit of place in 'the essential identity [understood as being] between the phenomenon's essence and the description that is proposed to discover it in its truth' (Henry 2008, 88). The phantastic is thus not other than the everyday, it is *just its* truth augured, made known, disclosed through the suspensive quietude afforded by the inventions of Hardyean Consciousness. The world takes place as it is, in all its quotidian strangeness.

V. 'SIGNIFICANT HOURS'

It might seem from certain perspectives that the phantasm is without any materiality whatsoever, even though I have argued that it can

emerge from the most basic material forms. However, it is salutary to remind ourselves that at the root of the phantasm or phantasy is that which is brought into the light, that which appears because it is unveiled to the light of day. Let me attempt to ground somewhat the apparition of the phantasm, as being countersigned by certain alternative historical signatures. The following passage from *Jude the Obscure* will serve this purpose:

> Old as it was, ... the well-shaft was probably the only relic of the local history that remained absolutely unchanged. ... Above all, the original church, hump-backed, wood-turreted, and quaintly hipped, had been taken down ... In place of it a tall new building of modern Gothic design, unfamiliar to English eyes, had been erected on a new piece of ground by a certain obliterator of historic records who had run down from London and back in a day. (*JO* I.I.12)

As we have encountered before, the material remnant bears imma-nently the spirit of place as well as its being the carrier of a site's historicity. In contrast to this sole remainder of a once-knowable past, the 'original church' has been obliterated, replaced with a faux-anachronism, foreign to the 'true' reader, whose perception is framed by a national identity, that identity presumably being deter-mined reciprocally by being formed and informed according to a native and organic epistemology, signalled in the materiality of the letter acknowledged as those equally obscure 'historic records'.

Much in *Jude* is marked by the temporal gathering or historical 'intensification' of cultural and epistemological obscurity, and this in turn informs Hardy's determination of Jude. Jude Fawley either ignores or knows little of his world, the world that can be said to be most properly his own. Ignorant of this world, and finding it therefore illegible, Jude looks beyond instead to the anachronistic modernity of Christminster, the university town in which the dead languages of Latin and Greek have more imaginative power, than the native Anglo-Saxon and, ironically, occasionally Roman traces of his own landscape. Hardy's narrator directs the reader to such obscure signs as these map the landscape, early in the novel: 'the hedgeless highway ... seemed to ascend and diminish till it joined the sky. At the very top it was crossed at right angles by a green "ridgeway" – the Icknield Street and original Roman road.'[4]

> This ancient track ran east and west for many miles, and down almost to within living memory had been used for driving flocks and herds to fairs and markets. But it was now neglected and overgrown. (*JO* I.III.19)

Archaic *genius loci* is conjured here by Hardy through an act of spatial and temporal mapping – note how the track 'runs' in different directions and also, it might be read, 'down *almost* to within living memory'. This is, simultaneously, also perceived in juxtaposition to stretch to a vanishing point, joining the sky. The topography bears history, and cultural memory is inscribed diagrammatically by direction and usage. At the same time, the road leads the eye to the limits of the world, to the meeting point between earth and sky, so that what one sees, where one dwells, is apprehended as *all* the world. One's being and one's dwelling is defined in this.[5] That *almost* is forcefully significant. It opens a gap between the living and the dead, which is only crossed, without being closed, through the memory of narrative told by others becoming reiterated as the narrative of memory. In this inversion, Hardy's vision of being is projected, addressed to the good reader. But the good reader is not Jude. Jude is, after all, 'reproached' by an illegible (to him) Greek text, 'like the unclosed eyes of a dead man' (*JO* I.VII.43, 48–9).

Such vision often occurs at liminal moments, significant hours in a day or at a time of year, when transition and suspension appear very similar to one another, and, furthermore, when space and time are interchangeable to a degree. As Sophie Gilmartin and Rod Mengham comment, '[p]aths and interludes, "spots of time", "timelines": space and time often stand in for each other metaphorically, and do so quite intensely in Hardy' (Gilmartin and Mengham 2007, 36). Turning to *The Woodlanders*, we find such an intersection or interlude as the inventive, inaugural disclosure of that novel's world. We see how, like *Under The Greenwood Tree*, it begins in the dark, in an isolated location. This is where the resemblance ends, however. We see very little. A wagon comes to a halt, someone dismounts, and heads off into the night, as does the cart, though in a different direction. The pedestrian takes a small by-road, leading nowhere other than a hamlet, isolated geographically from both the rest of Wessex and the rest of the world. This small collection of dwelling places can only be seen dimly in the dark, if at all. What can be seen is partial, fragmentary. The stranger can see into windows, poorly lit by whatever light sources the cottagers may possess. Unlike other Hardy novels, which begin with a panorama and the hypothesis of an encompassing view point, *The Woodlanders* is marked by the limit of the gaze, by circumscribed or partial perspectives, and by the sense that, though there are multiple perspectival lines and lines of sight, no-one can view everything. Partiality of vision, and therefore insight, is thus a structuring element that mediates and reflects

in however distorted a fashion, the perception that various characters have a limited consciousness – of their being, the world, time or the cosmos.

Yet within those limits, certain of Hardy's characters in *The Woodlanders* are given insight into the limits of their consciousness; they are self-conscious beings. Such self-consciousness frames being in a way that, allied with partiality of perspective and the limits or fragments of vision marks the novel as curiously proto- or pre-modern. Strange modernity though, given the often anachronistic grounding of being that Hardy presents, through rural ritual, archaic work practices, outmoded forms of legal entitlement, and the more pervasive, if diffuse sense that the village in question, Little Hinton, is somehow out of time, this being emphasized by its being accessible only through a 'forsaken coach-road' (W I.I.5). Belonging to no time in particular, it nonetheless gives the impression of being left behind, placed at a given hour beyond the boundary of a 'deserted highway', which, once being crossed by a hypothetical 'rambler', exchanges the uncomplicated sense of absence of human life for the much more eerie impression or consciousness of 'an incubus of the forlorn' (W I.I.5). Such an incubus only appears when one changes one's position 'by the act of a single stride', stepping 'at the place under notice, from the hedge of the plantation into the adjoining pale thoroughfare, [to] pause amid its emptiness for a moment' (W I.I.5).

Of this strange, liminal location, Hardy has already remarked that the 'spot is lonely, and when the days are darkening the many gay ones now perished who have rolled over the hill, the blistered soles that have trodden it, and the tears that have wetted it, return upon the mind of the loiterer' (W I.I.5). Apropos this sentence, not without interest is the fact that, for the Wessex edition, Hardy deleted everything after the factual statement that 'the spot is lonely', as if to exorcise to powerful a ghost or too painful a memory of rural loss. Consciousness of one's position is thus everything, and consciousness arrives as the internal apparition belonging to the physical relocation as a result of a step. In Hardy's introduction to Little Hinton with a step one exchanges worlds, finding oneself haunted by the dead. However fanciful such a vision might appear, there is a sense in which the narrative is also responsive to what might be called a spectral history here. Step into any old location, relatively unchanged, and you stand in a place through which generations have moved. Hardy is clearly aware of this, his prose poised as it is between that folkloric sensitivity, and a phenomenal sensitivity to the spirit of place, which is conjured through detail, through a pause

in narrative, which echoes, thereby doubling and supplementing, the pause of the rambler.

There are two Hardys, therefore, and the tension in the passage, that which is structured not so much as a dialectic as it is haunted by the sign of undecidability, resides in those two voices that mark the opening passage of *The Woodlanders*. As there are two voices (at least), so there are two times in the opening of *The Woodlanders*. On the one hand, we are at moments 'when the days are darkening', a cyclical inference haunting the single rambler and his step. On the other hand, there are all those phantom times of the 'many gay ones now perished'. In taking place, the step opens time from the single – and singular moment – into a visionary inauguration of recurrent, iterable and revenant temporality, the consciousness of the rambler being the screen on which the ghostly invention is projected. Yet, as is already implied, the flood of the past cannot be equated just with the sensitive mind, for place plays its part if one is receptive to reading the signs. The seer's ability is captured here, in a passage from *The Life*, on Hardy's birthday, as we read the interplay, the 'double-play of un-forgetting':

> At Bockhampton. My birthday – 44. Alone in the plantation, at 9 o'clock. A weird hour: strange faces and figures formed by dying lights. Holm leaves shine like human eyes, and the sky glimpses between the trunks are like white phantoms and cloven tongues. It is so silent and still that a footstep on the dead leaves could be heard a quarter of a mile off. (*LTH* 165)

Those readers having more than a passing familiarity with Hardy will recognize the ways in which this passage echoes with the disquiet and eerie monstrousness that is to be found in the author's fiction and prose. The phenomenal perception *and* possibly the reception of the landscape is all the more discomfiting because the viewing subject all but disappears from the scene, leaving only the reader to bear witness, as though he or she were in fact somehow transported to this location, placed within the frame of this vision. After that possessive pronoun, 'My', there is no discernible subject position, except for that of the implied reader. Even the reality of the footstep is questionable, for *could*, in conjunction with the present tense of the last sentence cited above, indicates nothing more than an imagined possibility. The countryside emerges for the reader through an uneasy prosopopoeic fragmentation of the landscape, which is arguably pagan in its daemonic resonances. This supposition is tendered in recognition of the sense of that which is archaic in the landscape, in but not of the experience and its present moment.

What is uncommon here is the fact that life of a kind, a manifestation of existence, is registered *in* the landscape itself, which is
uncanny precisely because it is presented as neither quite human
nor wholly other. Leaves are dead, lights are dying, but leaves shine
like *human* eyes, strange faces emerge, and the trees take on the
appearance of cloven tongues, while the glimpses of sky – and that
term 'glimpses' suggests that it is the sky which does the watching,
rather than merely being glimpsed – is spectral in its appearances.
Hardy's is a world that has a daemon existence, a quasi-life suspended liminally between life and death, all the more disturbing
because it does not, cannot, reflect upon its own condition, it has
no subject position. Yet it may be read as inviting us to *see*, as it
were, indirectly, to apprehend our own existence, and with that, our
own mortality, the fact of our being always already absent from this
location that we observe – that we have not yet or will, one day, no
longer, inhabit. We thus have the chance of coming to hear some
other's accent, the confession of the other.

Hardy's passage exemplifies such a strange life, a being without
body or material presence, or rather a being-without-being, that is to
say without any single or homogeneous material existence or, again,
ontological delimitation. The landscape in question clearly has being
or life of a sort, quasi-life if you will, albeit of a fragmented, heterogeneous, and phantasmic kind. There is an immanence in such
moments, or in remarks such as the following: '[t]here was now
a distinct manifestation of morning in the air, and presently the
bleared white visage of a sunless winter day emerged like a dead-
born child' (*W* I.IV.23). With its quality of 'manifestation' and
its disquieting 'face', early morning arrives still-born, that bleared
apparition appearing uncannily as the ghost of itself. Not dissimilar
to perception of the plantation on Hardy's birthday the moment and
the scene are neither wholly living nor dead, neither simply there nor
not there. Yet this entity we are naming landscape, this time we call
morning, is therefore all the more disruptive, violent, uncontainable
because it is neither has being entirely, nor is it without the traces
of some strange presence, arriving at a significant hour.

Hardy's language, his mode of representation, though not strictly
anthropomorphic, does, nevertheless, partake of what a spectral
autochthony, as a means to articulate that within and yet other to
the material world, and for which there is no precise language of
representation, or at least one which, in being primarily mimetic,
is adequate to the registration of the spirit of place. The cloven
tongues, human eyes and white phantoms, the incubus of the forlorn and the dead-born baby of a winter's morning: all imply an

atavistic persistence irreducible to what is *there*. And yet, in that illusion of the absence of any subject, the interpretation of place in terms suggestive of such other 'modalities of being', or a 'mode of actuality' (Husserl 1973, 299, 300), implies the phenomenological *as if* of some interpreting force, which can imagine, envision. However fictional, however *other*, the landscape has, therefore, what Edmund Husserl terms a '*quasi-existence*' (Husserl 1973, 300) for someone, which exceeds the perception of a single living being. We read such an effect in *The Woodlanders*. At an early hour, following the appearance of the visage of that winter's day already mentioned, one house in particular, is felt to be 'looking at you from the still distinct middle-distance of the early Georgian time'. Through its inanimate gaze, one gains perception of those 'great-great grandfathers and grandmothers who had been the first to gaze from those rectangular windows'. Through this instance of analogical apperception, one comes to apprehend how 'it was a house in whose reverberations queer old personal tales were yet audible, if properly listened for; and not ... silent beyond the possibility of an echo' (*W* I.IV.24). From feeling oneself gazed at, to the imagination of the phantoms of past generations of those who have dwelled there, one has the possibility, to hear echoes of narratives. In this a strange disjunction maintains a gap between location and subject, between sight and the trace of sound. Displaced within oneself through the displacement in registers that operate through the difference in their revenance, the subject has the possibility of access to the uncanny 'quasi-existence', as if one entered into a mode of actuality irreducible to, but issuing from material presence. That the phantasmic reveals itself in this manner, as if by chance, marks its event as ungovernable by any human subject, the implication being that it does not await human consciousness. Its force always already takes place in and as that which is given voice through the agency of the other.

VI. WHAT'S IN A NAME?

Such force may be found to reside in the proper name. Though many of Hardy's characters have names that serve a symbolic function, or else echo in particular ways, the registers of which have little to do with the concerns of realist fiction, it is *Tess* that draws our attention most particularly. *Tess of the D'Urbervilles* illustrates the high stakes involved in the use of the proper name, and the ways in which history, encrypted in the name, returns to leave the present in ruins. Indeed, we might even remark that the proper name is the site at

which ancient and modern collide, two distinct forces and their associated phenomena each bringing about the destruction of the other's boundaries, those limits by which temporal locus and identity are precariously enforced. *Tess* offers ample evidence also of how interpretation, once gone awry, is a prelude to disaster. Lastly, Hardy's twelfth novel presents the crisis of historical moment, as this crisis is suffered in the fate of the individual, namely Tess herself, who is subjected to cultural, material and phantasmic forces belonging to Wessex, which she can barely comprehend.

Any act of naming is a fraught process. Tess is both 'Tess Durbeyfield, otherwise D'Urberville, somewhat changed – the same, but not the same', as Hardy reminds us (*TD'U* II.XIV.89). There are two 'levels', two 'strata' at least by the historico-tectonic forces of which Tess is riven and rent in this seemingly plain statement. On the one hand, on the surface of this observation Hardy seeks to remind us that Tess is 'a stranger and an alien' in her home, though 'it was no strange land that she was in' (*TD'U* II.XIV.89). Her alienation, her becoming-estranged, deterritorialized from her proper sense of being, is a result of Alec's seduction. Even in this incident, however, name and land, being and dwelling, are closely interwoven. On the other hand, Tess, being both herself and no longer herself, bears in her body materially the effects of history. '[C]entrally concerned with the way the human past determines the present', as J. Hillis Miller argues, Tess and the novel which bears her name make undeniable how the 'idea of a present … is a repetition or reincarnation of the past', recurring 'through the novel like a refrain with many variations' (Miller 1970, 102).

Pregnant, violated, Tess is also rewritten, the force of her ancestors' Norman name[6] the signature that is also a countersignature bespeaking historical despoliation, dispossession, and displacement. Tess's is the body on which inscription is violently forced as the physical and symbolic re-enactment of one of English history's most decisive and irreversible transformations, the Norman conquest. The war of contested historical narratives takes place, written on Tess, the phantasms of Wessex, Anglo-Saxon, and Norman worlds striving for supremacy. To this is added the modernity of standard English. If this spectral reading seems not a little fanciful, it is arguable that Hardy's novels illustrate repeatedly and with a forceful determination the cultural consequences and legacies of various historical incursions on the English through more than two thousand years. More immediately, though, Alec, figure of the 'foreigner' or 'outsider', the *arriviste*, signifies for Hardy one more appropriation and colonization.

If Joan Durbeyfield's confused appellations, King Norman, Saint Charles, and Oliver Grumble (*TD'U* I.III.21) are historical indices in any significant manner, this is double: for, on the one hand, one's memory stands little chance of survival after one's death in anything but an adulterated form; on the other hand, how one receives a name can doom one despite efforts to control one's fate, as Tess makes one all too aware. The name is, though, just one manifestation of the impersonal power of language, of communication, address, inscription and articulation. *Tess*'s world is one where more than just the names of Durbeyfield and D'Urberville are the divided identities of a riven, disseminated and supplementary history. History is not, however, the trace and phantom manifestation of the past in the material present, with consequences for the future. Historicity marks Tess, dividing her identity and doubling her, specifically through the languages she speaks. Already cut adrift from her home somewhat by education, even though she has yet to leave, Tess speaks two languages: 'dialect was on her tongue to some extent, despite the village school' (*TD'U* I.II.15). The former is that which belongs to the district, and so identifies Tess's world. The other is that which is imposed on Tess from the outside. Hardy reenforces this point, and with it the generational, as well as cultural difference, by which Tess is becoming set adrift, as it were, from family, community, region and the past; while 'Mrs Durbeyfield still habitually spoke the dialect; her daughter, who has passed the Sixth Standard in the National School under a London-trained mistress, used it only when excited by joy, surprise, or grief' (*TD'U* I.III.21). The qualification suggests that Tess's authentic self speaks through her at moments of emotional intensity; or to see this in a broader context, that her 'world', Wessex, speaks through her, manifesting itself on her tongue, as though emotion conjures the spirit of place.

However, such moments are not common, and Tess's identity remains distanced from both her family, and, by inference, her home in the broader sense of the region of Wessex in which she lives. Through the difference that separates Tess and her mother, identity, definition, and epistemological and cultural stability remain riven, if not undecidable. Habitually, '[b]etween the mother',

> with her fast-perishing lumber of superstitions, folk-lore, dialects, and orally transmitted ballads, and the daughter, with her trained National teachings and Standard knowledge under an infinitely Revised Code, there was a gap of two hundred years as ordinarily understood. When they were together the Jacobean and the Victorian ages were juxtaposed. (*TD'U* I.III.23)

Here, the idea of generation is shown indirectly as an inadequate cultural measure. Standard and national transformations displace the worlds of mother and daughter, despite the fact that they belong to the same world, time, and place. While '[l]ike all the cottagers of in Blackmoor Vale, Tess was steeped in fancies and prefigurative superstitions' (*T'DU* I.VI.44), and although '[t]he Vale of Blackmoor was to her the world' (*T'DU* I.VI.44), she is all the more displaced through that nationalized standard inscription, which erases the regional cultural singularity of her identity and being. That which rewrites Tess, makes her unknowable to herself, and is as violent a 'translation' as is the unearthing of the D'Urberville/Durbeyfield affiliation. Tess's being has no proper dwelling place, driven from the homely at every moment, and unprepared by her modern, 'Standard' knowledge to read or have consciousness of what haunts her. Hardy is being only partly, if savagely ironic when his narrator observes through the suspension of parabasis '[s]o much for Norman blood unaided by Victorian lucre' (*TD'U* I.II.17), in a statement that yokes violently together genetic and capitalist inheritance.

It is important to acknowledge that though Tess is the focus of the novel, she is not alone in being in this haunted, divided condition. Place suffers equally. In the present moment of the novel, with regard to the naming of place, it is impossible to decide on whether it is the 'Vale of Blakemore, or Blackmoor' (*TD'U* I.I.7, I.II.12). That Hardy reiterates the same phrase within five pages hardly gives the reader confidence as to the correct identity. Another example of this is the undecidability that troubles the naming of 'Bulbarrow or Bealbarrow', the ancient burial site near Stourcastle (*TD'U* I.IV.30). Narrative keeps us at a distance through such acts of naming, leaving the reader always at a remove from greater knowledge of, or certainty concerning, particular regions in Wessex. *Tess* is very much a novel in which the reader remains an incomer, a tourist. At the same time, there are other reminders of one's being excluded. Hardy has occasion to refer to dialect expressions, access to which is all but impossible. An 'elderly boozer' observes shrewdly that Joan Durbeyfield '"must mind that she don't get green malt in flower"' (*TD'U* I.IV.28). We may guess at a meaning, but no footnote will render the immediacy of comprehension, the reader, whether in Victorian Manchester or London or in twenty-first century Leeds or Brighton, maintained outside the particular world and times to which such phrases are idiocultural singularities. Hardy's metanarrative affords no help: 'It was a local phrase which had a peculiar meaning, and there was no reply' (*TD'U* I.IV.28).

Thus, in part, Tess's world affirms itself in contingent, local surges, resisting erasure and overwriting; it remains in language and name, practice and belief, 'an engirdled and secluded region, for the most part untrodden *as yet* by tourist or landscape painter' (*TD'U* I.II.12; emphasis added). So precise and singular are the details of locality that, in a mere twenty mile separation between places, as 'soil and scenery' differ from one side of a hill to the other, so '[e]ven the character and accent of the two peoples had shades of difference, despite the amalgamating effects of a round-about railway' (*TD'U* II.XII.75). Here are worlds where traces of the past maintain themselves and persist in collective conscious-ness, to be remembered, and, so to speak, through memory and communal practice; these are worlds where people recollect hear-ing tales of visits by their grandparents to 'conjurors', in Egdon, Casterbridge and Owlscombe, such figures considered 'honest folk' who have disappeared from the modern world '"nowadays"' (*TD'U* III.XXI.133).

In bringing back, in inventing the traces of alterity, Hardy places himself as the latest, and possibly the last of such 'conjurors', prac-tising a weak magic that calls up the phantasms of past memory and 'unhistorical' (*TD'U* I.III.20) events, people and customs. In under-standing this, a strong reading might argue that *Tess* is the encrypted cipher of the *Complete Fortune-Teller* (*TD'U* I.III.22), itself likely to be an allusion to the *Universal Fortune-Teller*, an encyclopaedia of folk-lore, superstition and customary practices still very pop-ular' in parts of Victorian England (Firor 1962, 99). Whilst that old text is 'so worn by pocketing that the margins had reached the edge of the type' (*TD'U* I.III.22-23) – this image a material reminder of the way that time wears away at particular epistemes – *Tess* is marked everywhere with the 'marginalia' of semi-legible discourses and partially untranslatable knowledge. Indeed, Parson Tringham, the 'antiquary' (*TD'U* I.I.7), is one gatherer of such information, and can be taken as the shadow double of Hardy's narrator, thereby indicating the ambivalent status surrounding the consequences of historical recovery. Hardy's narrator has the saving grace, at least, of inventing the otherwise obscure, anonymous and unhistorical in the face of standardization and other forms of modern obliteration, as he figures through narration the clash of 'ideal and real' (*TD'U* I.II.13), and recovers what is unknown to those who practice 'the local Cerealia' (*TD'U* I.II.13).

There is a limit, though, even to a narrator's powers of conjuration. For, to come back to the question of the name, what becomes of those who pass out of history, becoming unhistorical as

it were, when a name, such as that belonging to the 'eclipsing girl', the one chosen over Tess by Angel Clare, whose name 'whatever it was, has not been handed down'? (*TD'U* I.II.17–18) Knowledge can never be absolute knowledge; consciousness can never encompass everything; and eventually in Hardy one is always confronted with the ironic reminder of this border, which excludes one, and confronts the reader with what can be known, and to what can be recovered. If, as Heidegger asserts, 'there is only "world" where there is language, that is', he contends, extending the ontological analogy, 'understanding of being' (Heidegger 2003, 32), then with Hardy we find that the world is never given to beings to comprehend as a totality. Representation thus unveils itself not as a bringing to presence but a perception of one's consciousness, and with that the historicity of one's being, as one finds oneself excluded from the times and worlds of Wessex, even at the level of language, and the return of phrases and words such as 'clipsing and colling', 'larry', 'plim', and 'vlee' (*TD'U* I.II.18, I.III.21). The absolute may be intimated as that which lies beyond the local; but consciousness as perception and perspective only serves to remind one that there is an horizon and frontier which encloses and determines one. Knowing of the D'Urbervilles or Standard English only shuts Tess out, from the 'home' of her past and her present 'homely' condition, consigning her to abjection and the uncanny condition of her being. And Tess is uncanny in Heidegger's sense, because the uncanny is not merely an impression or sensate apprehension, but in a 'more originary way (Heidegger 1996, 74); for she expresses, even if she does not have consciousness of this, a sense of 'seeking and searching out the homely, a seeking that at times does not know itself' and so causes to appear in Tess's wandering the 'not homely within whatever is homely' (Heidegger 1996, 74). Only when Tess fully comprehends her mortality can she remark "'Ah happy house – goodbye!'" (*TD'U* VII.LVIII.391).

VII.   DISCONTINUOUS APPREHENSION

Consciousness is thus limited; of this, there can be no doubt. Bounded and partial, it is occasionally represented by Hardy through the externalized image of a being embedded within a larger landscape, momentarily paused in representation like an insect in amber. Consciousness of one's being-in-the-world is consciousness that one does not have absolute consciousness. Alternatively, narrative 'consciousness' reveals, with oppressive clarity, the absence

of consciousness on the part of another that s/he is being observed. This can be taken to extremes in Hardy's worlds, as the following passage from *Tess of the D'Urbervilles* demonstrates:

> The swede field in which she and her companion were set hacking was a stretch of a hundred-odd acres, in one patch, on the highest ground of the farm, rising above stony lanchets or lynchets – the outcrop of siliceous veins in the chalk formations, composed of myriads of loose white flints in bulbous, cusped, and phallic shapes. The upper half of each swede-turnip had been eaten-off by the live-stock, and it was the business of the two women to grab out the lower or earthy half of the root with a hooked fork called a hacker, that it might be eaten also. Every leaf of the vegetable having already been consumed, the whole field was in colour a desolate drab; it was a complexion without features, as if a face, from chin to brow, should be only an expanse of skin. The sky wore, in another colour, the same likeness; a white vacuity of countenance with the lineaments gone. So these two upper and nether visages confronted each other all day long, the white face looking down on the brown face, and the brown face looking up at the white face, without anything standing between them but the two girls crawling over the surface of the former like flies. (*TD'U* V.XLIII.285)

In this, the human is reduced to the inhuman at both a macroscopic and microscopic level. Material conditions consume humanity, and the strange quasi-anthropomorphization of the land and sky is all the more uncanny for being so nearly human but held back from that. Human consciousness and reflectivity is erased from the earth. What we have here is an experience without the human, except as a condition of representation, in the choices made by the narratorial voice. This disembodied consciousness plays with the prosopopoeic, neither affirming it nor rejecting it outright, and mocking the registration of consciousness between one being and its other in those brown and white 'faces' of land and sky in a brutal and mute materialism that is almost entirely without history. The effect is primeval, atavistic, and, perhaps for some, monstrously engulfing.

I say the scene is without history *almost* advisedly; for there is in this bleak description the merest signs of human intervention, both diegetically, and in the narrative framing of the scene. This is farmland, of course, however poorly cultivated or maintained. Then, more subtly, there is the allusion to naming, and with that the intervention of a consciousness through language, the hooked fork being described as having been *called* a hacker. Then finally for now, there is the indecision over the choice of term, the 'stony lanchets or lynchets', which momentary indeterminability is resolved through

recourse to the more 'scientific' and classical determination of these outcrops as 'siliceous veins in the chalk formation'. A consciousness is there, beyond and above that of the women, who coming along after the cows, are merely perceived as insects, parasitical existences on the impoverished, and archaic world. And to a consciousness that can hesitate between dialect words (Old English in their derivation), before assuming the guise of the scientist in its discourse (inheriting the word from Humphrey Davy's *Elements of Agricultural Chemistry* [1813] or, perhaps from Darwin's *Journal of researches into the natural history and geology of the countries visited during the voyage of the Beagle* [1845]), and can, moreover, make the distinction that something is named, rather than merely being that object, as though there were no subjective intervention, these human figures are merely lower forms of life.

That there is a choice at all between dialect words, and the subsequent elevation into a distinterested classical taxonomy, implies a knowledge of such distinctions, and the relation without relation by which beings are cut off from one another. As with the matter of the proper or place name, language and the knowledge to which it gives access are problematized. What is odd in this given scene, additionally, is that knowledge, and the consciousness that manifests it, arrives without a subject *in stricto sensu*. The example thus serves economically to make the point about an architectonics of consciousness, wherein the distinguished and differentiated levels are structured in a manner analogous with the strata of land to which the passage refers. To push this point further, the passage is an analogical performative. It inscribes in the representation that which exceeds and is irreducible to representation of the landscape, or mimetic modes of representation in general. In doing so it enacts the condition of temporal sedimentation, as if the passage were the land it described. Historicity is here embedded in the contest for determination; bearing witness to the naming of traces, the historical trace itself is captured there, in the representation of the landscape, like a fossil or remnant of other civilizations. Old English or Anglicized Latin, the fragments signify the same thing but without reconciliation. The subjective consciousness registers historicity in its own articulation, an articulation aiming at representation but at a remove, disconnected, in a war-economy of difference. The field is thus the field of the historical, irrespective of local human agency or intervention. In this Hardy's narrative explores historical experience inasmuch as historical experience is registered as both an 'attribute' of the world 'and the attribute of the subject' (Ankersmit 2005, 8), however uncanny or ghostly that subject may be.

Stepping back from this particular scene, one should ask: in what way does the subject experience the world historically? This may be grasped if we perceive that one can 'ascribe to the mind the faculty of experience ... even though the mind does not possess any obvious equivalent to our eyes or ears for registering what is given to us' (Ankersmit 2005, 8). This faculty of experience is clearly of a different order, phantasmic in nature. What we register, therefore, is, in being subjective, of a different, and arguably more radically empirical order than any scientific empiricism would allow; for the very reason that, in being rooted in the experience, not of the subject but of the world, scientific empiricism relies for its validation on truths and data that are supposedly universal, constant, or transcendental. Hardy's rejection of such Truth and God affords his readers a momentary vision of the uncomprehending encounter between the material world in all its indifference and the subjective experience of the mind with its inescapably translative force, as it encounters the limits of the other's indifference. Only once can Tess be said to have a greater access to consciousness, beyond the material reality of the world:

> ... Tess fell more deeply into reverie than ever, her back leaning against the hives. The mute procession past her of trees and hedges became attached to fantastic scenes outside reality, and the occasional heave of the wind became the sigh of some immense sad soul, conterminous with the universe in space, and with history in time (*TD'U* I.IV.32).

In a momentary, partial loss of consciousness, Tess receives a phantasmal vision or visitation of some universal other, whilst driving the bee-hives to market. Lifted out of herself, Tess has no apprehension of the imminent danger and the chance occurrence that, after the revelation of the family's 'history', directs her to her fate through the suffering and death of the family horse. The material violence here is merely the expression of that which comes to Tess in the guise of reverie. For, while Hardy's choice of word implies daydream, it also signifies rage or wildness, a violent indifference on the part of the other to mere humanity. As *reverie* implies, it is as if an apparitional possession takes hold of Tess, manifesting the brute reality of a universe without sense of meaning, through her, and with Tess as its victim and plaything.

VIII.   WHEN WORLDS COLLIDE

There appears, therefore, an inhuman puissance that gives to Hardy's narratives both the potential for vision and the possibility

of destruction. As we have seen in previous chapters and in particular quotations considered in this chapter, Thomas Hardy's fictions
contain, if not multitudes, then 'worlds', which appear to exert their
power on the mortals who inhabit their disordered spaces. Hardy's
worlds-within-the-world are defined by their heterogeneous times,
and by the often conflictual condition produced through the clash
between visionary and real on the one hand, and by the past and
present, the archaic and modern, on the other. Different and differing, they inhabit, touch on, and occupy the same space, as in this
passage from *Tess*:

> Far behind the bright brick corner of the house ... stretched the soft azure
> landscape of The Chase – a truly venerable tract of forest land, one of
> the few remaining woodlands in England of undoubted primæval date,
> wherein Druidical mistletoe was still found on aged oaks, and where
> enormous yew-trees, not planted by the hand of man, grew as they had
> grown when they were pollarded for bows. All this sylvan antiquity,
> however, though visible from The Slopes, was outside the immediate
> boundaries of the estate. (*TD'U* I.V.38)

Multiple times, histories and cultures are written onto a single
space, artificially divided by modern distinctions concerning private
property. Pagan magic, inhuman prehistory, and echoes of early
modern England are thrown into relief by borders of the estate,
the various pasts placed and maintained at its margins. 'World'
is thus to be understood as the implied and signalled 'totality' of
elements, phenomena, and modes of communication that structure
this 'world'. Such a world is never comprehensible as absolute, however, as a finite or knowable totality. Representing one world only
serves to open that apparently closed world onto the possibility of
others.

Across a collection of poetry such as *Poems of the Past and
Present*, one apprehends connections between worlds and con-
sciousnesses, albeit discontinuously. Such connections have to do
with different temporal moments and their arbitrary interrelation,
as this comes to be disclosed to the consciousness of the reader, if
not to the perception of the characters, who within the chance and
often grimly ironic clash of worlds, come to suffer. To illustrate
this, we might turn to the dénouement of *Tess of the D'Urbervilles*,
where the pagan and the police close in on the fugitive Tess, con-
spiring to precipitate her end. Coming by chance to Stonehenge –
Tess calls it a '"monstrous place"' and a '"heathen temple"' (*TD'U*
VII.LVIII.392) – she and Angel stop at the place described by Clare

as '"[o]lder than the centuries; older than the D'Urbervilles"' (*T'DU*
VII.LVIII.393). Tess throws herself from tiredness on 'an oblong
slab' (*T'DU* VII.LVIII.393). Recollecting how Clare had called her
a heathen at Talbothays, Tess says, with not a little irony (though
more on Hardy's than on her part, perhaps), '"So now I am at
home"' (*TD'U* VII.LVIII.393), expressing a desire that there were
no-one else in the world, except for 'Liza-Lu (*TD'U* VII.LVIII.394).
The heathen home is all the world and the only home for Tess,
at least in her desires, in an almost complete if implicit rejection
of the modern. Desiring also that Angel marry her sister after
she is gone, Tess explains that Marlott people '"marry sisters-
in-law continually"' (*TD'U* VII.LVIII.394). Returning home, as
it were, becoming herself in some manner, which has failed to
happen through her wandering and encounters with the modern
and the world beyond the Vale of Blackmoor – or Blakemore –
Tess reverts to the expression of local knowledge and custom, to
what is homely, habitual and familiar. Her explanation to Angel
indicates knowledge of a world to which he does not have immediate access. Finally, Tess sleeps until dawn, when sixteen police
close around the altar stone and Tess (*T'DU* VII.LVIII.395). Tess
is taken, appearing to be a sacrifice in this meeting of the two
worlds, though whether her being given up is demanded by the
Druidical or the modern world remains undecidable. All that we
might venture is that it is impossible to be at home in two worlds
simultaneously.

Alternative Hardyean realities are also revealed through differing
temporal measures, whether time is understood as seasonal, pertaining to human life, structured by memory or historical events,
the division of days by horological means, various chronological
mappings, perhaps having to do genealogies or family histories,
the histories of a location or group of locations, or archaeological and paleontological time. Thus the difference between worlds
can be captured in the proper name, as in the difference that is
marked between Durbeyfield and D'Urberville (already observed,
above), between the world of the D'Urbervilles discovered in the
research of Parson Tringham, that of Tess and her family, and
that of the impostor D'Urbervilles, Alec and his mother. This is, in
relation to some of Hardy's mappings, a mere surface sketch, however, even if the story of a genealogical 'descent' propels the 'what
if' that defines historical and narrative chance. But if the name is
the device that sets Tess on a downward path, the confrontation
between the two worlds and their hitherto distinct times arrives
for her before the climax at Stonehenge, at the moment when

Tess arrives at the church in Kingsbere, to read, inscribed on a 'dark stone':

ostium sepulchri antiquae familae D'Urberville (*TD'U* VI.LII.363)

In the first volume edition, at least, Hardy has the typesetter employ a Gothic script to impress on the modern reader the full weight of age, the anachronistic resonance in this confrontation between the 'antique' family, and the 'daughter of the D'Urbervilles' (as one of Hardy's draft titles named the novel). There is, though, irony in this, given that the typeface and others like it would also, to some readers at least, have a then 'modern' resonance. This was of course as a result of its having been familiar for a generation at least since the rise of the Pre-Raphaelite Brotherhood in 1848, the Victorian fascination with the Gothic and medievalism inspired by Pugin's Gothic revival, and employed by, amongst others, William Morris's Kelmscott Press, established at Hammersmith in 1891, the same year as *Tess*'s publication. This aside, what Hardy gives us to read is that stress between ancient and modern, between the dead and the living, which finds itself concentrated through Tess's being.

IX. DIFFERENTIATED CONSTELLATIONS

It should be remembered finally, apropos the worlds of Hardy, that there are those connections, cartographies, traceries, or topographies that map a constellated network or mesh of social relations, as the term Wessex is meant to imply. More than implication though, Wessex names 'burden', responsibility certainly, but also motif, the principal motivating 'sentiment' or 'refrain', the undersong, as it were. Such constellated meshes are reproduced not only in representations of the world but in the doubling and division of consciousness. What each constellation suggests is itself the illusion of a totality, which, though gathered in the mediating place of subjective perception cannot be maintained. Hardy thus produces *quasi-totalities* in representations, events and instances of discontinuous consciousness, which touch on, or by analogy replicate or overlap other quasi-totalities, informing in turn larger and smaller totalities. And as already argued, an absolute totality in Hardy's world is a simulacrum by which thought seeks to orientate itself, but which remains only indirectly apprehended, if at all. Thus, it has to be said that there is no *one* totality, at least not one that could ever

be measured, grasped, represented or apprehended as such. Consciousness is thrown back on its failure to grasp the world and thus confronts the limits of its perceptions.

Hardy's quasi-totalities, the constellations of event, perception and trace, are composed of discontinuous ruins and fragments as we have seen, in which communication flows in interrupted measures in an effort to bring together and so reformulate the disparate parts of that world – spatially, topographically, historically – into a whole. Similarly, certain of Hardy's characters find themselves dispersed, divided, and unable to construct, either for themselves or in their desire for others, an ontology or identity that can assume totality unproblematically. Jude illustrates this in coming on the trace of himself as another, which trace initially returns to him as a memory. Recalling an inscription he had carved on the reverse side of a milestone when an apprentice, and wondering about the legibility of the sign after some years, he seeks it out:

> By the light of a match he could still discern what he had cut so enthusiastically so long ago:
>
> THITHER – J. F.
>
> The sight of it, unimpaired, within its screen of grass and nettles, lit in his soul a spark of the old fire. (*JO* I.XI.73)

Jude's sign confronts him with the external doubling, a prosthesis of the self, which materially will outlast Jude. In that use of the match to light the sign in so meagre and limited fashion, Hardy illuminates for the reader the narrow and temporary range of perspective. This fragment of Jude's other self appears from the dark, in an analogous reiteration of Jude's revenant memory, to disappear into the dark once more. Different times are connected momentarily, and Jude's attempt to gather himself to himself in this manner only serves to mark the difference between himself as he was and as he appears to himself – and to us.

Attempted connection, reformation and reformulation paradoxically lead to further foregrounding of the disconnecting, dividing, *differing and differentiating* modes of representation already implicit in Hardy's world. Phillotson's collection of photographs of Sue demonstrates this. Opening a draw, in which he finds 'therein an envelope', Phillotson takes out 'a photograph of Sue as a child, long before he had known her' (*JO* III.VI.161). This is not the end of matters. He also finds 'another of her as a young woman. ... It was a duplicate of the one she had given Jude, and

would have given to any man' (*JO* III.VI.161). There is no true Sue here, only a potentially endless iterable series of figures, typical modern reproductions that do not lead to the person they figure. Despite kissing the image, Phillotson's actions only remind the reader that communion or communication fail. The simulated experience of presence and the desire for an absolute presence or the present serve to remind one this is reformation or reformulation is impossible, strictly speaking. For as there are two photographs at least, two Sues of different ages, so that one photograph, given to Jude and hypothetically available for 'any man', implies an uncanny fragmentation of the self and, with that of the impossibility that haunts Phillotson's desire.

What we may perceive here is that if Hardy's world can be read as a 'realm of emergence, mediation, the *intra-ctive* [and] ... the compounded reflection', that realm of consciousness or world of emergence and mediation is staged in such a manner that it denies the possibility of the production, or apprehension, of a 'the balanced whole' (Bhaskar 1993, 271). There is always, as Hardy expresses it, 'the Unfulfilled Intention, which makes life what it is' (*W* I.VII.52). It is what disillusions, demystifies, disabuses one of any sense of harmony or homogeneity. The vegetable world gives Hardy's reader ample evidence of this, as well as of the 'Unfulfilled Intention' in the deformed leaf, the parasitical lichen, the destructive ivy (*W* I.VII.52). Hardy's representations present no balanced – if by that term one suggests harmony – whole, but instead forms haunted by the immanence or promise of their own deformity. Seasonal coherence is also internally disordered, Hintock's plantations and copses being touched in *The Woodlanders* by 'here and there an apparent mixture of the seasons' in the 'change from the handsome to the curious', as '[a]ngles were taking the place of curves, and reticulations of surfaces – a change constituting a sudden lapse from the ornate to the primitive on Nature's canvas' (*W* I.VII.51).

At an extreme, Nature's 'natural' and material demystification of aesthetic presumption of harmonious whole assumes, for the same consciousness desirous of the picturesque, an oddity bordering on the uncanny. As with seasonal transience, there is a temporal significance in Hardy's making-strange, as this is filtered through Grace Melbury's perception: 'The plantations were always weird at this hour of eve – more spectral far than in the leafless season, when there were fewer masses and more minute lineality' (*W* II.VII.299). Hardy's alliteration and consonantal echoes played in the iterability of *f*s, *m*s, *l*s and *s*s; the undulating and sinuous cross rhythms that create the impression of the parts of the sentence entwining itself as

it unfolds – such formal, material devices structure the image, creating a performative utterance from within the scrupulously attempted mimetic fidelity of the sentence. He does not leave this disquieting representation at this, though; for 'there were strange faces and figures from expiring lights . . . while now and then low peeps of the sky between the trunks were like sheeted shapes, and on the tips of boughs sat faint cloven tongues' (W III.VII.299). The differentiated constellation of tropes and figures, images and metaphors direct us to a world within the natural world, a world where 'stout-trunked trees' appearing '[w]rinkled like an old crone's face, and antlered with dead branches' (WII.XI.197) is infested with a strange life, which cannot quite be explained away through discussion of figurative language. Nature is more – and less – than natural, if one perceives its inhuman vitality with that sense of intimate apprehension that Hardy's narrator and certain of his characters are afforded.

We see into a folkloric world in *The Woodlanders* where modernity in the guise of the somewhat jejune scientist and doctor, Fitzpiers, and the return of Grace Melbury from school eventually cause catastrophe. The world of Little Hintock is a place where fear of an elm tree eats away at the health of Marty's father, John South, rather 'than any organic disease' (WI.XIII.91). So intimately is folkloric belief interwoven in particular lives that Fitzpiers' 'remedy' of cutting down the elm tree precipitates South's death (W I.XIV.102). If *Tess* keeps the reader at the borders of Blakemore – or Blackmoor – Vale, *Woodlanders* immerses its readers in its powerfully strange, illogical world. While the walking and dance with which *Tess* begins is carried on largely for tradition's sake, the Midsummer ritual, carried on on 'old Midsummer Eve' (24 June), appears invested with a far greater pagan vitality. Traditionally a time of processions and love divination, as well as the lighting of bonfires 'particularly tenacious in the West Country' since at least the sixteenth century (Roud 2008, 303), Midsummer Eve is connected, as we read in *The Woodlanders* 'with the sowing of hemp-seed, a handful of which was carried by each girl' into the woods (W II.IV.146). Once more, then, Hardy gives expression to a 'significant hour' (W II.IV.148) at which young women engage in a folkloric practice for the purpose of conjuring images of the men they will marry. This, of course, leads to Suke Damson and Fitzpiers spending the night in the hay-cock, discussed in Chapter One.

Crossing that road at the beginning of *The Woodlanders*, then, we are immersed in alternative modes of perception and consciousness, as well as finding ourselves in a world of different behaviours,

practices and beliefs. At certain points, the distance between the reader and the disquieting strangeness of Wessex is closed between the rational and superstitious, the modern and archaic, as the phantastic supplements the real as its spectral other perhaps more than in any other novel by Hardy. Or say instead that *The Wood-landers* comes closest to being the prose manifestation of Hardy's poetry, and also therefore his poetic vision. The text is a threshold at which we meet archaic and irrational Wessex most immediately, in the first volume of the novel at least, much as Marty South is 'met' at night 'flatly on the threshold, like the very brink of an absolute void, or the ante-mundane Ginnung-Gap believed in by her Teuton fathers' (W I.III.16). But with the cutting of the tree, and the ending of leases, which loses Winterborne his house, modern times break up Hardy's odd world, it leaves those who have dwelt there for a long time without a home, and it leads in the end to the death of Giles Winterborne.

* * *

After this, Hardy never came quite so close to the spirit of Wessex again. *Tess of the D'Urbervilles* holds its reader at a certain distance, intimating that by the 1880s and 1890s, there was no going home, one's condition was always to be homeless, unto death. Perhaps the irony in this resides in the fact that Hardy had to move back to Dorset to discover this, building Max Gate, and calling this home but constantly tampering with its form, until his death; whereupon his own body was, if not divided, then split in burial, his heart being buried in Dorset, the rest of his remains being interred in Westminster Abbey. Whatever the case, before he abandoned novel writing, following *Tess* he wrote just two other novels, both phantasies of desire in their own way, *The Pursuit of the Well-Beloved* and *Jude the Obscure*. While *Tess* insists on the homeless condition as the essence of being in Modern England of the nineteenth century, *Jude* shows the consequences of another form of homelessness, that of being a stranger in one's own land, unable to read its signs, and always seeking another home, which will always be denied.

Afterword

I. UNTIMELY ARRIVALS

Texts, ideas, the traces of historical and cultural forces: all take time to arrive. If they arrive at all, they are never on time. The arrival of the trace is radically disordered from the start. If interpreted precipitately, texts miss being read and so remain to be received. Yet the reader cannot help but be precipitate, overly anxious; otherwise, the reader is laggardly, moving in the wake of delivery or transmission. Moreover, any reception of some past trace always involves loss in translation, impoverishment through transmission, even if there is some other gain. We have seen such effects: Bathsheba's valentine to Farmer Boldwood, Tess's letter of confession to Angel Clare. There is also, perhaps most heartbreaking of all, a note written by a suicide, A Sergeant-Major Holway, in one of Hardy's most disturbing short stories, 'The Grave by the Handpost' (1897). 'On the table in the cottage', Holway 'had left a piece of paper, on which he had written his wish that he might be buried at the Cross [the cross-roads] beside his father'. However, 'the paper was accidentally swept to the floor, and overlooked till after his funeral, which took place in the ordinary way in the churchyard' (*DPOT* 342). This 'last post' can only ever be received by the reader, who must live with the belated knowledge that another's desire remains unfulfilled – and perhaps the awfulness of the situation is not in our consciousness of this, but in our awareness that Sergeant-Major Holway will have died in the mistaken belief that his will would be carried out, and that he can never know that it was not.

To be modern in Hardy appears to gain self-reflexive insight into all that one has received or missed, particularly when one realizes that reception is belated, or that whatever one has gained comes at a price and a limit is imposed on translation or comprehension. The

message arrives either to condemn one or to remind one that one has no access to the full meaning of the message. Such an experience in *Tess* occurs when Tess' witnesses the writing the scripture painter's two 'tex's' (*TD'U* 80), both of which are, unconsciously, deliveries destined for Tess. First:

THY, DAMNATION, SLUMBERETH, NOT
2 PET . ii. 3. (*TD'U* II.XII.79)

and then

THOU, SHALT, NOT, COMMIT – (*TD'U* II.XII.80)

The untimely arrival of the second text is haunted by its own future conclusion. Tess does not need the sign-writer to complete the quotation, being able to anticipate for herself the completion of the sentence, in both senses of that word. The other mode of transmission, where one is made abject by signification, takes place in *Jude the Obscure*, when the 'predestinate Jude' (*JO* I.VII.44) confronts the same legible-illegible text twice – H K A I N H Δ I A Θ H K H (*JO* I.VII.43, 49) – a text described uncomfortably as having a haunting power, regarding Jude as it does 'with fixed reproach . . . like the unclosed eyes of a dead man' (*JO* I.VII.48-49). Jude thus reads, and so develops, 'a general consciousness of his neglect . . . written on the face of all things confronting him' (*JO* I.VII.48). In the case of both Tess and Jude, dead languages come alive in particular ways, Jude and Tess becoming, inadvertently, the recipients of anachronistic and haunting messages. That which returns therefore appears with an ironic, mocking inevitability.

Hardy understood this more than most. His language is 'peppered' with such revenant scraps. To see it from this perspective, though, is to miss the directions from which Hardy receives the various transmissions. The worlds he constructs are structured through such transmissions, arrivals, conversions, and renovations. His 'literary language' is 'influenced by his sense of the way words are knitted to a dark and controlling past' (Taylor 1993, 277). That 'sense' is, however, an openness on Hardy's part to the innumerable fluxes of alterity. If his language is, then, a 'deliberately heterogeneous assortment of words from many layers of historical usage . . . its mixture of vocabularies drawn from various classes, regions, and languages'; if, in turn, these are 'drawn from these sources again and again at different times' (Taylor 1993, 277), this is doubtless the affirmation of what Hardy perceived to be self-evident: who one is, culturally and historically, comes about as a result of anachrony,

transmission, translation, gain and loss, in the structuring of being. One knows oneself, however belatedly, to be modern, because one perceives finally, indirectly, the extent to which one is haunted and burdened by the traces of the past that leave their impression on the modern subject.

'Wessex' offers a collective name for one's identity, illustrating the condition of one's not being on time with oneself, as it were, through a 'teeming linguistic universe of growth and decay' (Taylor 1993, 277). This is more than merely linguistic, however; for Hardy apprehended this to be the condition of any individual organism, which was 'a unity aggregated from multiplicity' (Hardy cit. Taylor 1995, 278). And there is in this also a sense of Hardy's perception of particular examples of architecture, and by extension, the built environment as these are represented through towns such as Christminster and Casterbridge. Indeed, Hardy had made the analogy between poetry and architecture in *The Life*:

> He had fortified himself in his opinion [of the necessity of irregularity and heterogeneity in art] by thinking of the analogy of architecture, between which art and that of poetry he had discovered ... that there existed a close and curious parallel .... He knew that in architecture cunning irregularity is of enormous worth, and it is obvious that he carried on into his verse, perhaps in part unconsciously, the Gothic art-principle ... the principle ... resulting in the 'unforeseen' (as it has been called) character of his metres and stanzas ... (*LTH* 301)

Whilst the immediate analogy operates between one aesthetic form and another, there is given here an epistemological principle, and with that a sense of temporal and historical structuring as the concomitant force beyond the merely formal aspects of Hardy's writing. What arrives from the past, what remains in the present field of vision, whether literary text, language-trace, material structure such as a barrow or barn, church or castle; even natural phenomena – all are capable of producing in Hardy's subjects, all are informed by the immanence of, the 'unforeseen'.

Amongst the many aspects of his awareness of the significance of such traces in their detail and irregularity, those elements that determine the singularity of Hardy's text and which risk being lost to an aesthetic consciousness seeking unity, there is Hardy's 'tender sensitivity to the human voice at the core of his imagination' (Paulin 2005, xix). Whether or not it is the human voice only to which Hardy is attuned, as opposed to the 'voices' in all creatures, things, phenomena is open to question. However, he gives particular expression to this astute perception apropos transmission, translation and loss in a commentary on the Dorset dialect poetry

of William Barnes. Interpreting, explaining or annotating dialect words Hardy claimed, provided only 'a sorry substitute for the full significance the original words bear ... without translation' (Barnes 1908, vii). From another perspective, therefore, Hardy knew that words and signs arrive with a velocity that inevitably produces indirect, sensuous apprehension, thereby causing 'a feeling before it gets defined' (Taylor 1983, 306). In this apprehension, Hardy marks a distance, once more, from realist forms of narrative. Instead, he announces himself a novelist of, and for, future generations. Hardy is only ever available as other to the times in which he wrote. In this, he remains the novelist of the nineteenth century who, more than any other, affirms the past as always arriving. He is the novelist and poet of cultural memory and the times of the other. In this we have the signs, ironically, of the fortunes of Hardy's own texts. In seeing this, we understand how the historical and 'postal' chance of Hardy's novels, in their transmission and critical reception, act on certain of their readers in a manner analogous with the effect that the many missives, telegrams, signs, paintings and other modes of communication that make their appearances in his texts. Hardy's texts make of his readers – some of them at least – unwary doubles of his characters, thereby proving the epistemological truth that has been misread as aesthetic flaw.

The historicized, historicizing modes of representation inform Hardy's writing through the revelation of the times of their having taken place. They thus record both representation of the world, and mental reflection on, or image of, that world. In this, Hardy's historicizing records are themselves the traces of so many *memento mori*, so many archived and archiving (re)collections of heterogeneous traces. They are researches into, remembrances of, times past. They affirm the ruins of the innumerable pasts that crowd the present of so many of Hardy's novels, signalling and sending themselves into an unprogrammable future, and risking everything on reading or unreadability.

II. VISION AND TRAIT

Whilst it has become something of a commonplace to speak of Hardy as a cinematic novelist, it is more accurate to remark that he shares with photographic technology the ability to bear the burden of memory through the inscription of the haunting trace, as Tim Armstrong makes clear. Of photography, Armstrong observes: 'alongside its status as an index of the real, the photograph itself becomes ghostly; it comes to represent mourning, abstracting and

estranging its subject-matter' (Armstong 2000, 59). One might regard this work as being also that of the nominal or genealogical trait, on which Hardy plays – and equally frustrates – in novels such as *A Laodicean*, with its narrative of the De Stancys; there is the question of the Luxellian line also in *A Pair of Blue Eyes*, and in the apparent declension from D'Urberville to Durbeyfield in *Tess*. The trait is carried, furthermore, in *The Well-Beloved*, through three generations. The trace and trait in all their manifestations serve simultaneously as indexical markers of the real and forces that abstract or estrange from within the reality and present they serve to construct. Such estrangement and abstraction give one the sense of how intimately close and yet impossibly far Hardy is from our time, from the time we consider ours.

Additionally, not only does Hardy employ material resources, anachronistic and recovered linguistic elements, and a tropic play generated from the very idea of biological inheritance, he also invents visions of the past from within the present, as the response to a sympathetic resonance received within the real, as in the image of the poet-swimmer from 'In Front of the Landscape', 'plunging and labouring on in a tide of visions' that threaten to engulf 'the customed landscape / Yonder and near' (*CP* 303). Vision and landscape contest with one another, the latter reduced to little more than a 'ghost-like gauze' as material substance is transformed into an evanescent screen for 're-creations', 'speechful faces, gazing insistent'. Of the spectres, the subject remarks 'I could see them, feel, them, hear them, address them' (*CP* 303). Other phantoms, images and scenes, so many 'lost revisiting manifestations' (*CP* 304), subject to 'misprision' return to demand 'fuller translation than rested on them / As living kind' (*CP* 304). The poet-seer thus receives out of the landscape and its material presence the revenants of those who have inhabited the land, and who, misinterpreted, return in order that poetry translate the vision into the materiality of the letter, and so transmit beyond itself the vision translated into another medium for those readers in the future to bear witness. To make us feel and gain insight, rather than simply to make us 'see' the visible world, except by that indirect vision made available through the trace, this it might be said is Hardy's desire, his narrative and historical obsession. Hence, a complex textual weave emerges, comprising so many folds, and threads, so many echoes in different registers. As Jacques Derrida observes, '[t]he memory without memory of a mark returns everywhere' (Derrida 1995, 42). Once a note is sounded in Hardy, an impossible number of others resonate for the patient reader, attentive to the difference of historicity, its signs and traits.

If we are to be attentive to the signs, traces, and marks of history and the ways in which the past leaves its remainders on our identities and our memories, we would do well to acknowledge that 'We two kept house, the Past and I', as Hardy puts it in 'The Ghost of the Past' (*CP* 308–9), a poem where the form of the text doubles through the materiality of the letter, the ghostly form of Hardy's 'house', that is to say the 'structure' of mind and memory wherein he habitually dwells and where the revenant traces making up his being surface in iterations and echoes:

We two kept house, the Past and I,
   The Past and I;
I tended while it hovered nigh,
   Leaving me never alone.
It was a spectral housekeeping
   Where fell no jarring tone,
As strange, as still a housekeeping
   As ever has been known.

As daily I went up the stair
   And down the stair,
I did not mind the Bygone there –
   The Present once to me;
Its moving meek companionship
   I wished might ever be,
There was in that companionship
   Something of ecstasy.

It dwelt with me just as it was,
   Just as it was
When first its prospects gave me pause
   In wayward wanderings,
Before the years had torn old troths
   As they tear all sweet things,
Before gaunt griefs had torn old troths
   And dulled old rapturings.

And then its form began to fade,
   Began to fade,
Its gentle echoes faintlier played
   At eves upon my ear
Than when the autumn's look embrowned
   The lonely chambers here,
The autumn's settling shades embrowned
   Nooks that it haunted near.

And so with time my vision less,
   Yea, less and less
Makes of that Past my housemistress,
   It dwindles in my eye;
It looms a far-off skeleton
   And not a comrade nigh,
A fitful far-off skeleton
   Dimming as days draw by.

Hardy calls the species of haunting at work here a 'spectral house-keeping', which is 'as strange, as still a housekeeping / As ever has been known'. There is nothing, apparently, of the uncanny in the 'companionship' that exists between the 'Bygone' and the speaker of the poem, until the phantom form 'began to fade, / Began to fade'. That absolute iteration, also an echo, is a structural device used in three of the five stanzas, drifting in each case from the first to the second lines. The other two stanzas alter the repetition into iterable forms, the second stanza pairing 'I went up the stair' with 'And down the stair', the fifth, and last stanza reading 'And so with time my vision less, /Yea, less and less'. In these iterable forms, Hardy's poem becomes performative; moving from statement to statement it enacts its own condition of being-haunted, its own spectral echoing, and emphasizes through structural play how in order for there to be a ghost, there has to be a structure. As Derrida puts it, 'haunting implies places, a habitation, and always a haunted house' (Derrida 1995, 86). That strange stillness speaks of the law of the house for Hardy, which law dictates that no house is properly a house unless it is haunted; which is to say that the house as architecture and structure is also an archive; it is an archive, furthermore, for the spectre, being of the past, being the trace of the past itself, is stored, remains harboured as the memory of that which it once was. The structural relation, a structure which is as temporal as it is spatial, is mapped in those iterations and in the correlation between the 'Past', the 'Bygone', that which was the 'Present once', and the speaker.

That the formal echoes of the poem's text return from line to line, whether altered or not, intimates doubling, something return-ing the same and yet not the same; there is thus about the iterable form a displacement within and as the condition of the structure, in short that which haunts form. This in turn informs both the rela-tion between that which is spectral and other than the narrator and the relationship of speaker and reader, at least structurally and tem-porally. For, that 'I', the 'me', the 'my', who moves throughout the poem *and* the house bearing witness to its other, reiterates the motions of its other, even as, in that, it also serves as one of the two

'subjects' of the poem. On the one hand, the past or the 'Bygone' is one subject; on the other hand, 'I' is an other. House and poem further reiterate the dimorphic dyad. The 'present' moment is thus always already in disarray, as is presence, opened within themselves through the disequilibria in forms and identities. Because so much depends in this poem on repetition and its other the future to come is admitted (in the ghostly possibility of every reader, of every other reader and the other of every reader). 'Repetition is thus inscribed at the heart of the future to come' as that which carries the archival trace and also the possibility, the 'violence' of 'forgetting' (Derrida 1995, 79). Indeed, Hardy affirms as much in the last stanza, with the diminution of his 'vision', which 'dwindles in my eye', to loom 'a far-off skeleton', a 'fitful far-off skeleton'. Memory carries in itself its own precarious loss, 'Dimming as days draw by'.

Thus, the title begins to fulfil its double genitival promise, where the ghost apprehended as 'The Past', 'The Bygone', and so personified, passes away, leaving only its ghost, the ghost of a ghost. Nothing, neither more nor less, than a poem, that which *makes* appear in the time of its reading *mutatis mutandis*. 'The Ghost of the Past' confesses to nothing less than the fact that ours is a ghost-ridden culture therefore, however ambiguous such a confession might be, and however ambivalent we may feel in response to such an assertion. We inhabit and share a modernity and a collective identity in which we dwell and which we find to be haunted everywhere, by what Hardy is pleased to call 'the persistence of the unforeseen'. That persistence, Hardy realizes, is part of the very work of literature, the text considered as a structure of reproduction; for, 'when the very *first* perception of an image is linked to a structure of reproduction, then we are dealing with the realm of phantoms' (Derrida 1989, 61). It is precisely this realm that Hardy exploits; it is also this, which Hardy's work, on every page, confesses, even as, in assuming responsibility for this realm, he responds to its call.

This is Hardy's secret.

III. PHANTASMAL CULTURE

The culture of phantoms and phantasms that Hardy registers marks its transition and upheaval through formal signs of instability, rupture, disruption and, to return to a word of Hardy's, 'disproportioning'. As paradoxical as it may seem, the spectral or phantasmic trace bears witness to the material conditions of history

more immediately than any historical or merely factual record. Perceiving this, we come to see how Hardy's novels are less constative statements about 'traditional way[s] of life' than they performative enactments of singular events that express the historicity and condition of being of 'trapped between aspiration and anxiety, and therefore typical of some of the central contradictions of the age' (Eagleton 2005, 188). There is nothing universal about Hardy, 'there is nothing timeless about the rural order which these men and women [of Hardy's fiction] inhabit' (Eagleton 2005, 189). That the twinned poles of aspiration *and* anxiety are readable as, inescapably, the signs of historical overdetermination may perhaps help towards explaining Hardy's critical reception. For such instability in, and as a constitutive element in the formation of, narrative, when produced performatively in the grammatical and semantic planes of a novel are always likely to generate in the reader a concomitant sense of anxiety, without the possibility of stilling the contradictions or mobility that may find all too uncanny echoes in the reader's own being or identity.

Thus, what I have described as the haunting of Hardy's text by those confessions of the other: this is the secret utterance of nothing other than the materiality of history itself, whereby a spectral necessity emerges in articulation, allowing, as Jacques Derrida has it, 'what does not arrive to arrive . . .. This constituting structure is a destructuring fracture . . .. Here, in any case, the border between literature and its other becomes undecidable' (2000, 91–2). Hardy's novels disturb some of his readers, or remain misread even today, precisely because, in registering instability and undecidability, they return to their readers a heart of darkness all too uncannily familiar.

What is all the more difficult to come to terms with is that Hardy's novels speak not so much from a single, identifiable place or voice as from some form of phantom narrating machine, speak[ing] with (at least) three different accents' (Gatrell 2000, 56). Such complexity maps for the reader's perception the numerous layers of narrative form. It also invites – or perhaps demands of – us that we accommodate ourselves to different perspectives and, with that, to a recognition that any perspective is always positioned, partial, and open to realignment, distortion, interpretation, and so on. In active interanimation, Hardy's complex narrating and envisioning machines map, even as they generate, the intercalation of that network of places constituting the partly real, partly dream country of Wessex. In doing so, they trace the footsteps of those who, thought of less today as the dead than as yesterday's living, inhabit and haunt both this country of Wessex, and, *still*, the world we misapprehend

as ours, today. Hardy demands we apprehend our being haunted, that we dwell on this condition, even as it dwells in us, speaking in secret, and leaving everywhere the partly erased-partly legible signs of its past lives. History is, after all, what T. S. Eliot called in *Four Quartets* 'a pattern / Of timeless moments'. And History, as Hardy perceived, is therefore 'now and England' (Eliot 1963, 222), although that 'now' is always already spectral, always the place of the perceiving subject, the addressee, the recipient and reader. Imploring that we perceive this also, Thomas Hardy insists that we apprehend the significance of a phantasmal cultural. Every page bears a demand that we have to recognize, and so respond to, taking responsibility for

. . .those invisible ones of the days gone by. (W II.I.124)

Notes

INTRODUCTION

1. I use the terms 'dwell' and 'dwelling' specifically, following Martin Heidegger. Dwelling arises from how one lives on the earth, rather than being determined by the material structures one builds: 'dwelling is the manner in which mortals are on the earth' (Heidegger 1993, 350). Building is what we do because we dwell on the earth, rather than being that which defines dwelling. For Heidegger, not having a true relation to the earth means that one is alienated from the truth of one's being. The Heideggerian 'fourfold' is the organic coalescence of earth and air (Hardy's landscapes and the subject's place within these), mortals (figured in Hardy through 'living memory' and those who had driven flocks and herds, as well as in the fairs and markets), and 'divinities'. It is not immediately clear where this last category might be located in Hardy, other than through vague rhetorical references to the fates or gods, or specifically in the passage quoted above. However, given that Heidegger speaks of the unconcealment or withdrawal of the divinities in thinking earth, air and mortal together in the 'simple oneness of the four' (1993, 352), I would read the dis-enclosure of the Heideggerian divinities in Hardy's sense of temporal dwelling and spatial perception. Merely visual or realist examination is transformed through visionary perception into an apperception of some immanent or transcendent force. Dwelling is thus perceived as that which perception maintains through the careful reading of the traces of the past, dwelling and being intimately enfolded in Hardy's narrative act of what Heidegger calls 'preserving', which 'keeps the fourfold in that with which mortals stay: in things' (Heidegger 1993, 353).

1. APPREHENSION, SUSPENSION, ABSTENTION: *DESPERATE REMEDIES* (1871)

1. 'Realism' and 'realist fiction' are umbrella terms throughout this book. While there is a danger that the terms are taken for granted, I am not

227

implying that there is a single practice identified by that name. Although Dickens, Eliot, Thackeray, Trollope and other novelists of the first generation of Victorian fiction are loosely termed realists, they all write very differently from each other. With some caution – and, doubtless, this will still be insupportable – I am using 'realist', 'realism' and so on, to refer to those modes of narrative where the 'average experience' of the middle orders of society are presented with the implicit understanding that this is how the world comports itself, and that what is represented is, if not all the world, then all the world that matters. Whilst the everyday is 'derailed' in small, local ways, all events creating detours and departures from the norm are understood as being within a more or less realistic paradigm. So, for example, someone may die of a disease, be run over by a train, lose a fortune, or prohibit a daughter to marry for love, but rarely do the characters in realist fictions stare intently at the minutiae of pond-life and speculate on the universe, or reflect on the craze for restoring medieval churches to their original state. The characters in realist fictions rarely become involved in any narrative strand that is odd, disquieting, or overly exciting. Additionally, their tales are told in a prose, which, whilst capable of delving into the minds of its characters, nevertheless maintains, on the one hand, an omniscient position over the world that is created, and, on the other hand, a narrative distance. Hardy may employ such devices, but he also frequently departs from them in different formal ways as well as in a manner that invites one to question what is going on. Events in Hardy are not always probable.

As Roger Fowler argues, 'all theories of realism, however sophisticated, rest on the assumption that the novel imitates reality, and that reality is more or less stable and commonly accessible'. However, he does go on to admit that all definitions 'prove unsatisfactory' (1987, 201). Of course, it can be said that Hardy – more or less – conforms to realist practices so understood. There are several problems with this however, and it is the problematic 'interruptions' that are to be found everywhere in Hardy's writing, which, when read aesthetically, are taken to be flaws, failures, inconsistencies. As I mention elsewhere, Hardy is seen as at fault for his generic mixing, the instability of representation, the failure to adopt a moderate and consistent tone, his use of 'inappropriate' modes of speech in particular contexts, or the impossibility of certain situations, given the discourse framed by the events. In 'realism', so-called, prose style remains consistent in order to give the suggestion of authenticity in representation. Regardless of their differences, Dickens et al are hardly likely to speak of Spring as a time of Dryads; were they to do so, it is equally unlikely that they would connect Dryads to pulsing, bursting, straining, and thrusting of vital juices, as does Hardy. Again, whilst a realist narrative might describe trees in winter as 'skeletal', it

is less likely that the trees would be personified as weird skeletons, each species having an individual voice. Ultimately though, the terms 'realist' and 'realism' are largely unhelpful, hindrances at worst, while, at best, prompts for critique and departure into a discussion of singularity and difference, and why the realist novel, if such a thing exists, cannot, by example, be exemplified, every example differing from every other.

2. DISTORTIONS AND TRANSFORMATIONS: *UNDER THE GREENWOOD TREE* (1872), *A PAIR OF BLUE EYES* (1873)

1. Charles Johnson, *The Country Lasses or, The Custom of the Manor: A Comedy in Five Acts, with Prose* (1715). *The Country Lasses* was Johnson's most successful play, and was performed, more or less continuously, until 1813. Also, see the next sentence, in the body of the chapter, above: Marianne Harriet Mason, *Nursery Rhymes and Country Songs, Both Tunes and Words from Tradition* (1877).

   In the note to 'Rosebud in June', Tim Dolin, editor of the Penguin edition draws on Jackson-Houlston (1989, 324–5). In Jackson-Houlston's article the song is renamed or misnamed 'the Sheep-Shearing Song'. The earliest evidence of collecting and printing is found by Jackson-Houlston between 1905 and 1908. Dolin fails to mention either Cecil Sharp, who was instrumental in collecting many traditional songs, or Gustav Holst, who produced an arrangement of the tune. Sharp's version (1916) was collected by him from William King from West Harptree, Somerset, 1904.

2. On the subject of sheep-shearing songs in Hardy, see Ruth Firor (1962, 142–5, 187–9). Sheep shearing and sheep-shearing songs appear elsewhere in Hardy, notably in *Far from the Madding Crowd*, when Joseph Poorgrass sings at Bathsheba's shearing party, and in *The Dynasts*, in which the Duke of Bedford refuses to defer the sheep-shearing dinner. In response to a query from the Prince Regent concerning the Duke's last-minute arrival at the Regent's fête, Bedford replies: '"Well, it so happened that my sheep-shearing dinner was fixed for this very day, and I couldn't put it off. So I dined with them there at one o'clock, discussed the sheep, rushed off, drove the two-and-forty miles, jumped into my clothes at my house here, and reached your Royal Highness's door in no very bad time"' (*D* II.VI.vii.) There is in Bedford's priorities an allegiance to tenants before the Prince, and in that a mildly subversive intimation of the duty owed to rural community before monarchy.

3. On the significance of Schopenhauer, see Asquith (2005, 36–42, 106–7, 159—60).

5. CONFESSIONS OF THE OTHER: *THE WOODLANDERS* (1887), *TESS OF THE D'URBERVILLES* (1891), *JUDE THE OBSCURE* (1895)

1. J. Hillis Miller points to both *A Pair of Blue Eyes* and *Far from the Madding Crowd*, commenting that, in Hardy's third and fourth novels, published immediately before *Ethelberta*, Hardy first presents 'the sequence of Bathsheba's loves'. Elfride Swancourt is, though, also 'a woman loving three men in sequence'. Taking his cue from Proust, Miller remarks that such serial desire 'reverses the pattern of Jocelyn's life' (Miller 1970, 168). Importantly, this assigns Hardy's fascination with a Platonic or Shelleyan ideal, its relation to love and desire, to a much earlier date than composition for *The Well-Beloved* would imply. Also, it takes away the context of artistic imagination, condenses the time-frame and thus diminishes or rationalizes the persistence of obsession within the shorter time-frame, whilst also problematizing feminist and psychoanalytic readings of *The Well-Beloved* in their interests in male desire.

2. A strong reading could argue that generic mixing is Hardy's formal means of illuminating for us the unhomely nature of the novel itself, at the end of the nineteenth century: there is no 'proper' form, the novel is without its own properties or proprieties. It is expelled from the homely conditions it once assumed, recovery, marriage, closure, the retreat into a quiet harmonious life signalled either by marriage, the announcement of children, the reward of wealth and comfort, or all of the above.

3. A diary entry from 1926 finds Hardy referring once more to Proust, apropos *The Well-Beloved* and the French author's development of the theme. Hardy also gives two citations from Proust's *A l'ombre des jeunes filles en fleurs*, the first of which is particularly pertinent in the context of the present chapter: '. . . peu de personnes comprennent le caractère purement subjectif du phénomène qu'est l'amour, et la sorte de création que c'est d'une personne supplémentaire, distincte de celle qui porte le même nom dans le monde, et dont la plupart des éléments sont tirés de nous-mêmes' (*LTH* 432) ['very few people comprehend the purely subjective character of the phenomenon that is love, and the sort of creation that is a supplementary person, distinct from the one who bears the same name in the world, and one most of whose elements are drawn from ourselves'; Proust 1996, 46; trans. modified]

4. Hardy appears to conflate Icknield Street and Icknield Way, the former being a Roman road running from Gloucestershire to South Yorkshire, the latter being the 12th-century name given to an Iron Age road that runs from Norfolk to Dorset, ending in Lyme Regis. Another name, used by Hardy in this passage, is the Ridgeway. The name, originally Celto-British, and possibly a reference to the Iceni tribe, brings to Hardy's landscape a temporal layering, dating place back as far as the first century BC. With the reference to the Roman road, to the

markets and fairs, Hardy thus layers the representation in a kind of spectro-archeological mapping, which gathers invisibly within it the phantasm of a broad continuous cultural identity, broken only shortly before *Jude*, as that remark 'down almost to within living memory' attests.

5. Hardy's representation captures a poetic anticipation of the Heideggerian definition of authentic being and dwelling, gathered in and comprehended through what the philosopher calls the fourfold, which comprises earth, air, human mortal and divinities (Heidegger 1993, 343–64). On this, see the Introduction.

6. Hardy draws in his history on the de Turberville family. Sir Payn, or Pagan de Turberville, who, coming over with William, assisted specifically in the conquest of Glamorganshire, as Parson Tringham reveals to John Durbeyfield. The details Hardy gives to Tringham concerning the family name appearing in the Roll of Battle Abbey are also accurate.

Bibliography

WORKS BY THOMAS HARDY

Collected Letters of Thomas Hardy. Eds Richard Little Purdy and Michael Millgate, 7 vols. Oxford: Oxford University Press, 1978–88.

The Complete Poems. Ed. James Gibson. Basingstoke: Palgrave, 2001.

Desperate Remedies. Ed. Mary Rimmer. London: Penguin, 1998.

The Distracted Preacher and Other Tales. Ed. Susan Hill. London: Penguin, 1979.

The Dynasts: An Epic-Drama of The War With Napoleon and The Famous Tragedy of the Queen of Cornwall. London: Macmillan, 1931.

Far from the Madding Crowd. Ed. Rosemarie Morgan, with Shannon Russell. London: Penguin, 2000.

The Hand of Ethelberta. Ed. Tim Dolin. London: Penguin, 1997.

Jude the Obscure. Ed. Dennis Taylor. London: Penguin, 1998.

[Hardy, Florence Emily] *The Life of Thomas Hardy 1840-1928*. London: Penguin, 1962.

A Laodicean. Ed. John Schad. London: Penguin, 1997.

The Literary Notebooks of Thomas Hardy. Ed. Lennart A. Björk, 2 vols. Basingstoke: Macmillan, 1985.

The Mayor of Casterbridge. Ed. Keith Wilson. London: Penguin, 1997.

The Mayor of Casterbridge. Ed. Norman Page. Peterborough, Ontario: Broadview Press, 1997.

The Mayor of Casterbridge. Ed. Dale Kramer. Oxford: Oxford University Press, 1987.

The Personal Notebooks of Thomas Hardy. Ed. Richard H. Taylor. Basingstoke: Macmillan, 1978.

A Pair of Blue Eyes. Ed. Pamela Dalziel. London: Penguin, 1998.

The Pursuit of the Well-Beloved and The Well-Beloved. Ed. Patricia Ingham. London: Penguin, 1997.

The Return of the Native. Ed. Tony Slade, Int. Penny Boumelha. London: Penguin, 1999.

Selected Poems. Ed. Harry Thomas. London: Penguin, 1993.

'Studies, Specimens &c.' Notebook. Ed. Pamela Dalziel and Michael Millgate. Oxford: Clarendon Press, 1994.

Tess of the D'Urbervilles. Ed. Tim Dolin, Int. Margaret R. Higgonnet. London: Penguin, 1998.

Thomas Hardy's 'Facts' Notebook: A Critical Edition. Ed. William Greenslade. Aldershot: Ashgate, 2004.

Thomas Hardy's Public Voice: The Essays, Speeches, and Miscellaneous Prose. Ed. Michael Millgate. Oxford: Oxford University Press, 2001.

The Trumpet-Major. Ed. Linda M. Shires. London: Penguin, 1997.

Two on a Tower. Ed. Sally Shuttleworth. London: Penguin, 1999.

Under the Greenwood Tree. Ed. Tim Dolin. London: Penguin, 1998.

Wessex Tales. Ed. Kathryn R. King. Oxford: Oxford University Press, 1991.

The Withered Arm and Other Stories 1874–1888. Ed. Kristin Brady. Harmondsworth: Penguin, 1999.

The Woodlanders. Ed. Patricia Ingham. London: Penguin, 1998.

HARDY CRITICISM, VICTORIAN CRITICISM, AND OTHER SECONDARY SOURCES

Andersen, Carol Reed. 'Time, Space, and Perspective in Thomas Hardy'. *Nineteenth-Century Fiction*, 9:3 (December 1954): 192–208.

Ankersmit, F. R. *Sublime Historical Experience*. Stanford: Sanford University Press, 2005.

Anon. Review of *The Mayor of Casterbridge* (29 May, 1882). Rpt in Thomas Hardy, *The Mayor of Casterbridge*. Ed. Norman Page. Peterborough, Ontario, 1997. 404.

Armand, Louis. *Incendiary Devices: Discourses of the Other*. Prague: Univerzita Karlova v Praze / Nakladatelstvi Karolinum, 2006.

Armstrong, Tim. *Haunted Hardy: Poetry, History, Memory*. Basingstoke: Palgrave, 2000.

———— 'Player Piano: Poetry and Sonic Modernity'. *Modernism/Modernity*, 14:1 (2007): 1–19.

Asquith, Mark, *Thomas Hardy, Metaphysics and Music*. Basingstoke: Palgrave, 2005

Bäckman, Sven. *The Manners of Ghosts: A Study of the Supernatural in Thomas Hardy's Short Poems*. Göteborg: University Press of Sweden, 2001.

Ball, David. 'Hardy's Experimental Fiction'. *English: The Journal of the English Association*. 35 (1986): 27–36.

Barnes, William. *Selected Poems*. Ed. Thomas Hardy. London: Henry Frowde, 1908.

Bayley, John. *An Essay on Hardy*. Cambridge: Cambridge University Press, 1973.

Benjamin, Walter. 'A Small History of Photography'. *One Way Street*. Trans. Edmund Jephcott and Kingsley Shorter. London: NLB, 1979. 240–57.

———— 'Perception is Reading'. *Selected Writings. Vol. I, 1913–1926*. Ed. Marcus Bullock and Michael W. Jennings. Cambridge, MA: Belknap Press, 1996a. 92.

———— 'On Perception'. *Selected Writings. Vol. I, 1913–1926*. Ed. Marcus Bullock and Michael W. Jennings. Cambridge, MA: Belknap Press, 1996b. 93–6.

———— *Illuminations*. Trans. Harry Zohn, Int., Hannah Arendt. London: Pimlico, 1999.

Bennett, Brandon B. 'Hardy's Noble Melancholics'. *Novel: A Forum on Fiction*. 27:1 (Autumn 1993): 24–39.

Berger, Sheila. *Thomas Hardy and Visual Structures: Framing, Disruption, Process*. New York: New York University Press, 1990.

Bhaskhar, Roy. *Dialectic: The Pulse of Freedom*. London: Verso, 1993.

Bivona, Daniel. *Desire and Contradiction: Imperial Visions and Domestic Debates in Victorian Literature*. Manchester: Manchester University Press, 1990.

Blanchot, Maurice. *The Writing of the Disaster*. (1980) Trans. Ann Smock. Lincoln: University of Nebraska Press, 1986.

———— *The Work of Fire*. (1949) Trans. Charlotte Mandell. Stanford: Stanford University Press, 1995.

Bonica, Charlotte. 'Nature and Paganism in Hardy's *Tess of the D'Urbervilles*'. *ELH*, 49:4 (Winter 1982): 849–62

Boumelha, Penny. *Thomas Hardy and Women: Sexual Ideology and Narrative Form*. Brighton: Harvester Press, 1982.

Bourassa, Alan. 'Literature, Language, and the Non-Human'. *A Shock to Thought: Expression after Deleuze and Guattari*. Ed. Brian Massumi. London: Routledge, 2002. 60–76.

Brooks, Jean. *Thomas Hardy: The Poetic Structure*. New York: Cornell University Press, 1971.

Brown, Joanna Cullen. *Hardy's People: Figures in a Wessex Landscape*. London: Allison and Busby, 1991.

Bullen, J. B. *The Expressive Eye: Fiction and Perception in the Work of Thomas Hardy*. Oxford: Oxford University Press, 1986.

Butler, Lance St. John, ed. *Thomas Hardy after Fifty Years*. Totowa, NJ: Barnes & Noble, 1977.

——— ed. *Alternative Hardy*. New York: St Martin's Press, 1989.

Casagrande, Peter J. *Hardy's Influence on the Modern Novel*. Totowa, NJ: Barnes & Noble, 1987.

Chapman, Raymond. *The Language of Thomas Hardy*. New York: St Martin's Press, 1990.

Clark, T. J. 'Phenomenality and Materiality in Cézanne'. In Tom Cohen et al., *Material Events: Paul de Man and the Afterlife of Theory*. Minnesota: University of Minneapolis Press, 2001. 93–113.

Clements, Patricia, and Juliet Grindle, eds. *The Poetry of Thomas Hardy*. Totowa, NJ: Barnes & Noble, 1980.

Coleridge, Samuel Taylor. *Biographia Literaria or, Biographical Sketches of My Literary Life and Opinions*. Ed. James Engell and W. Jackson Bate. Princeton: Princeton University Press, 1984.

Dave, Jagdish Chandra. *The Human Predicament in Hardy's Novels*. Atlantic Highlands, NJ: Humanities Press International, 1895.

Davidson, Donald. 'The Traditional Basis of Thomas Hardy's Fiction'. *Southern Review* 6 (Summer 1940): 163–78.

Davie, Donald. *With the Grain: Essays on Thomas Hardy and Modern British Poetry*, ed. and int., Clive Wilmer. Manchester: Carcanet, 1998.

Davies, J. V., ed. *Lawrence on Hardy and Painting: 'Study of Thomas Hardy' and 'Introduction to these Paintings'*. London: Heinemann, 1973.

Davis, Jr., William A. 'The Rape of Tess: Hardy, English Law, and the Case for Sexual Assault'. *Nineteenth-Century Literature*, 52:2 (September 1997): 221–31.

de Laura, David J. '"The Ache of Modernism" in Hardy's Later Novels', *ELH*, 34:3 (September 1967): 380–99.

Deleuze, Gilles. *The Logic of Sense*. Trans. Mark Lester. New York: Columbia University Press, 1990.

────── *Empiricism and Subjectivity: An Essay on Hume's Theory of Human Nature*. Trans. and Int. Constantin V. Boundas. New York: Columbia University Press, 1991.

──────, and Félix Guattari. *What is Philosophy?* Trans. Hugh Tomlinson and Graham Burchill. New York: Columbia University Press, 1994.

de Man, Paul. *Romanticism and Contemporary Criticism: The Gauss Seminar and Other Papers*. Ed. E. S. Burt, Kevin Newmark, and Andrzej Warminski. Baltimore: The Johns Hopkins University Press, 1993.

────── *Aesthetic Ideology*. Ed. Andrzej Warminski. Minneapolis: University of Minnesota Press, 1996.

Derrida, Jacques. 'Foreword: *Fors*: The Anglish Words of Nicolas Abraham and Maria Torok', trans. Barbara Johnson. *The Wolf-Man's Magic Word*, Nicolas Abraham and Maria Torok. Minneapolis: University of Minnesota Press, 1986. xi–il.

────── 'The Ghost Dance: An Interview with Jacques Derrida', trans. Jean-Luc Svoboda. *Public* 2 (1989): 60–73.

────── *Archive Fever: A Freudian Impression*. Trans. Eric Prenowitz. Chicago: University of Chicago Press, 1995.

────── *Demeure: Fiction and Testimony*. Trans. Elizabeth Rottenberg. Stanford: Stanford University Press, 2000.

Devereux, Joanna. *Patriarchy and Its Discontents: Sexual Politics in Selected Novels and Stories of Thomas Hardy*. New York: Routledge, 2002.

Dewitt, Anne. '"The Actual Sky is a Horror": Thomas Hardy and the Arnoldian Conception of Science'. *Nineteenth-Century Literature*, 61:4 (2007): 479–506.

Durham, Scott. *Phantom Communities: The Simulacrum and the Limits of Postmodernism*. Stanford: Stanford University Press, 1998.

Eagleton, Terry. *Walter Benjamin or, Towards a Revolutionary Criticism*. London: Verso, 1981.

────── *The English Novel: An Introduction*. Oxford: Blackwell, 2005.

Ebbatson, Roger. *Hardy: The Margin of the Unexpressed*. Sheffield: Sheffield Academic Press, 1993.

Eliot, T. S. *Four Quartets*. *Collected Poems 1909-1962*. London: Faber & Faber, 1963. 187–224.

Elliott, G. R. 'Spectral Etching in the Poetry of Thomas Hardy'. *PMLA*, 43:4 (December, 1928): 1185–95.

Enstice, Andrew. *Thomas Hardy: Landscapes of the Mind*. New York: St Martin's Press, 1979.

Fayan, Jr., George S. 'Hardy's *The Woodlanders*: Inwardness and Memory'. *Studies in English Literature, 1500–1900*, 1:4 (Autumn 1961): 81–100.

Federico, Annette. 'Thomas Hardy's *The Well-Beloved*: Love's Descent'. *English Literature in Transition, 1880–1920*, 50:3 (2007): 269–90.

Ferris, David S. 'Introduction: Aura, Resistance, and the Event of History'. *Walter Benjamin: Theoretical Questions*. Stanford: Stanford University Press, 1996. 1–26.

Firor, Ruth A. *Folkways in Thomas Hardy*. (1931) New York: A. S. Barnes & Co., 1962.

Fisher, Joe. *The Hidden Hardy*. New York: St Martin's Press, 1992.

Fowler, Roger, ed. *A Dictionary of Modern Critical Terms*. Rev. ed. London: Routledge and Kegan Paul, 1987.

Freud, Sigmund. The "Uncanny." *Writings on Art and Literature*. Ed. Neil Hertz. Stanford: Stanford University Press, 1997. 193–224.

Gallagher, Shaun. *The Inordinance of Time*. Evanston: Northwestern University Press, 1998.

Garson, Marjorie. *Hardy's Fables of Integrity: Woman, Body, Text*. Oxford: Oxford University Press, 1991.

———— 'The Mayor of Casterbridge: The Bounds of Propriety'. In *The Mayor of Casterbridge*. New Casebooks. Ed. Julian Wolfreys. Basingstoke: Macmillan, 2000. 80–115.

Gatrell, Simon. *Hardy the Creator: A Textual Biography*. Oxford: Clarendon Press, 1988.

———— *Thomas Hardy and the Proper Study of Mankind*. Basingstoke: Macmillan, 1993.

———— 'The Mayor of Casterbridge: The Fate of Henchard's Chararcter'. In *The Mayor of Casterbridge*. New Casebooks, Ed. Julian Wolfreys. Basingstoke: Macmillan, 2000. 48–79.

———— *Thomas Hardy's Vision of Wessex*. Basingstoke: Palgrave, 2003

Gilmartin, Sophie, and Rod Mengham. *Thomas Hardy's Shorter Fiction: A Critical Study*. Edinburgh: Edinburgh University Press, 2007.

Gittings, Robert. 'Introduction'. Thomas Hardy. *The Hand of Ethelberta*. London: Macmillan, 1975.

Goode, John. *Thomas Hardy: The Offensive Truth*. Oxford: Basil Blackwell, 1988.

Goodheart, Eugene. 'Thomas Hardy and the Lyrical Novel'. *Nineteenth-Century Fiction*, 12:3 (December 1957): 215–25.

Gossin, Pamela. *Thomas Hardy's Novel Universe: Astronomy, Cosmology, and Gender in the Post-Darwinian World*. Aldershot: Ashgate, 2007.

Greenslade, William. *Degeneration, Culture and the Novel*. Cambridge: Cambridge University Press, 1994.

Grossman, Julie. 'Thomas Hardy and the Role of Observer'. *ELH*, 56:3 (Autumn 1989): 619–38.

Grundy, Joan. *Hardy and the Sister Arts*. Basingstoke: Macmillan, 1979.

Hagan, John. 'A Note on the Significance of Diggory Venn'. *Nineteenth-Century Fiction*, 16:2 (September 1961): 147–55.

Hawkins, Desmond. *Hardy at Home: The People and Places of His Wessex*. London: Barrie and Jenkins, Ltd, 1989.

Heidegger, Martin. *History of the Concept of Time: Prolegomena*. Trans. Theodore Kisiel. Bloomington: Indiana University Press, 1992.

———— 'Building Dwelling Thinking'. *Basic Writings: Revised and Expanded Edition*. Ed. David Farrell Krell. London: Routledge, 1993. 343–64.

———— *Hölderlin's Hymn "The Ister"*. Trans. William McNeill and Julia Davis. Bloomington: Indiana University Press, 1996.

———— *Four Seminars*. Trans. Andrew Mitchell and François Raffoul. Bloomington: Indiana University Press, 2003.

Helfer, Martha B. *The Retreat of Representation: The Concept of Darstellung in German Critical Discourse*. Albany: State University of New York Press, 1996.

Henry, Michel. *Material Phenomenology*. Trans. Scott Davidson. New York: Fordham University Press, 2008.

Herbert, Lucille. 'Hardy's Views in *Tess of the D'Urbervilles*', *ELH*, 37:1 (March 1970): 77–94.

Higonnet, Margaret R., ed. *The Sense of Sex: Feminist Perspectives on Hardy*. Urbana: University of Illinois Press, 1993.

Hirooka, Hideo. *Thomas Hardy's Use of Dialect*. Tokyo: Shinozaki Shorin, 1983.

Hughes, John. *'Ecstatic Sound': Music and Individuality in the Work of Thomas Hardy*. Aldershot: Ashgate, 2001.

Hume, David. *A Treatise on Human Nature*. Ed. L. A. Selby-Bigge. Oxford: Clarendon Press, 1975.

Husserl, Edmund. *Experience and Judgement*. Rev. ed. Ludwig Landgrebe, trans. James S. Churchill and Karl Ameriks, Int., James S. Churchill, Afterword Lothar Eley. Evanston: Northwestern University Press, 1973.

—— *Cartesian Meditations: An Introduction to Phenomenology.* Trans. Dorion Cairns. Dordrecht: Kluwer Academic Publishers, 1995.

Hyman, Virginia R. *Ethical Perspective in the Novels of Thomas Hardy.* Port Washington, NY: Kennikat Press, 1975.

Hyppolite, Jean. *Logic and Existence.* Trans. Leonard Lawler and Amit Sen. Albany: State University of New York Press, 1997.

Ingham, Patricia. *Thomas Hardy.* Atlantic Highlands, NJ: Humanities Press International, 1990.

Irwin, Michael. *Reading Hardy's Landscapes.* Basingstoke: Macmillan, 2000.

Jackson-Houlston, C. M. 'Thomas Hardy's Use of Traditional Song'. *Nineteenth-Century Literture*, 44:3 (December 1989): 301–34.

Jedrzejewski, Jan. *Thomas Hardy and the Church.* Basingstoke: Macmillan, 1996.

Johnson, Bruce. *True Correspondence: A Phenomenology of Thomas Hardy's Novels.* Tallahassee: University Presses of Florida, 1983.

Johnson, Charles. *The Country Lasses or, The Custom of the Manor: A Comedy in Five Acts, with Prose.* London: np, 1715.

Johnson, Michael L. 'From Hardy to Empson: The Swerve of the Modern'. *South Atlantic Review*, 50:1 (January 1985): 47–58.

Johnson, Trevor. *A Critical Introduction to the Poems of Thomas Hardy.* New York: St Martin's Press, 1991.

Jones, Lawrence. 'Thomas Hardy's "Idiosyncratic Mode of Regard"'. *ELH*, 42:3 (Autumn 1975): 433–59.

Keen, Suzanne. *Victorian Renovations of the Novel: Narrative Annexes and the Boundaries of Representation.* Cambridge: Cambridge University Press, 1998.

Kiely, Robert. 'Vision and Viewpoint in *The Mayor of Casterbridge*'. *Nineteenth-Century Fiction*, 23:2 (September 1968): 189–200.

King, Jeanette. *Tragedy in the Victorian Novel: Theory and Practice in the Novels of George Eliot, Thomas Hardy, and Henry James.* Cambridge, 1978.

Knoepflmacher, U. C. 'Hardy Ruins: Female Spaces and Male Designs'. *PMLA*, 105:5 (October 1990): 1055–70.

Koepnick, Lutz. 'Aura Reconsidered: Benjamin and Contemporary Visual Culture'. *Benjamin's Ghosts: Interventions in contemporary Literary and Cultural Theory.* Ed. Gerhard Richter. Stanford: Stanford University Press, 2002. 95–120.

Kramer, Dale. *Thomas Hardy: The Forms of Tragedy*. London: Wayne State University Press, 1975.

Krell, David Farrell. *Daimon Life: Heidegger and Life-Philosophy*. Bloomington: Indiana University Press, 1992.

Lacoste, Jean-Yves. *Experience and the Absolute: Disputed Questions on the Humanity of Man*. Trans. Mark Raftery-Skehan. New York: Fordham University Press, 2004.

Langbaum, Robert. *Thomas Hardy in Our Time*. Basingstoke: Macmillan, 1995.

Leavis, F. R. *The Great Tradition: George Eliot, Henry James, Joseph Conrad*. New York: New York University Press, 1963.

Lorentzen, Eric. 'Reading Hodge: Preserving Rural Epistemologies in Hardy's *Far from the Madding Crowd*'. *Victorian Newsletter* 110 (Fall 2006): 1–10.

Lothe, Jakob. 'Variants on Genre: *The Return of the Native*, *The Mayor of Casterbridge*, *The Hand of Ethelberta*'. In Dale Kramer, Ed. *The Cambridge Companion to Thomas Hardy*. Cambridge: Cambridge University Press, 1999. 112–29.

Lucas, John. *The Literature of Change: Studies in the Nineteenth-Century Provincial Novel*. Hassocks: Harvester Press, 1977.

Lukacher, Ned. *Time-Fetishes: The Secret History of Eternal Recurrence*. Durham: Duke University Press, 1998.

Mallett, Phillip, ed. *The Achievement of Thomas Hardy*. Basingstoke: Macmillan, 2000.

——— ed. *Thomas Hardy: Texts and Contexts*. Basingstoke: Macmillan, 2002.

Mason, Marianne Harriet. *Nursery Rhymes and Country Songs, Both Tunes and Words from Tradition*, illus., Miss E. M. S. Scannell. London: Metzler and Co., 1877.

Matz, Aaron. 'Terminal Satire and *Jude the Obscure*'. *ELH* 73:2 (Summer 2006): 519–47.

Maxwell, Donald. *The Landscape of Thomas Hardy*. London: Cassell and Co., 1928.

Maynard, Katherine Kearney. *Thomas Hardy's Tragic Poetry: The Lyrics and* The Dynasts. Iowa City, IA: University of Iowa Press, 1991.

Miller, J. Hillis. *Thomas Hardy: Distance and Desire*. Cambridge, MA: Harvard University Press, 1970.

——— *Fiction and Repetition: Seven English Novels*. Cambridge, MA: Harvard University Press, 1982.

—— *The Linguistic Moment: From Wordsworth to Stevens*. Princeton, NJ: Princeton University Press, 1985.

—— *Topographies*. Stanford, CA: Stanford University Press, 1995.

—— *Reading Narrative*. Norman: University of Oklahoma Press, 1998.

Millgate, Michael. *Thomas Hardy: His Career as a Novelist*. Basingstoke: Macmillan, 1994.

—— *Thomas Hardy: A Biography*. New York: Random House, 1982.

Mistichelli, William J. 'The Comedy of Survival in Thomas Hardy's *The Hand of Ethelberta*. *Modern Language Studies*, 22:4 (Autumn 1992): 88–104.

Moore, Kevin Z. *The Descent of the Imagination: Postromantic Culture in the Later Novels of Thomas Hardy*. New York: New York University Press, 1990.

Morgan, Rosemarie. *Women and Sexuality in the Novels of Thomas Hardy*. London: Routledge, 1988.

—— *Cancelled Words: Rediscovering Thomas Hardy*. London: Routledge, 1992.

Musselwhite, David. *Social Transformations in Hardy's Tragic Novels: Megamachines and Phantasms*. Basingstoke: Palgrave Macmillan, 2003.

Nancy, Jean-Luc. *Dis-Enclosure: The Deconstruction of Christianity*. Trans. Bettina Bergo, Gabriel Malenfant, and Michael B. Smith. New York: Fordham University Press, 2008.

Natarajan, Uttara. 'Pater and the Genealogy of Hardy's Modernity'. *Studies in English Literature, 1500–1900*, 46:4 (Autumn 2006): 849–61.

Niemeyer, Paul J. *Seeing Hardy: Film and Television Adaptations of the Fiction of Thomas Hardy*. Jefferson NC: McFarland & Co Inc., 2002

Nishimura, Satoshi. 'Thomas Hardy and the Language of the Inanimate'. *Studies in English Literature, 1500–1900*, 43:4 (Autumn 2003): 897–912.

Orel, Harold. *The Unknown Thomas Hardy: Lesser-Known Aspects of Hardy's Life and Career*. Brighton: Harvester Press, 1987.

—— *The Final Years of Thomas Hardy*. Basingstoke: Macmillan, 1976.

O'Toole, Tess. *Genealogy and Fiction: Family Lineage and Narrative Lines*. Basingstoke: Macmillan, 1997.

Page, Norman, ed. *Oxford Reader's Companion to Hardy*. Oxford: Oxford University Press, 2000.

—— ed. *Thomas Hardy: Family History*, 5 vols. London, 1998.

Paulin, Tom. *Thomas Hardy: The Poetry of Perception*. Basingstoke: Macmillan, 1975.

—— 'Introduction'. *Thomas Hardy: Poems Selected by Tom Paulin*. London: Faber and Faber, 2005. ix–xxii.

Pite, Ralph. *Hardy's Geography: Wessex and the Regional Novel*. Basingstoke: Macmillan, 2002.

Plotnitsky, Arkady. *In the Shadow of Hegel: Complementarity, History, and the Unconscious*. Gainesville: University Press of Florida, 1993.

—— 'Algebra and Allegory: Nonclassical Epistemology, Quantum Theory and the Work of Paul de Man', in Tom Cohen et al., *Material Events: Paul de Man and the Afterlife of Theory*. Minneapolis: University of Minnesota Press, 2001, 49–92.

Potolsky, Matthew. 'Hardy, Shaftesbury, and Aesthetic Education'. *Studies in English Literature, 1500–1900*, 46:4 (Autumn 2006): 863–78.

Proust, Marcel. *In Search of Lost Time. Vol. 2. Within a Budding Grove*. Trans. C. K. Scott Moncrieff and Terence Kilmartin. Rev. D.J. Enright. London: Vintage, 1996.

Purdy, Richard Little. *Thomas Hardy: A Bibliographical Study*. Oxford: Clarendon Press, 1954.

Ray, Martin. *Thomas Hardy: A Textual Study of the Short Stories*. Aldershot: Ashgate, 1997.

Reilly, Jim. *Shadowtime: History and Representation in Hardy, Conrad and George Eliot*. London: Routledge, 1993.

Ricciardi, Alessia. *The Ends of Mourning: Psychoanalysis, Literature, Film*. Stanford: Stanford University Press, 2003.

Richards, Jill. '"The History of Error": Hardy's Critics and the Self Unseen'. *Victorian Poetry*, 45:2 (Summer 2007): 117–33.

Richter, Gerhard. *Walter Benjamin and the Corpus of Autobiography*. Detroit: Wayne State University Press, 2000.

Robbins, Ruth. *Pater to Forster, 1873–1924*. Basingstoke: Palgrave Macmillan, 2003.

Robson, Catherine. '"Where Heaves the Turf": Thomas Hardy and the Boundaries of the Earth'. *Victorian Literature and Culture*, (2004): 495–503.

Rogers, Shannon L. 'Medievalism in the Last Novels of Thomas Hardy: New Wine in Old Bottles'. *ELT (1880–1920)*, 42:3 (1993): 298–316.

—— '"The Historian of Wessex": Thomas Hardy's Contribution to History'. *Rethinking History*, 5:2 (July 2001): 217–32.

Ronen, Ruth. *Possible Worlds in Literary Theory*. Cambridge: Cambridge University Press, 1994.

Roud, Steve. *The English Year: A Month-by-Month Guide to the Nation's Customs and Festivals, from May Day to Mischief Night*. London: Penguin, 2008.

Royle, Nicholas. *After Derrida*. Manchester: Manchester University Press, 1995.

Salter, C. H. *Good Little Thomas Hardy*. Totowa, NJ: Barnes & Noble Books, 1981.

Scarry, Elaine. *Resisting Representation*. New York: Oxford University Press, 1994.

Schmidt, Dennis J. *The Ubiquity of the Finite: Hegel, Heidegger, and the Entitlements of Philosophy*. Cambridge, MA: MIT Press, 1988.

Schopenhauer, Arthur. *The World as Will and Representation*. Two vols. Trans. E. F. J. Payne. New York: Dover Publications, Inc., 1966.

―――― *Parerga and Paralipomena: Short Philosophical Essays. Vol. 2*. Trans. E. F. J. Payne. Oxford: Clarendon Press, 2000.

Scott, James F. 'Thomas Hardy's Use of the Gothic: An Examination of Five Representative Works'. *Nineteenth-Century Fiction*, 17:4 (March 1963): 363–80.

Seel, Martin. *Aesthetics of Appearing*. Trans. John Farrell. Stanford: Stanford University Press, 2005.

Sherman, G. W. 'Thomas Hardy and the Agricultural Laborer'. *Nineteenth-Century Fiction*, 7:2 (September 1952): 111–18.

Siebenschuh, William R. 'Hardy and the Imagery of Place'. *Studies in English Literature, 1500–1900*, 39:4 (Autumn, 1999): 773–89.

Simpson, Helen. 'Wives for Sale'. *Times Literary Supplement*. December 24 & 31, 2004 (5307/8): 7.

Springer, Marlene. *Hardy's Use of Allusion*. Basingstoke: Macmillan, 1983.

Squillace, Robert. 'Hardy's Mummers'. *Nineteenth-Century Fiction*, 41:2 (September 1986): 176–89.

Stewart, Susan. 'Lyric Possession'. *Critical Inquiry*, 22:1 (Autumn 1995): 34–64.

Stone, Donald D. 'House and Home in Thomas Hardy'. *Nineteenth-Century Fiction*, 39:3 (Dec., 1984): 292–304.

Tague, Gregory. *Character and Consciousness: George Eliot, Thomas Hardy, E. M. Forster, D. H. Lawrence*. Palo Alto, CA: Academia Press, 2005.

Tandon, Bharat. '"... Among the Ruins": Narrative Archaeology in *The Mayor of Casterbridge'*. *Studies in the Novel*, 35:4 (Winter 2003): 471–89.

Taylor, Dennis. *Hardy's Poetry, 1860–1928*. New York: Columbia University Press, 1981.

———— *Hardy's Metres and Victorian Prosody: with a Metrical Appendix of Hardy's Stanza Forms*. Oxford: Clarendon Press, 1988.

———— *Hardy's Literary Language and Victorian Philology*. Oxford: Clarendon Press, 1993.

Taylor, Richard H. *The Neglected Hardy: Thomas Hardy's Lesser Novels*. Basingstoke: Macmillan, 1982.

Thomas, Jane. *Thomas Hardy, Femininity and Dissent: Reassessing the 'Minor' Novels*. Basingstoke: Macmillan, 1999.

Vigar, Penelope. *The Novels of Thomas Hardy: Illusion and Reality*. London, 1974.

Vrettos, Athena. 'Displaced Memories in Victorian Fiction and Psychology'. *Victorian Studies* (Winter 2007): 199–207.

Weber, Carl J. 'Chronology in Hardy's Novels'. *PMLA*, 53:1 (March 1938): 314–20.

Weber, Samuel. *Mass Mediauras: Form, Technics, Media*. Stanford: Stanford University Press, 1996.

———— *Benjamin's – abilities*. Cambridge, MA: Harvard University Press, 2008.

White, R. J. *Thomas Hardy and History*. Basingstoke: Macmillan, 1974.

Wickens, G. Glen. *Thomas Hardy, Monism and the Carnival Tradition: The One and the Many in* The Dynasts. Toronto: University of Toronto Press, 2002.

Widdowson, Peter. *Hardy in History: A Study in Literary Sociology*. London: Routledge, 1989.

———— *On Thomas Hardy: Late Essays and Earlier*. Basingstoke: Macmillan, 1998.

Wigley, Mark. *The Architecture of Deconstruction: Derrida's Haunt*. Cambridge, MA: MIT Press, 1993.

Williams, Merryn. *Thomas Hardy and Rural England*. Basingstoke: Macmillan, 1972.

Williams, Raymond. *The English Novel from Dickens to Lawrence*. London: Hogarth Press, 1970.

Wittenberg, Judith Bryant. 'Early Hardy Novels and the Fictional Eye'. *Novel: A Forum on Fiction*, 16:2 (Winter, 1983): 151–64.

Wotton, George. *Thomas Hardy: Towards a Materialist Criticism*. Totowa, NJ: Barnes & Noble, 1985.

Wright, T. R. *Hardy and the Erotic*. Basingstoke: Macmillan, 1989.

Zietlow, Paul. *Moments of Vision: The Poetry of Thomas Hardy*. Cambridge, MA: Harvard University Press, 1974.

Index

Note: Principal discussions of novels are indicated in bold; 'n.' and a number after a page number indicates a note number on that page.